Europe's Deadly Century

Perspectives on 20th century conflict heritage

Europe's Deadly Century

Perspectives on 20th century conflict heritage

Edited by Neil Forbes, Robin Page and Guillermo Pérez

LANDSCAPES OF WAR

Remembering conflict in twentieth-century Europe

The editors gratefully acknowledge the support provided under the
EU Commission's Culture 2000 programme.

The Partners in the Landscapes of War project are:

- Regione Calabria, Italy, lead partner
- CoNISMa, National Inter-University Consortium for Marine Sciences, Rome, Italy.
- Federación Valenciana de Municipos y Provincias (FVMP), Valencia, Spain
- Consell Valencià de Cultura, Valencia, Spain.
- Centre de Conservation du Livre, Arles, France
- English Heritage, Swindon, Great Britain
- Coventry University, Coventry, Great Britain
- Hansestadt Rostock, Rostock, Germany
- Bluimage productions, Catanzaro/Rome, Italy

ENGLISH HERITAGE

Education and Culture

Culture 2000

Published by English Heritage, Kemble Drive, Swindon SN2 2GZ
www.english-heritage.org.uk
English Heritage is the Government's statutory adviser on all aspects of the historic
environment.

First published 2009

ISBN 978-1-84802-039-9
Product code 51483

British Library Cataloguing in Publication data
A CIP catalogue record for this book is available from the British Library.

The National Monuments Record is the public archive of English Heritage. For more
information, contact NMR Enquiry and Research Services, National Monuments
Record Centre, Kemble Drive, Swindon SN2 2GZ; telephone (01793) 414600.

Brought to publication by Robin Taylor, Publishing, English Heritage.
Typeset in Charter 9.5pt

Edited by Janet Hadley
Page layout by Simon Borrough

Printed in Belgium by DeckersSnoeck.

Front cover
Carabanchel Prison, Madrid © Alfredo González-Ruibal

CONTENTS

ABOUT THE CONTRIBUTORS

Geert Baert Geert Baert is Assistant Professor at the University College of Ghent, where he is teaching soil science, GIS and landscape genesis; he is involved in research on soil fertility and on soil-landscape relationships in temperate, semi-arid and humid tropical countries. He graduated at the University of Ghent in earth sciences in 1979 and soil science in 1981.
Contact: Geert.Baert@hogent.be

Angus Boulton Angus Boulton is a visual artist working in photography and film. The DG Bank Kunststipendium of 1998/99, and subsequent residency in Berlin, created an opportunity to turn his attention towards aspects of the Cold War and begin investigating the European legacy of the Soviet military. Until 2008 he was engaged in an AHRC [Arts and Humanities Research Council] research fellowship at Manchester Metropolitan University. The photographic series and films arising from various projects have been exhibited internationally.
Contact at: www.angusboulton.net

Martin Brown Martin is Archaeological Adviser to Defence Estates, acting as an internal consultant and both advising and supporting the management, preservation, recording and understanding of the estate's cultural heritage. Before joining Defence Estates he worked as an archaeological fieldworker and as a curator. He is a founder member of No-Man's-Land, the European Group for Great War Archaeology and is co-director of the Plugstreet Project, which is exploring conflict landscapes in the UK and Belgium.

Gillian Carr Gillian Carr is Lecturer in Archaeology at the Institute of Continuing Education at the University of Cambridge. Although her background is in the British Iron Age and the Roman occupation of Britain, her current area of expertise is in pioneering and developing the archaeology of occupation, based on the case study of the German occupation of the Channel Islands during the Second World War.
Contact: gcc20@hermes.cam.ac.uk

Wayne D Cocroft Wayne Cocroft is a Senior Archaeological Investigator with English Heritage's Archaeological Survey and Investigation team. Since the early 1990s he has specialised in the investigation of modern military sites and is the author of Dangerous energy: *The archaeology of gunpowder and military explosives manufacture* and co-author of *Cold War: Building for nuclear confrontation 1946–1989*, and many articles on these topics. In this field his particular interests are munitions production, military research and development sites, and the archaeology of rocketry.
Contact: wayne.cocroft@english-heritage.org.uk

Benjamin Gilles Benjamin Gilles is currently Director of the university library of Saint-Charles in Marseilles (University of Provence). He works with the Centre de Conservation du Livre/ Centre Interrégional de Conservation on the digitisation of the Norton Cru collection. He is preparing a thesis in the Ecole des Hautes Etudes en Sciences Sociales, supervised by Professor Stéphane Audoin-Rouzeau. He works on the genesis of Norton Cru's book, Témoins.
Contact: benjamin.gilles@univ-provence.fr

Fleur Hutchings Fleur Hutchings completed her architecture degree in Sydney, Australia and worked for Norman Foster in Hong Kong and London. She joined the World Heritage Studies programme at BTU Cottbus where she received her Master of Arts with a thesis on the Cultural Significance of Bletchley Park.

Axel Klausmeier Axel Klausmeier is Director of the recently established Berlin Wall Foundation. He was formerly an Assistant Professor at Brandenburg University of Technology, Cottbus, Germany. He has been involved in the documentation and listing of historic cultural landscapes for many years. Since April 2007, he has been working for the research project, 'The Berlin Wall as Symbol of the Cold War: From an Instrument of the SED Home Policy to an Architectural Monument of International Rank'. He has produced numerous publications on all aspects of the conservation of historic landscapes and troubling heritage.
Contact: klausmeier@berliner-mauer-gedenkstaette.de

Jeremy Lake Since 2002 Jeremy Lake has been a member of the English Heritage Characterisation Team, which has worked at developing new methods for understanding and managing the historic environment, including landscapes and rural buildings. Previously he worked with English Heritage's Listings Team and the National Trust.

Jeremy Lake has published extensively on a range of subjects. Since the mid-1990s he has developed thematic listing surveys on chapels, military and industrial sites and farmsteads that have connected designation to guidelines for reuse and management.
Contact: jeremy.lake@english-heritage.org. uk

Harlind Libbrecht Harlind Libbrecht graduated as a landscape architect at the Horticultural Institute Melle in 1981 (now University College Ghent). He started teaching at the same institute in 1989. He teaches design studies in landscape architecture and also teaches survey methods in historical landscapes. Lately he has also been involved in landscape research.
Contact: harlind.libbrecht@telenet.be

Joseph Magro Conti Joseph Magro Conti is manager of the heritage planning unit in the Malta Environment and Planning Authority. His responsibilities include policy development, consultancy, and monitoring development within heritage-sensitive areas. He graduated as an archaeologist at the University of Malta and holds a postgraduate certificate in Mediterranean culture and heritage management from the Universita' del Mediterraneo (La Sapienza, Rome), and a MA in heritage management from the University of York, UK.
Contact: Joe.MagroConti@mepa.org.mt

Gabriel Moshenska Gabriel Moshenska is a post-graduate student at University College London Institute of Archaeology, working on the archaeology, material culture and memory of World War II. His fieldwork has focused on a range of sites and collections relating to the London Blitz. He is currently researching the history and archaeology of air-raid shelters.
Contact: g.moshenska@ucl.ac.uk

Christian Mühldorfer-Vogt Since 2006 Christian Mühldorfer-Vogt has been Director of the Historisch-Technische Informationszentrum at the V-weapon site of Peenemünde. His main focus is the management of the museum. Most of his publications deal with problems in presenting the history of the Third Reich in museums.
Contact: hti@peenemuende.de
HTI, Im Kraftwerk, 17449 Peenemünde, Germany.

David Parham David Parham is Senior Lecturer in Marine Archaeology at the School of Conservation Science at Bournemouth University. His research interests include seafaring during the later prehistoric period, wooden ship construction of all periods and the archaeology of seafaring in the late-post-medieval to modern period.
Contact: DParham@bournemouth.ac.uk

Chris Patrick Chris Patrick is a planning archaeologist for Coventry City Council. He has worked in Coventry as the city's archaeology officer since 2004. Although his current role is chiefly concerned with the protection of Coventry's medieval archaeology, he has recently become heavily involved in the researching of the city's 20th century heritage. He has recorded many of Coventry's industrial complexes before their demolition with a particular interest in their role in wartime production.
Contact: Christopher.Patrick@coventry.gov.uk

Monica Petrillo Monica Petrillo works at the National Inter Universities Consortium for Marine Sciences (CoNISMa), where she is responsible for the cartographic laboratory, producing cartography and geographic information systems (GIS) for research projects. She graduated in building engineering and has worked as an independent professional in many building planning, restoration and urban development projects. She is currently involved in national and international research programmes, due to her expertise in the management of geodatabases and in the realisation of GIS, which are mainly concerned with the identification of geomorphic-geologic processes, sediment dynamics and to the mapping of the seabed and habitat.
Contact: petrillo@conisma.it

Andrew Rigby Andrew Rigby is Professor of Peace Studies and the Founding Director of the Centre for Peace and Reconciliation Studies at Coventry University. He has taught peace studies in a number of countries and published widely, most recently focusing on how

communities and societies emerging out of destructive conflict deal with the legacy of human rights abuse.
Contact: a.rigby@coventry.ac.uk

Alfredo González Ruibal Alfredo González Ruibal teaches at the Department of Prehistory of the Universidad Complutense de Madrid. His research, focused on the archaeology of the contemporary past, ethnoarchaeology and material culture, has been published in several international journals. He is also the editor of a volume on the archaeology of the Spanish Civil War (*Arqueología de la Guerra Civil Española,* Madrid, 2008) and has conducted fieldwork on conflict, colonialism and dictatorship in Spain and Ethiopia.
Contact: a_ruibal@yahoo.co.uk

Alessandra Savini Alessandra Savini is a temporary researcher (marine geologist) at the National Inter Universities Consortium for Marine Sciences (CoNISMa). Her main scientific interests deal with seafloor mapping and processes of sedimentation and their interaction with marine habitats. She has been involved in numerous national and international research programmes, due to her expertise in seabed data interpretation. Her geographic areas of interest lay mainly in the Mediterranean. She works at the Department of Geological Sciences and Geotechnologies of Milano-Bicocca University, where she lectures in marine geology and laboratory of coastal marine geology.

José Ramón Valero Escandell José Ramón Valero Escandell teaches human geography at the University of Alicante. He was awarded a PhD in geography and history and received a Master of Geography, History and Arts Didactics and has lectured at universities in Italy and Cuba. He is an expert on migration and local studies, he has written many books about the Spanish Civil War, including, *Territory of defeat. The last days of the II Republic Government in the Vinalopó County* (2004). In 2007 he led the joint team that edited the report, *Inventory of sites and resources related to the Civil War in the municipalities of Vinalopó County.*
Contact: jose.valero@ua.es

Sylvie Van Damme Sylvie Van Damme studied geography and spatial planning at Ghent University. She teaches landscape planning at the University College Ghent, Faculty of Biosciences and Landscape Architecture and is working on a PHD on the integration of landscape in spatial design in Flanders.
Contact: sylvie.vandamme@hogent.be

Joris Verbeken Joris Verbeken teaches geographical information systems and various landscape management courses at the University College of Ghent. Before that he was involved in various cartographic and GIS activities at the University of Ghent's Department of Geography, where he had graduated in geography in 2003.
Contact: joris.verbeken@hogent.be

Angus Wainwright Angus Wainwright is the archaeologist for the National Trust's East of England Region. He covers all periods of archaeology advising on the care, management and interpretation of archaeological sites and landscapes. He has worked in the east of England for the last 15 years and has had a particular responsibility for Orford Ness.
Contact: Angus.Wainwright@nationaltrust.org.uk

ABOUT THE EDITORS

Neil Forbes Neil Forbes is Professor of International History, and Director of Postgraduate Research at Coventry University. His publications are in the international political, economic and business history of the inter-war period, with a special emphasis on Britain's relations with Europe. His current research projects include the process of financial stabilisation in Europe after the First World War, the ways in which the ideological divisions of the 1930s interacted with the commercial operations of multinational enterprise, and the memorialisation of war in the 20th century. Contact: n.forbes@coventry.ac.uk

Robin Page Robin Page works in the Heritage Data Management team of English Heritage based at the National Monuments Record. His primary area of interest is in the production, curation and dissemination of digital data covering a wide range of archaeological sites and historic buildings. He has worked on a number of desk-based projects to enhance this data, particularly those relating to 20th-century military sites. Before joining English Heritage he worked as a field archaeologist in the UK, Central Europe and Syria.
Contact: robin.page@english-heritage.org.uk

Guillermo Pérez Guillermo Pérez was born in Valencia, Spain. He received degrees in biological and environmental sciences from University of Valencia and Polytechnic University of Valencia. He has been working for eight years for Consell Valencià de Cultura (Valencia Council of Culture), a consultation and advisory institution of the Valencia Regional Government for heritage and cultural affairs, where he advises, cooperates and assists in researching and producing reports published by the institution about promoting and preserving Valencian cultural and environmental heritage. He is also editor of CVC's website and manager of the European Programme Culture 2000-funded project Landscapes of War.
Contact: cvc@gva.es

ACKNOWLEDGEMENTS

The editors are especially grateful to Sarah Britton, Research Fellow, Coventry University and Daniel Miles, of the Projects Team at English Heritage, for their invaluable help in preparing the text for publication.

Introduction

NEIL FORBES, ROBIN PAGE AND GUILLERMO PÉREZ

At the end of the first decade of the 21st century, it is possible to look back on the history of Europe in the previous century with some detachment. The century commenced with some optimism – the promises of la belle époque – that the tensions generated around the world by the imperialist ambitions of the European powers, and by the rise of mass electorates within those states, would be lessened by improving living standards. What no one was able to foresee was the way technological and scientific advance would, in the course of the century, be harnessed in warfare and conflict with such barbaric and tyrannical results. The conflicts of Europe's deadly century set countries, classes, ideologies and ethnic groups against one another across the continent on an unparalleled scale. European boundaries, society and even ideas and beliefs were remade three times over in a series of great convulsions – the two world wars, the Cold War and an interrelated series of geographically more limited, but no less bitter conflicts, such as the Spanish Civil War. These conflicts left their mark on the physical and mental landscape of Europe: barriers to keep people out of or within allotted zones; the scars of trenches, chains of fortifications stamped out of the ground with desperate energy; the seas around Europe studded with wrecks that are in effect submerged war graves; vast tracts of land taken up by airfields; bunkers and research stations full of weapons capable of throwing Europe back into the stone age; and memorial landscapes created to commemorate the conflicts (or the prevailing version of them).

The extent to which history does or does not repeat itself, and the extent to which it is instructive to coming generations, will always be a matter for debate. Certainly, any commentator would always be well advised to avoid the claim that history has come to an 'end'. At the dawn of the 1990s with the fall of the Soviet bloc, the unwary or the complacent may have congratulated themselves that an uncomfortable history could soon be marginalised, even forgotten. After a delicate shudder, Europeans could turn away from the obsolete ferro-concrete of the bunkers and look forward to the dividends of a durable peace – swords turned into ploughshares – within a continental cordon sanitaire.

The viciously fought, tragic wars among the Yugoslav successor states shattered this illusion almost as soon as it appeared. The images and reportage conveyed around the world had a sickening and shocking familiarity: once more in Europe villages burned, refugees fled for their lives, and emaciated figures looked through the wire of camps. The ideological wars of the century had ended only to be replaced by ancient and deep-rooted ethnic and religious conflict.

Considerable political tensions remain, particularly at the sub-state level in Europe, and the economic challenges for the international system are formidable. But for the first time most Europeans are able to feel confident that the chauvinistic rivalries and extremist ideologies that propelled nation to take up arms against nation and also divided the citizens within nations are historical phenomena, rather than contemporary evils. In this sense, Eric Hobsbawm referred to the 'short twentieth century' – an era of 'religious' wars the most militant and bloodthirsty of which involved secular ideologies – but also presciently pointed to the global challenges that lie ahead (Hobsbawm, 1994). Similarly, after eloquently describing the terrible events that took place in the Dark Continent, Mark Mazower concludes optimistically that societal and cultural diversity in Europe is a way to recapture traditions of civilisation rather than a source of tension to be feared (Mazower, 1998).

Indeed, the European Union was itself born from a determination to prevent future conflict between its constituent nations; it now facilitates collaborative work, where old enemies can together reflect upon the past and use the traces of previous conflicts to learn lessons for the future. To entertain the idea that this family of nations will once more find themselves at war with each other seems faintly ludicrous; no sooner is the thought formed than it may be dismissed as inconceivable. Likewise, while only limited progress has been made in dismantling arsenals of nuclear weapons, it is possible to begin to hope that with the end of the Cold War, the threat of mass destruction has greatly receded.

For the populations of Europe, therefore, there is the promise of a new era. For the first time in the modern history of the continent, hardly any of its citizens will have direct experience at any time in their lives of war and warfare. This presents, it need hardly be said, tremendous opportunities. It also brings unexpected challenges. There is a widespread recognition that it is necessary to safeguard against complacency; the enjoyment of democratic freedoms across Europe and conditions of peaceful coexistence among states must never be assumed to be irreversible rights.

In recent years, a number of projects and publications have reflected a great surge of interest expressed by the general public in memory and reminiscence, remembrance and commemoration in relation to 20th-century conflict and war (Wood, 1999). The welling up among the public of this desire to commemorate continues to stimulate scholarly debate. One theory recently advanced is that commemoration is a particular act of externalisation to bring about the vital combination of closure and perpetuation – the complement of burial – especially necessary in cases where there is either an 'excess' or 'absence' of memory (Runia, 2007).

Occasionally, critical voices are raised against the rituals of remembrance. There is a risk that ceremonies, developed at times of mass grieving and mourning for the fallen, may become institutionalised in order to help cultivate myths of statehood. One writer suggests that memorialisation of war tends to reproduce stories of national glory and heroism (Edkins, 2003). The practice of remembering may facilitate the development of cults around victims or even help to keep old hatreds alive. For many

in Europe, the scars left by war and conflict are still raw and will never heal. Political extremists, especially the European far right, have also reinterpreted some aspects of 20th century conflicts for their own ends, reducing complex and painful realities to yelled slogans. A spectrum of socio-political influences has acted to condition memories in post-war Europe, and will continue to operate in the construction and reconstruction of memory (Lebow, 2006). Clearly, symbols honouring barbaric regimes have no place in a civilised world. But the purposes of truth and reconciliation cannot be served by neglecting the physical remains of war, conflict and ideological struggle that lie everywhere around us.

Another approach to researching and representing sensitive issues concerning the remembrance of conflict is to foster what is called 'inter-generational learning', whereby oral history and personal testimony, verified as far as possible by existing knowledge, offers contextual detail about specific sites of remembrance. Exploring individual and collective identities and the history of localities provides a platform to promote peace and reconciliation between communities, and tolerance and sensitivity towards minority groups. In recent historical literature it is possible to see the emergence of a critique arguing that the writing of history should analyse how identity is constructed and demonstrate how identities are in a constant flux (Berger, 2007).

Certainly, there is a tendency for historical writing, based around progressive national narratives, to be exploited for the broad political purpose of extolling the virtues of coherence and unity. Some in Europe have sought to draw a veil of obscurity over the events (and thus the remains) of the past, in the name of promoting intra- or international harmony. But what is increasingly evident is how historiography has acquired a new focus on transnational factors. This includes a wide variety of groups beneath the level of the state, ranging from elites of one kind or another to those discriminated against, marginalised or victimised – especially during times of war and conflict. Similarly, in the field of archaeology, 'conflict archaeology' has emerged as a discrete discipline based on the study of the diverse physical remains of recent wars, and increasingly reflecting cross-disciplinary approaches (for example Schofield et al 2006; Schofield and Cocroft 2007).

It is encouraging that most European states continue to reflect on the less praiseworthy episodes in their recent history. Studies have revealed, for example, collaboration and complicity on a wide scale with even the most barbaric acts perpetrated during World War II (discussed in Forbes, 2007). Engaging with the historical record and facing up to responsibility is inevitably painful and difficult. But, in the longer term it is not possible to see how democratic values can otherwise be immutably established.

This collection of essays is concerned with why it is important to give adequate and appropriate recognition to the heritage of Europe's conflicts and how that heritage should be preserved and managed. The papers assembled here derive from a series of themed workshops held in 2007–09 under the auspices of *Landscapes of war: remembering conflict in 20th century Europe* – a project funded under the European Commission's Culture 2000 Programme. The partners represented in the project were drawn from a number of European states; that constituency is reflected in the geographical or territorial focus of the essays.

The first section, *Methods of investigation: textual, visual, material*, deals with different approaches to investigating the heritage of 20th century conflicts, and what are often extensive, contested and sometimes enigmatic and ambiguous buildings and monuments. This presents particular challenges to archaeologists, historians and the local communities who live in areas characterised by past conflict. These landscapes exist in all spatial and geographical dimensions: on land, underground, in the air and at sea; even – for the Cold War – in space. Many of these places are well known – others have remained closely guarded secrets. This is now a common past, in which all share an interest. The question of how best to document and describe these places for the benefit of this and future generations lies at the centre of this book.

The *textual* element here is strongly represented by Benjamin Gille's paper on Norton Cru's classic interwar analysis of French literature about World War I, *Témoins*. The paper presents a perceptive landscape archaeology of the mind, that is of Norton Cru's personal perspective of World War I captured in his book, of the contrasting evidence of his wartime letters, and the effect his work had on wider perceptions of that war. With his meditative style, the

innovative film maker Angus Boulton provides the *visual* element, with a fresh viewpoint on the interpretation of abandoned Cold War bases, which although apparently simple and sparse, subtly allow the viewer to explore the sites for themselves as they slowly reveal their original purposes.

An overview of best practice in the investigation of the material or physical evidence of modern conflict is given by one of its leading English exponents, Wayne Cocroft, while Alessandra Savini and Monica Petrillo focus on the benefits of recent advances in underwater survey techniques. Gillian Carr examines new ways of looking at the meanings (and countermeanings) of sites and artefacts of the German occupation of the Channel Islands during World War II from the point of view of both occupiers and the occupied. Such remnants tell stories of passive resistance and resilience that are little known outside the islands.

Martin Brown's paper, *Strange meetings*, looks at different scales of approaching the archaeology of the Western Front that can encompass the previously unprecedented vastness of that conflict or that can focus on the sharp poignancy of the fate of individual soldiers, as real people. Case studies of cross-disciplinary surveys of the evidence applied to specific conflicts and locations are given by JR Valero (the Spanish Civil War) and David Parham (the Battle of the Atlantic).

In the second section, *Defining values and significance: memory, commemoration and contested landscapes*, contributors deal with some of the most complex and often controversial aspects of study in this field: essentially the issues around why and how the heritage of 20th-century conflicts should be valued. The question of what to do with sites of conflict and military heritage gives rise to a range of views. In general terms, the significance and value placed on landscapes of war and conflict is related to education and knowledge; they remind us that the freedoms that are associated with civil society have been won at the cost of struggle and terrible sacrifice. The intention must be to develop accurate histories of sites based on scientific investigation, thorough research, and a careful analysis of the documentary record.

How, then, is it best to contextualise and locate different sites, in terms of international and national histories and regional and local historical narratives? Should different sites be remembered and preserved in different ways? How is it possible to deal with different groups' interpretations of the same heritage sites or artefacts, or with situations where too often only one (biased) version of the past has been presented, excluding all others? When is it appropriate to use sites for alternative purposes? How are the competing pressures of marketing, 'commodification' and education to be balanced? Should sites that are especially sensitive be exempt from commercialisation?

These concerns form the backdrop of Alfredo Gonzàlez Ruibal's paper on the monuments of Franco's Spain. He argues cogently and passionately for a radical revaluation of the way such sites are interpreted to the public in Spain, in what amounts to a manifesto for their democratisation and an overt deconstruction of former Francoist myth-making. The dynamic nature of the subject matter is demonstrated by the fate of the former Carabanchel Prison, used as a case study in this paper of how a previously fascist monument could be turned into a site to promote democracy and benefit the community. Since the paper was submitted, despite protests from academics and local residents, the building was demolished to use the land for development. Gabriel Moshenka carries on the theme of contested spaces and explores how 'public', community-based projects can operate in contested environments – as opposed to the 'public' face of large heritage organisations. Andrew Rigby compares strategies for the commemoration of the terrible heritage shared between Coventry and Dresden and how these have gradually changed.

Jeremy Lake presents a case study of how significance and value can be attributed to Bletchley Park: a site that is defined neither in terms of its architectural merits, nor the uniqueness of the surviving fabric, but instead for its historical significance as a major centre for signals intelligence, specifically code-breaking, during World War II and through this as the birthplace of the computer and of information technology.

The final section *Public archaeology, public history: case studies in conservation and management* is concerned with approaches to the preservation and presentation or 'interpretation' of conflict archaeology, along with the management of its relationship with the wider environment. Themes that are covered include best practice – or cautionary tales – in presenting and managing sites or areas, problems and limitations that potentially dangerous sites can present, and looking at when/how far to manage and when to let alone.

This section focuses on the idea of 'public history' – how to make available, to the widest possible audience, knowledge about the heritage of conflict in 20th century Europe. The objective should be to open up intellectual and physical access to a wide variety of conflict heritage sites whilst remembering, at the same time, how important it is to interpret such heritage sensitively. Public history frequently stimulates debate – questions about who 'owns' the past, the ambiguities over how people identify with the local community or nation state, and whether or how to make moral judgements. But whatever the complexities and diversity involved, it is of fundamental importance to formulate and pursue conservation and management strategies.

Axel Klausmeier discusses the project to record and display the remnants of that symbol par excellence of a divided Europe, the Berlin Wall, initially in the face of public incomprehension or outright hostility to the idea. Christian Mühldorfer-Vogt describes the interpretation of the famous V-weapon site at Peenemünde by the use of a sensitively constructed heritage trail, and notes the difficulty of reconciling the technological achievement of the rocket programme with the terrible human cost of its production and warlike use. At a higher level of management and conservation, Chris Patrick narrates the story of Coventry's rise as an industrial centre, the destruction of its historic centre in the Second World War, and the post-war strategies to rebuild the city in a new mould and latterly to conserve or record the remaining fragments of the pre-war city. Angus Wainwright sets out the National Trust's management strategy for the former Atomic Weapons Research Establishment site at Orford Ness on the east coast of England, which combines important man-made features (and man-made problems) with important natural landscapes. The lightness-of-touch management strategy will be controversial for some. Finally Harland Libbrecht looks to the future with a bold potential strategy for displaying the First World War landscape of Flanders in its wider historical setting for the 21st century.

The book's afterword is the poignant speech given by the President of the Consell Valencia de Cultura. An eye-witness to the horrific effects of 20th century warfare, his comments stress the achievement of a worthwhile state of relative peace, the need to guard against complacency and thus the ongoing duty of Europeans to actively communicate and share knowledge about the physical and emotional heritage to avoid future conflicts. This speech was made specifically at the opening of the *Landscapes of war exhibition* in the city of Valencia, but its words could serve as a rationale for this book.

The authors contributing to this volume come from a variety of professional backgrounds – historians, archaeologists, curators, as well as experts in peace studies, conservation and heritage. In bringing together the skills and knowledge embodied in both academic and policy-practitioner traditions, the book offers a trans-disciplinary and international perspective on conflict heritage. The intention underlying this collection is that the values, methods and approaches discussed by the contributors should be applicable and debated in a wide range of contexts, and that expertise which is demonstrated here may help to inform both further study and good practice. It is to be hoped that the debates and discussions set out here will be of interest to a wide range of professional practitioners, academics and policy-makers, as well as the general reader, and will open the way to a deeper understanding of the significance of Europe's conflict heritage.

Bibliography

Berger, S (ed) 2007 *Writing the Nation: A Global Perspective*. Basingstoke: Palgrave

Edkins, J 2003 *Trauma and the Memory of Politics*. Cambridge: Cambridge University Press

Forbes, N 2007 'Multinational Enterprise, "Corporate Responsibility" and the Nazi Dictatorship: The Case of Unilever and Germany in the 1930s'. *Contemporary European History*, **16**, 149–167

Hobsbawm, E 1994 *Age of Extremes: The Short Twentieth Century 1914 – 1991*. London: Abacus

Lebow, R N *et al* 2006 *The Politics of Memory in Postwar Europe*. Durham, NC: Duke University Press

Mazower, M 1998 *Dark Continent: Europe's Twentieth Century*. London: Penguin

Runia, E 2007 'Burying the dead, creating the past'. *History and Theory*, **46**, October, 313–325

Schofield, S *et al* 2006 *Remapping the Field: New Approaches in Conflict Archaeology*, Berlin/Bonn: Westkreutz Verlag

Schofield, S and Cocroft, W (eds) 2007 *A Fearsome Heritage: Diverse Legacies of the Cold War*. Walnut Creek: Left Coast

Wood, N 1999 *Vectors of Memory: Legacies of Trauma in Postwar Europe*. Oxford: Berg

1. Methods of investigation: textual, visual, material

Understanding a literary site of remembrance : *Témoins*, by Jean Norton Cru

BENJAMIN GILLES

'The First World War appears less and less understandable to the modern man.' The words of the French historian François Furet, have a particular resonance today in light of the death of the last French soldier of the First World War, Lazare Ponticelli, in March 2008 (Furet 1995, 64).

The First World War is singular for its duration, its totality and its violence. The war lasted five years and profoundly marked both people and territories. It signalled the birth of modern propaganda and mobilised entire populations. Men were enrolled for long months and women performed work in their absence. Children also played an important role (Audoin-Rouzeau 1993). The war caused great trauma for whole societies. The importance of this shock is illustrated by the number of men killed daily. In France, 860 French soldiers died every day, while on the German side the average was 1300 (Audoin-Rouzeau and Becker 2000, 32–33). Scarcely a single family was spared mourning.

These exceptional characteristics explain why many soldiers needed to recall their stories. The 20th century has been described as the era of witnesses. This label mainly stems from the many and varied testimonies of Second World War concentration camp survivors (Wieviorka 1988). The First World War represents a major change, however, in that it was the first time – and the last – that veterans talked in such numbers about any conflict. The improvement in literacy levels in this period was obviously an important factor, but so too was the need to bear witness to the unthinkable. The war constituted a central experience for these men: an experience that needed to be put into words. In other words, war became experience when it could be told. Consequently, many testimonies were built around

two complementary ideas: war as tragedy and soldiers as victims (Smith 2007, 1).

The concepts of tragedy and its victims created a mental landscape of the war for many years. If, for example, we read *Under Fire (Le Feu)* by Henri Barbusse, written in 1916 (Barbusse 1916) or *Les suppliciés* by René Naegelen, published 11 years later (Naegelen 1927), we find the same analysis of the war. This analysis had political and moral relevance in inter-war France. The expression 'no more war' became a leitmotiv. These veterans' testimonies raise the question as to whether the witness should be seen as entirely neutral.

Are these stories a true representation of the war? The question is an important one. For civilians, novels or memoirs were the only way to imagine the conflict and to draw its outlines. Writing served as a way to rebuild the sense of community destroyed by the war; giving civilians and soldiers the opportunity to create a new social link (Waintrater 2004, 67).

The study of testimony then, is haunted by the question of authenticity and empirical truth. Tim O'Brien, a Vietnam war veteran, explains this problem clearly. In his book, *The things they carried*, he writes about the difficulty of telling a true war story: 'In any war story, but especially a true one, it's difficult to separate what happened from what seemed to happen. What seems to happen becomes its own happening and had to be told that way' (O'Brien 1998, 71).

However hard these difficulties between reality and its perception might have been, some veterans of the First World War did try to provide a true landscape of war. Jean Norton Cru was one of these veterans. A professor of French literature in Williamston College, USA before the war, he served in the French

Territorial Army between 1914 and 1917, supplying the front lines and repairing trenches after battles or bombardments. Only twice did he take any direct part in combat. From February 1917 onward, he served as an interpreter in the British and US armies.

Norton Cru had a lot of time during the war to read war novels. Indeed, the French Territorial Army often worked at night and stayed far away from the front-line during the day. During the war, Norton Cru used this reading to differentiate true stories from false ones and to establish an objective knowledge. This ambition – or mission – emerged again after the War. For him, literature represented a complete landscape.

The telling of the true war shaped this landscape – a war without legend or heroic emphasis, and where fear played a leading role. This meant the creation of disillusionment with the traditional romantic image of the war (Harari 2005, 43) and its presentation in objective terms. Such was the purpose of Norton Cru's book project, *Témoins* (Norton Cru 1929). Many veterans recognised their own experience in this book – an experience they did not often find in official or military histories. As such, the work quickly became the literary equivalent of a 'site of remembrance'. *Témoins* was published in 1929 and was the result of the criticism of 251 French war novels.

This paper aims to show how Norton Cru created his landscape of war. The analysis will be concentrated on the process of creation. How did Norton Cru build his critical work? Methodological options will be defined in order, first, to understand how Norton Cru read a war novel; and second, to find out if his own experience of war was present in his work.

How did Norton Cru read a war novel? *Wooden Crosses* as a case study

Norton Cru classified the testimonies he read as diaries, memories, thoughts, letters and novels. He favoured war books written by fighting men. For each document, Norton Cru gave a short biography of the author. He made a point of noting his military and war career. How did Norton Cru collect this information? After the reading of a book, he would send his author a questionnaire that requested personal information (name, job, date of birth) and details about life in the trenches. He expected information

about dates and places to be given in minute detail.

Precision about dates and places was especially important for Norton Cru as it was the basis for, or the foundation of, his search for truth. Indeed, the author of *Témoins* was influenced by the literary school of French criticism, which was prominent at the end of the 19th century. This school had the scientific ambition – in the context of Positivism – of looking for truth in novels. Norton Cru acquired this methodological heritage and it was a key starting point in his charting of the landscape of war. So, the work of Norton Cru is a work based on truth. For him, the witness has a moral duty: to tell a true war story. But how did the author of *Témoins* distinguish good testimony from bad?

The analysis of the construction of his criticism paves the way to new interpretations. It is our objective to make an archaeological reading of the book *Témoins* by tracing our way back to the primary documents on which it was based, focusing on the famous novel by Roland Dorgelès, *Wooden Crosses (Les Croix de Bois)*, published just a year after the end of the war (Dorgelès 1919). Norton Cru made many readings of this book, from several perspectives. The first reading consisted in underlining the places and the dates that Dorgelès mentioned. He underlined, for example, the name of the city of Charleroi, and used a red crayon in order to note down everything related to fighting conditions. On another page he underlined a passage describing the consequences of a shell explosion.

The most important thing for Norton Cru was to find the way the story was shaped and told. In looking for the description of places, dates or war events, however, we meet the first problem in his methodology. A significant part of the analysed corpus is constituted by novels. Yet the novel is a literary genre which does not really lay great store by accuracy. His search for the true elements is written down in the book. Norton Cru wrote the different stages of the story on the table of contents. His goal was to restore the coherence and to reintroduce meaning into a logical narrative. This first stage is a deliberate search for the factual truth. He synthesised this search on the first pages of the book, where he wrote all the topographic data and their page references.

Norton Cru followed this methodological approach by identifying all the errors contained in the text. This second step of the criticism probably came during the analysis of a second book. Here, Norton Cru introduced intertextuality in his work. He linked all the descriptions inside the book and used external references. He also linked the novel by Dorgelès to *Under Fire* written by Henri Barbusse. We can characterise this method of reading as a network reading.

He then listed all the factual errors. He noted 50 errors in *Wooden Crosses*. They are not classified but counted page by page. The published critique, *Témoins,* has the same shape. In *Témoins*, Norton Cru picked out all the errors and sometimes gave a commentary. So, ostensibly, there is no difference between the primary work and the published version. But, in fact, it is more complicated than this. The errors noted in *Wooden Crosses* can be grouped into three types: technical, literary tropes and experience of war.

The technical errors are errors about armament (for example, an anachronistic reference to the presence of a steel helmet in the French army in February 1915), military events, places, or technical impossibilities (the length of a shot for example). Such errors can be easily checked. They express the methodological approach of Norton Cru, inherited from the French literary movement. The literary turns are the literary fantasies of the author. This refers to unlikely scenarios created in order to catch the attention or the emotion of the reader. Metaphors or symbols were often part of this category. Because they looked untrue or unbelievable, Norton Cru classified them as lies. He found a deep inconsistency between telling the truth and writing novels. For Norton, novels could not access the truth in and of itself.

The last group of mistakes consists of war experience. The author of *Témoins* used his own experience to tell the truth from the lies. This method, however, had no objectivity. It was founded on his individual perception of the war, which was based on his own feelings and on his own culture of war. Theoretically, this latter category is less present in the critic's work than the other two. Indeed, Norton Cru did his best to explain his objective method in *Témoins*. The following analysis, however, illustrates how Norton Cru faced a dilemma. The proportion of errors noted by referring to his own war experience made up most of the mistakes that he noted.

The idea of *Témoins* as a 'true' landscape of war collapsed. So how did he turn his experi-

ence from a personal point of view to objectivity? What he did was to translate his own war experience through the category of technical errors. The number of technical inconsistencies suddenly increased. So the errors by Dorgelès could not be questioned because all veterans of the First World War were able to say that one thing or another was not true. Norton Cru succeeded here in transforming individual experience into collective agreement. Our analysis of the methodological approach used by Norton Cru reveals an original conception of the reading. The 251 testimonies contained in the novels contributed to the creation of a landscape of war. In this landscape, Norton Cru tried to say what was true and what was an error, as if the culture of war could be one and only, and as if all soldiers shared the same vision or the same analysis of the war.

This methodological approach – and this question of how Norton Cru read a war book – raises another issue. Despite his hard work and his intention to be objective, the filter of his personal experience gave him a perspective from which it was impossible to escape. What was his personal experience of war?

The prism of the war experience

We have seen how Norton Cru created a literary landscape of war based on a specific methodology, in which his own experience played a major part. In *Témoins*, however, he preferred to play down his role as critic by highlighting a scientific approach. Many veterans agreed on this depiction of the war. As a result, *Témoins* has become a symbolic site of remembrance and offers a homogeneous vision of war.

In this paper we have described the foundations of this vision. By following Norton Cru's methodology, we have attempted to understand his experience of war, and through this approach have been able to use some of the same techniques he himself used. Questions remain, however, about how Cru actually put together his own landscape of war. How was it created? What was Norton Cru's experience of war? These questions have been made easier to address by the recent publication of his war letters (Norton Cru 2007).

The letters give us an opportunity to link the war to the creation of the book. It is important, however, that the letters are not read as the basis of *Témoins*. The book may appear simple but is actually a formidable and ambitious endeavour; singular and unique in its attempt to cover all French testimonies of the war. Before Norton Cru, no one had done this and no one has attempted it since. Furthermore, the personality of the author contained in *Témoins* may differ significantly from the author contained in the letters. The book was published 11 years after the war and in this context, Norton Cru's understanding and vision of events could have changed considerably.

How then, do we read the wartime letters without being contaminated by this latter vision? One must focus on the soldier's experience and not be confined merely to a search for traces of the genesis of the book. Why apply this method? Because *Témoins* was not rooted in the trenches. It was in fact a little while later, in 1922 when Norton Cru came back to Verdun, that he was struck by the site of remembrance of the First World War (Vogel 1961, 50–51).

Norton Cru wrote 243 letters or postcards between August 1914 and April 1919 to his family in France. Almost two-thirds of these letters were written during his period in the trenches. This part of the correspondence is very interesting. It tells us that Norton Cru was rarely directly involved in combat. Only twice – once in June 1916 in Verdun, and once in Champagne in January 1917 – did he participate in battle. These experiences represent a real break in his correspondence. The analysis of the writing shows that Norton Cru changed his expression. He used the word 'we' less and less and replaced it with 'I' instead. Indeed, the perception of the war became more individual and less collective.

As well as the content of the correspondence, we have also examined the nature of the subject and his attitudes toward the war. Did his feelings change between mobilisation in August 1914 and the end of the war? Like many French soldiers Norton Cru expressed consent, but unlike others this did not waver during the course of the war. He never questioned his involvement in the conflict and consistently believed he had a part to play in obtaining victory for the Allied forces: there is no evidence of the increasing demoralisation that affected many of his comrades in the French army or on the home front. In his letters we see a separation between the home front and the soldiers' world. This separation, however, is not always clear and pure. His letters are full of allusions to rumours coming from the home front and propagated by newspapers, such as the German atrocities committed in Belgium in 1914. The integration of the rumour is probably a way of reconciling French brutalities. Dehumanising of the enemy made up for our own atrocities. This is perhaps a way of accepting and condoning the killing in 1915 of German prisoners of war (Norton Cru 2007, 102).

The narrative process used here is very telling. It illustrates how some dimensions of the war such as violence and brutalisation were referred to in euphemisms. But was Norton Cru's wartime perception and experience unique or did it parallel that of other soldiers? The comparison with the correspondence of another territorial soldier, the French historian, Jules Isaac, is instructive here and helps us understand the soldier Norton Cru (Isaac 2004). A count of names of peers quoted in the letters of both men suggests that Norton Cru had little social life in the trenches. While Isaac regularly mentions eight associates, Cru speaks of only two. Comparison also highlights the significance of the Protestant faith of the author of *Témoins*. Norton Cru lived the war as an intense personal experience. His Protestantism was strengthened in war. In almost three-quarters of the 249 letters written during the period he alluded to religion. It is deeper than a revival caused by the war. It is the result of a particular vision of the conflict: he sees a redeeming dimension to the fighting and considers it is a divine test. It seems that Norton Cru certainly had his own very specific perspective and interpretation of the conflict.

Did this perspective change? By analysing the themes developed in the letters (and the language used), it is clear that there was indeed a marked change in 1917. Before this date, the letters were full of observations about the living conditions in the trenches: he emphasised the mud, the food and the cold. After he had been involved in battle, however, nature, walking and his personal meditation became the new emphasis. Norton Cru became less materialistic and more spiritual. This exploration of his own faith had major consequences after the war. The author can be recognised as a moral witness because his vision of the war was filtered through his Protestantism (Winter 2007, 470).

The correspondence of Norton Cru clearly reveals that Norton Cru changed during the time he spent as a participant in the war. Two characteristics did remain constant though: consent and faith. Significantly, these are two features that we do not find in *Témoins*. They are totally suppressed from the book, although they represent his conceptual mapping of the war.

The methodology we have adopted in this analysis is based on a precise reading of the correspondence. In identifying a clear narrative break, we can conclude that 1917 is a landmark. The chronological break marks a defining experience for Norton Cru. Norton Cru fought in only two actions, this direct experience of combat amounted to less than one month out of 29 months spent in the trenches. It was, however, enough to significantly affect the mapping of his landscape of war. When he participated in combat, he entered the soldier's world. With this experience, he could build a collective culture of war that was shared by all soldiers. This is reflected in the inclusion in *Témoins* of a critique of Erich Maria Remarque's *All quiet on the western front* (Remarque 1929). Norton Cru wanted to make the landscape of war clear. For him literary criticism was the way to build a European soldiers' history.

This analysis has offered some insights into the relationship between individual experience and the narrative process led by objectivity. *Témoins* is an extraordinary example of this contradiction. Norton Cru's war experience certainly plays more of a leading role in the creation of *Témoins* than the methodological construction inherited from the French literary school. The book's vision of the war aims to describe the true face of the war to civilians and veterans. There is, however, another agenda. Norton Cru never belonged completely to the veterans' community and the book appears to provide him with an opportunity to realise this link – to integrate into this world. Fear and duty are the main components of this realistic drawing of the war. This mixing explains the success as well as the controversial place of *Témoins* in modern history.

Many veterans found their stories in this book. During the inter-war period, the French official history denied a role for ordinary soldiers in recounting the war. Only strategic or diplomatic views counted, as shown in Pierre Renouvin's 1927 study (Renouvin 1927). The objective of *Témoins* was to recall the soldiers' history and to differentiate the true from the false. This explains why *Témoins* has become a real site of remembrance for the veterans' community – one which holds the brainwashing of official versions of history in contempt. The book helped foster a collective identity, particu-

larly for the soldiers who were unable to verbalise or otherwise convey their experience of war. It was an attempt to resolve the problem of the unspeakable and to reconcile individual testimony and public collective memory.

Témoins has an ambiguous status today, because testimony is often regarded as a stumbling block in the French modern history of the First World War. The discussion revolves around whether testimony is in fact the best way to understand soldiers and their culture. One of the questions is to determine whether resilience of the men in the trenches was the result of consent or of military constraint. For some historians though, the work of Norton Cru is an important historical object. He is seen as representative of his era, and regarded as a war witness like any other. Whatever the view of the scholar, the book is clearly considered an important reference for many historians (Rousseau 2003).

This French debate cripples the analysis and understanding of *Témoins*. In order to get past this discussion, the book should no longer been seen as an icon. This way of contemplating history undermines the fact that every literary work is the result of the singular experience of its author, especially when it deals with an intimate experience, such as war. The studies of the American veterans' Vietnam war testimonies prove that, behind the form of the telling, similarities exist between stories of war (Herzog 1992). These similarities – such as the search for truth – are ways to read *Témoins*. So, to introduce a 'cross-chronological' approach is fundamental if we want to understand how Norton Cru's testimonial landscape of the Great War was constructed.

Resumé

Comprendre un lieu de mémoire: une archéologie de *Témoins* de Jean Norton Cru

La Grande Guerre fut rapidement perçue par les contemporains comme un événement exceptionnel tant par sa durée, sa violence que par son caractère total. Acteurs directs du conflit, les hommes mobilisés ont alors ressenti le besoin de narrer leur expérience par le biais de la littérature. La guerre 1914-1918 rend ainsi inédite l'ampleur de la diffusion du témoignage combattant, inaugurant à la même occasion l'ère du témoin qui caractérise tout le XXème siècle. Afin de démêler les vrais récits des faux et dans un souci de construction historique, un ancien soldat français mobilisé dans les troupes territoriales, Jean Norton Cru, s'est attaché dans son essai *Témoins* à la critique de plus de deux cent cinquante ouvrages de guerre publiés en France entre 1915 et 1928. Son ambition consiste à présenter le combat sous son aspect le plus réaliste, dénué de toute légende ou héroïsation. Mais, l'analyse de l'ouvrage conduit à nuancer la portée de cette volonté, et invite à intégrer l'expérience combattante de Norton Cru comme prisme de la critique.

Dans cette perspective d'étude, *Témoins* constitue un paysage de guerre unique en son genre. Norton Cru crée, à travers son œuvre, un paysage mental, lequel donne accès à une représentation de l'expérience de la guerre des tranchées. Celle-ci s'appuie la littérature de guerre, conçue comme une géographie symbolique. S'inscrivant dans le contexte politique et historiographique des années 1920 qui occulte la parole combattante, l'ouvrage entend dégager, derrière le propre vécu de son auteur, une expérience uniforme, communément partagée. La réalisation d'une histoire européenne des combattants de 14-18 est au cœur des préoccupations de Norton Cru. Cela explique pourquoi *Témoins* est devenu un lieu de mémoire pour nombre d'anciens soldats, pour lesquels la guerre demeure une expérience indicible. Ainsi, au travers de l'analyse critique de l'ouvrage de R. Dorgelès, *Les Croix de Bois*, notre contribution s'interroge sur les modalités de création de ce paysage que *Témoins* à la volonté de cartographier.

Notre approche impose de travailler, en quelque sorte, à la manière d'un archéologue. Elle consiste à éliminer d'abord la couche de surface, ici l'œuvre sous sa forme publiée, pour atteindre et restituer le paysage mental de Norton Cru. Cette méthode met en lumière les pratiques de lecture et d'annotations de l'auteur. Sa culture de guerre affleure régulièrement lors de l'analyse critique des ouvrages, mais se trouve pourtant complètement gommée dans *Témoins*. Cette tentative d'objectivation originale – car elle ne passe par le témoignage individuel, modèle classique de la narration – n'est pas sans annoncer l'autre grande ère testimoniale combattante, la guerre du Vietnam.

List of references

Audoin-Rouzeau, S 1993 *La guerre des enfants. 1914–1918*. Paris: Armand Colin,

Audoin-Rouzeau, S and Becker, A 2000 *Comprendre la Grande Guerre*. Paris: Gallimard

Barbusse, H 1916 *Le Feu (Journal d'une escouade)*. Paris: E. Flammarion

Dorgelès, R 1919 *Les croix de bois*. Paris: Albin Michel

Furet, F 1995 *Le passé d'une illusion*. Essai sur l'idée communiste au XXe siècle. Paris: Robert Laffont

Harari, Y N 2005 'Martial Illusions: War and Disillusionment in Twentieth-century and Renaissance Military Memoirs', *The Journal of Military History*, **69**, n° 1, 43–72

Herzog, T 1992 *Vietnam war stories: Innocence lost*. New York: Routledge

Isaac, J 2004 *Jules Isaac, un historien dans la Grande Guerre: lettres et carnets. 1914–1917*. Paris: Armand Colin

Naegelen, R 1927 *Les suppliciés*. Paris: Editions Baudinière

Norton Cru, J 1929 *Témoins: essai d'analyse et de critique des souvenirs des combattants édités en français de 1915 à 1918*. Paris: Les Etincelles

Norton Cru, J 2007 *Lettres du front et d'Amérique: 1914–1919*. Aix-en-Provence: Publications de l'Université de Provence

O'Brien, T 1998 *The things they carried*. New York: Broadway Books

Remarque, E-M 1929 *A l'ouest rien de nouveau*. Paris: Stock

Renouvin, P 1927 *La Crise européenne et la Grande guerre (1904–1918)*. Paris: Presses Universitaires de France

Rousseau, F 2003 *Le procès des Témoins de la Grande Guerre: L'affaire Norton Cru*. Paris: Editions du Seuil

Smith, LV 2007 *The embattled self: French soldiers' testimony of the Great War*. Ithaca: Cornell University Press

Vogel, H 1961 citing letter of Jean Norton Cru (22/08/1922) in 'Jean Norton Cru', *Annales de la Faculté des Lettres et Sciences Humaines d'Aix*, **35**, 50–5

Waintrater, R 2004 'Le pacte testimonial' in. Chiantaretto, J-F (ed) *Témoignage et trauma. Implications psychoanalytiques*. Dunod: Paris

Wieviorka, A 1998 *L'ère du Témoin*. Paris: Plon

Winter, J 2007 'The "moral witness" and the two world wars', *Ethnologie française*, **3**, XXXVII, 467–74

1. Methods of investigation: textual, visual, material

'Cood bay Forst Zinna': Film, art and archaeology

ANGUS BOULTON

The prolonged Cold War conflict was played out principally in secret, with major decisions taken behind closed doors and training routinely undertaken inside the numerous military complexes throughout Europe and beyond. The overriding need to build for nuclear confrontation has left a legacy of redundant buildings, installations and damaged landscapes. To this day, these sites remain loaded with significance.

Artists have recently become familiar contributors to the practice of recording the contemporary environment, and the places of conflict within it, so it is perhaps inevitable that a search for unusual locations eventually led them to some of the decommissioned installations from the Cold War. As inquisitive people, artists frequently seek to focus on the world around them, often creating interpretations from previously unforeseen perspectives. The question here is how might these 'artistic' appraisals add to the varied interpretations of sites from this period of history.

Does the inherent freedom and curiosity that artists embrace preclude them from academic discourse? Although I am not uncomfortable with the opinion that artists are separate practitioners, sometimes working alone towards personal goals, their input is becoming increasingly appreciated as having equal validity, and is regarded as a challenging antidote to those methods with more established historiographical justifications.

As a filmmaker and photographer engaged in examining the Soviet legacy in eastern Europe, my projects are merely findings that attempt to unravel the reality I encounter. The purpose of this chapter is to comment on an example of my own artistic practice, discussing the aims and methodologies I adopted to create the short film *Cood bay Forst Zinna*, a personal interpretation of one particular Soviet barracks complex. It is hoped that through the following explanation, we might gain a range of insights into alternative approaches to investigating this rich subject matter. While acknowledging the less restrictive constraints an artist is able to work within, the text also reflects on some of the questions and problems that arise as a result. Following a short film synopsis and description of the location, I will explain the reasons for undertaking such a project through the medium of film.

Film synopsis

Viewed from the window of a passing train, an installation momentarily becomes visible in a forest clearing. Approached on the ground, this large site, obscured by a grey concrete wall, appears abandoned, cut off from the outside world (*see* Figures 1.1–1.21).

Inside, one encounters a bewildering complex of accommodation blocks, exercise areas and assault courses. A neglected children's playground and forlorn fountain, a group of farm buildings and animal enclosures all lie unused and overgrown. Walking further, towards the perimeter wall, various sports and recreational facilities become recognisable. An empty, crumbling swimming pool with faded Olympic rings, a football pitch overgrown with birch saplings, assorted gymnasia with peeling murals; all facilities that might indicate the site of a derelict sports academy.

However, as the camera continues to explore, a stranded armoured personnel carrier appears, parked outside the gates of a large garage and workshop area surrounded by curious teaching aids and murals in a Cyrillic script. Finally, on entering a vandalised room bedecked with faded black and white

Fig 1.1 (far left) Forst Zinna.
© Angus Boulton

Fig 1.2 (left) Approach road, perimeter fence.
© Angus Boulton

Fig 1.3 (far left) Children's playground.
© Angus Boulton

Fig 1.4 (left) Farm enclosure.
© Angus Boulton

Fig 1.5 (far left) Accommodation.
© Angus Boulton

Fig 1.6 (left) Gymnasium I.
© Angus Boulton

Fig 1.7 (far left) Swimming pool.
© Angus Boulton

Fig 1.8 (left) Mushroom cloud mural.
© Angus Boulton

Fig 1.9 (far left) Barrack blocks.
© Angus Boulton

Fig 1.10 (left) Outdoor cinema.
© Angus Boulton

13

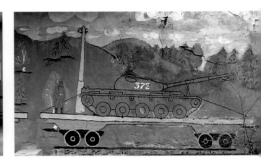

*Fig 1.11 (above)
Gymnasium II mural detail.
© Angus Boulton
Fig 1.12 (above centre)
Gymnasium II.
© Angus Boulton
Fig 1.13 (above right) Tank
training mural.
© Angus Boulton
Fig 1.14 (right) Underwater
tank training.
© Angus Boulton
Fig 1.15 (far right) Garage
complex.
© Angus Boulton*

*Fig 1.16 (right) Library.
© Angus Boulton*

*Fig 1.17 (far right) History
of the unit museum.
© Angus Boulton*

*Fig 1.18 (right) Officers
saluting, museum.
© Angus Boulton*

*Fig 1.19 (far right) Podium,
parade ground.
© Angus Boulton*

*Fig 1.20 (right) Soviet
Armed Forces mural.
© Angus Boulton*

*Fig 1.21 (far right) 'Cood
bay Forst Zinna'. © Angus
Boulton*

photographs, the initial impression begins to appear misleading as the full nature and actual purpose of Forst Zinna becomes apparent.

Historical background

The Land of Brandenburg, surrounding Berlin, contained more than half the total number of Soviet military bases inside the former East Germany (GDR), accommodating some 250,000 troops and additional personnel. While almost all these locations originally date from the Prussian or Nazi periods, many underwent further expansion once in Soviet hands. Indeed, over 200,000 hectares within Brandenburg were requisitioned for military use, so that by 1990 almost 9 per cent of the region appeared on maps as *Sperrgebiete*, 'restricted areas' (Brandenburgische Boden Gesellschaft mbH, 1996).

Many bases, within or next to towns, have been converted into housing, offices or centres of light industry. Installations in more remote locations have simply been closed off and left to slowly decay. Initial development was further complicated by the absence of any form of occupational records for the barracks following handover to the German authorities by the departing troops. Most sites had been in military hands for much of the last century and although the buildings are frequently of historic value, much of the outlying land remains dangerous and problematic. The vast training areas and firing ranges have been fenced off as prospective nature reserves, to which access may eventually be permitted along a few designated safe footpaths, and only after the lengthy and expensive task of munitions clearance has been thoroughly undertaken – usually to a depth of four metres.

One of the largest restricted areas lies south of Berlin, and formed the northern border to a complex of bases in and around the Prussian garrison town of Jüterbog. The main element stationed here was the 32nd Poltava Armoured Division, part of the 20th Guards Army. The division contained roughly 11,600 people, with not only motor-rifle and armoured regiments along with the normal ancillary and support services, but also everything from missile, artillery, transport, and signals units to catering, schools, shops and a hospital. The 172nd and 439th Special Helicopter Regiments were based at Damm, west of Jüterbog, To the north, at Altes Lager, there was a Flying Academy and large adjoining airfield for the 833rd Fighter Regiment (Dimitriev et al 1994).

Forst Zinna

At the eastern edge of this cluster of bases are the barracks at Forst Zinna, until 1992 home to the 57th Construction Brigade and 118th Armoured Training Regiment. Both units formed an integral part within the overall group, and although directly subordinate to the main headquarters in Wünsdorf, they were administered to some extent by the authorities in Jüterbog.

The training regiment was responsible for instructing the new conscripts (six monthly intakes) and NCOs to operate tanks as drivers, commanders and gunners, using the large training area opposite the base. The construction brigade was responsible for major projects throughout the GDR for the Western Group of the Soviet Armed Forces, including accommodation blocks, training facilities and command bunkers, and was divided into project teams that varied in size, depending on the tasks involved. All told, the combined military force in this particular region was believed to be around 40,000. Having spent several months photographing the other buildings and compounds within the region, I walked along the railway tracks towards Berlin one morning in October 2000, and arrived outside the remote and remarkably intact barracks of Forst Zinna.

Artistic practice

The depiction of 'trace' appears as a recurring theme running through most of the film and photographic projects I have undertaken. It is the representation of these traces of human presence, whether past or present, that frequently forms the focus of a style of photography, and more recently film, aiming to interpret aspects of recent history, memory, and a sense of place. The still imagery is formal, often symmetrical and could be viewed as architectural or documentary in nature, a recognised style that lends itself to the process of recording. However, by creating collections of similar images, and exhibiting them in series, the intention is to use repetition as a means of exploring further this sense of place. The deceptively simple results aim to draw more from the viewer than a basic visual document might allow, whether by the triggering of personal memory or other, frequently unforeseen, associations.

Military bases, by their nature unfamiliar to most of us, provide intriguing locations in which to experiment within this field of artistic practice. Initially, my aim was to raise awareness in the West of this largely forgotten legacy. The Soviet military left behind vast expanses of damaged land. Many of the restricted areas that lie at the heart of the hundreds of bases scattered throughout Europe remain, almost two decades after the end of communism. Following repeated visits to a variety of different locations, it became apparent that one universal feature was becoming increasingly difficult to convey through still imagery alone; the ever present and overwhelming dead atmosphere one encounters while picking through the detritus of other peoples' lives. A move into film, and the opportunity to explore the dimension of sound, whether ambient or by the addition of music, was a logical step to take in the pursuit of a more thorough appraisal. With this medium one could lead audiences on a tour through a Soviet military installation.

To begin with I adopted a style I was already familiar with, one in which the equipment is used primarily like a still camera, mounted on a tripod and left to run, ostensibly to record the location and capture 'atmosphere'. The reduced field of view means panning is necessary, both to convey more information and to move the narrative forward. The final film intercuts static scenes with sequences of movement, and intentionally engages with a more meditative approach, one that deliberately withholds the clear answers more often found in mainstream documentaries. Scenes unfold before the viewers' eyes, the wind might rustle through the leaves and trees, rain drips from a collapsing ceiling or a garage door slams, but usually very little in the form of what might be recognised as 'action' takes place. The intention is solely to show what lies in front of the camera lens with minimal intervention. Scenes cross-dissolve into one another slowly yet continuously.

Hopefully, the cumulative effect of this meditative approach is to reach a point at which the viewer forgets the presence of the camera and imagines the recent past and those who once lived and worked in Forst Zinna. In essence, therefore, this is deliberately pared down film-making. Dispensing with the captions or dialogue present in documentary film, it challenges the audience to create their own stories from viewing what may be an unfamiliar location. My overriding intention is to inform through the act of simply showing what is there, using a style that is part of growing field of film-making – somewhere between strict documentary and artist film and video.

Exhibiting photographs allows the viewer to take in images at their leisure, perhaps returning to those of interest for closer inspection, a process referred to by Roland Barthes in *Camera Lucida* as the punctum (Barthes, 1980). By contrast, the sometimes didactic nature of film can prove a more difficult medium in which to work, being both productive and limiting in equal measure. Although film enables artists to construct specific narratives, with this style of minimal, linear film-making, it is essential to be able to hold the viewers' attention throughout. Assuming that the audience arrives with a degree of visual sophistication, and will search for clues and signifiers within the various scenes as the film unfolds, finding a preferred level of information dissemination becomes fundamental. Having spoken to security guards, questioned locals and researched the history of Forst Zinna in detail before filming commenced, the resulting piece is understandably informed and influenced by this background knowledge. Therefore, not only is *Cood bay Forst Zinna* an exercise in exploring the recent past by revealing the present, but also a subjective appraisal of a particular location, albeit one that strives merely to observe.

Following careful planning and using notes made during a detailed photographic survey undertaken during the preceding October visit, filming took place over two days in March 2001. Working to a tight schedule and making use of the fortuitous contrast in weather conditions, I deliberately shot footage of the extensive sports and recreational facilities in the pleasant spring sunshine, saving the more overtly militaristic imagery for the rainy gloom of the following day. By adopting a quasi forensic style, one that both replicates my methodical process of investigation and reflects my initial exploration, I planned to mix carefully chosen restricted views, akin to still imagery, with the short panning sequences. In this way, I could steer the viewer through a succession of unfolding scenes, primarily in an effort to trigger a more personal interpretation through memory and association. Although the film is initially misleading to those unfamiliar with the landscape of a Soviet military base, the final sequence and musical accompaniment reflects what actually came to my mind, while I stood alone in silence, contemplating the photos peeling from the walls of the unit's small museum.

It was during the editing process, while compiling sections of the static footage and calculating the specific length of individual scenes, that another positive aspect of a filmic approach became apparent. Although it can be argued that filming or photographing an empty military base can never produce an authentic impression of its former occupancy, what actually remains can contribute to the creation of a valuable interpretation, admittedly representative of a certain moment in time, but often exhibiting unexpected results.

A photograph is recognised as a representation of an instant in time and is therefore rooted in the moment of registration, whereas this style of filming is concerned with the subject of time through an exploration of the tension between the 'then and now'. The carefully selected views and vistas, both interior and exterior, moving and static, could be said to loosely comment on the relationship between time halted and continuous time, reflecting the past and present. Therefore, while the static scenes correspond to the documentation of recent history, the periods of movement, the panning sequences, equate more to the present day experience, to the 'now'; the end result can be viewed as both an historical document and a contemporary interpretation.

When artists choose to address sites from the Cold War, a wide range of interpretations will result. Their projects employ alternative methodologies and are undertaken from somewhat oblique and often unforeseen standpoints. These differing approaches to the question of how and why places of conflict are recorded, prove worthy of consideration within an important and growing field of study. Artists are, however, frequently more concerned with the philosophical questions a site imparts rather than the physical nature it exhibits.

A visual document of an intriguing location, recognisably military in origin, overloaded with metaphors and yet largely forgotten now, Cood bay Forst Zinna is my impression of a place and the small part it played in recent history. The film could be seen as a comment on the death of an ideology. In hindsight, the Cold War can now be viewed as a dangerous game played out in secret, with set rules, at certain times and at specific locations. Moreover, in the light of global events today, and at a time when the rulebook appears all but torn up, witnessing such places allows us the opportunity to reflect on the recent past, perhaps with an equivocal tinge of sadness.

This feeling just might have been uppermost in the mind of the soldier who poignantly wrote 'Goodbye' [Cood bay] in pencil on a bedroom wall, shortly before setting off for home and an uncertain future.

List of references

Barthes, R 1980 *Camera Lucida*. Paris: Editions du Seuil

Boulton, A 2001 *Cood bay Forst Zimma*. DV film, colour, 19 mins, private distribution

Brandenburgische Boden Gesellschaft mbH 1996 *Geschäftsbericht 1995*

Dimitriev, S, Fadin, K, Fjodorov, V, Furs, A, Potapov, A and Timachkov, D 1994 *Sowjetische Truppen in Deutschland 1945–1994*. Moscow: Junge Garde Verlag

1. Methods of investigation: textual, visual, material

Recording landscapes of war

WAYNE D COCROFT

As a first principle, public understanding of any historical site, group of monuments or landscapes is fundamental to their future survival (English Heritage 2003, 3). An appreciation of historic worth should encourage people to value and care for the historic environment, leading to a greater interest and a desire for deeper knowledge. To many people, recent military monuments have negative connotations or are perceived as ugly, yet they have a strong following and many are open to the public. While we might have strong affection for historic townscapes and countryside, many military bases were closed places, where the local populace had little knowledge about their activities. One of the first tasks of any recording project is to document a site so that its historical significance may be understood and assessed.

Discovery

During the 20th century, the century of total war, European states increasingly appropriated large areas of land for military purposes. As mechanised warfare transformed the pace and scale of battle, airfields, a multitude of camps, munitions factories, airfields, test ranges, and ever larger training areas were required. In Britain, by the end of the Second World War, the military directly controlled about 20 per cent of the total land area (Childs 1995, 186). Elsewhere, there was little escape from the traces of war, with ubiquitous civil defence structures and with nearly every factory and workshop given over to the war effort.

Compared to some other types of monuments, modern military sites are some of the best documented places, through written records, maps and plans, ground and air photographs, and the memories of people who served within them. To aid the study of recent military remains, documentary sources can provide a short cut for locating many sites. In the United Kingdom, the National Archives is an invaluable source, providing information on location and historical context.

Many of the methods used to record archaeological monuments are derived from military practice. In England, modern archaeological field recording techniques may be traced back to the founding of the Ordnance Survey in 1791 (Roy 1793; Harley 1975, 145). Similarly, aerial archaeology grew from techniques developed during the world wars and the satellite imagery of the Cold War. The concept of gradual evolution and sequential type series for artefacts was derived from the ideas of Lieutenant-General Pitt Rivers (1827–1900) through his work on the development of the musket (Bowden 1991, 14–22, 95–102, 162).

The archaeological techniques used for recording modern military sites are similar to those used to record the monuments of earlier periods. It is, however, their scale, complexity, and the myriad of secondary sources relating to them, that make them some of the most challenging monuments to document. Many are so large that they might be regarded as designed landscapes in their own right, often comprising hundreds of buildings and other features. They were often closed and secret places with little published information on their past activities. Some buildings may have architectural merit or represent the remains of complex technological systems, where, in rare instances, plant and machinery might survive. In some cases there may be a seemingly overwhelming amount of documentation, as well as the possibility of speaking to former service personnel.

Recording levels

At the outset of any research, a clear understanding of a project's aims will inform the level of recording to be undertaken. English Heritage (England's statutory heritage protection body) has recording guidelines for historic buildings and landscapes that use the concept of staged levels (English Heritage 2006, 13–16 and 2007, 23–24). The simplest level of record is a basic identification record that may form part of wider national or regional studies. The highest level of records will often include detailed drawings, descriptions, extensive research and historical contextualisation.

In considering modern defence sites these guidelines may need to be adapted. Often original drawings may be available and if these can be obtained they represent a considerable saving in time and effort, although they may need to be redrawn to bring out key constructional, chronological or functional details. They may also need to be updated to record any modifications to a site or structure. Reduced to its essence a good record will comprise a combination of description, interpretation and analysis (English Heritage 2006, 3).

Photos from the air

Aerial survey is one of the most effective methods for locating many former military sites. During the First World War, air photography underwent a rapid evolution, and many of the early archaeological practitioners learnt their skills in military service. Likewise, during the Second World War, there was a massive growth in the application of air photography (Hegarty and Newsome, 2007, 4–10). In Britain, large collections of oblique and vertical photographs are readily available through the National Monuments Record. These are being used by English Heritage's National Mapping Programme to plot all known archaeological sites, including traces of wartime activity.

Where detailed stereographic photography (a technique whereby two images are combined to produce a three-dimensional view) is available, it may be used to build up detailed plots of defensive landscapes (Hegarty and Newsome, 2007, 54–62). It is particularly valuable where no maps are available, but it also forms an important check against documentary sources that may represent proposed, rather than completed, schemes.

Air photographs have also been used to esti-mate the current survival of various monument types. Using documentary sources it has, for example, been possible to locate the 981 heavy anti-aircraft gunsites constructed between 1939 and 1945 (Anderton and Schofield 1999, 11–13). By locating these on air photographs, it was shown that only 57 (5.8 per cent) remained in a relatively complete condition, and this is probably an overestimate as the latest available photography was sometimes 10 or 20 years old. Air photographs have also been invaluable in confirming which post-war anti-aircraft sites were actually built.

TARA – The Aerial Reconnaissance Archive – of air photographs taken by the Allies during the Second World War, now at the Royal Commission on the Ancient Historical Monuments of Scotland in Edinburgh, is a remarkable record of around 10 million images of the effect of the war on the European landscape. Wartime German aerial reconnaissance photography is another source, which was eagerly seized by the Allies, especially for its coverage of eastern Europe (Going 2002, 23–32).

Another valuable source of information for the future study of Cold War sites will be declassified satellite photographs, especially the investigation of the installations of the Soviet Union and her allies (Fowler 2008, 714–731). Modern satellite imagery – readily available online – is increasingly becoming a key resource for the rapid assessment of current survival.

Archaeological field recording

Landscape archaeology emphasises the importance of understanding the evolution of the landscape through time, without giving undue weight to a single period or theme. Archaeologists might expect to find traces of 20th century conflict virtually anywhere they work. Most surveys of upland and coastal landscapes will reveal traces of military activity.

At Dunstanburgh Castle, Northumberland, for example, extensive remains of Second World War anti-invasion defences were found around the castle, including pillboxes, weapon pits and a minefield (Oswald et al 2006, 87-91). In Wiltshire, the Salisbury Plain Training Area was acquired by the military in the late 19th century. This has protected it from large-scale cultivation (see Figure 1.22). Restricted access has resulted in a high degree of preservation across its 37,000 hectares, an area roughly

Fig 1.22 Perham Down, Salisbury Plain, Wiltshire: military practice trenches dug into a landscape of prehistoric 'Celtic' fields. © English Heritage CCC 11757/7834

the size of the Isle of Wight. Within it are remains of prehistoric, Romano-British and later field systems, settlements and ritual sites (McOmish *et al* 2002, xv). Here, the archaeologists' initial interest was in the earlier periods. As the survey progressed through aerial reconnaissance and ground survey, however, it was recognised that a century of military training had left its own distinctive and significant marks on this ancient landscape (McOmish *et al* 2002, 137–148).

Despite the wealth of documentary evidence, detailed knowledge about individual sites is often lacking. Elsewhere, records were never created or have subsequently been lost or destroyed. In all these cases, the landscape, and the sites and structures themselves may be our only source of evidence. Even where documentation is available, it often has to be backed up in order to make information accessible to a variety of users.

RAF Perranporth, Cornwall, is a well-preserved Second World War fighter airfield where a number of the fighter pens are designated as scheduled monuments. Here, a survey was required to help decide how to manage the airfield in the future. The existing 1:2500 scale Ordnance Survey map was used as the base plan, to which missing features were added. More detailed diagrams were also produced of the protected fighter pens, and the 1945 building inventory was used to compile a list of the surviving features and their condition (Fletcher and Newman 2002).

In an army range at Chatham, Kent, is an unusual survival of a pre-First World War anti-aircraft site; we believe it may be the world's first purpose-built anti-aircraft position. Exceptionally, given the significance of this site, a specially commissioned reconstruction drawing was produced.

Cold War, people and places

For a few sites, a combination of factors may come together to justify the highest level of recording. These reasons include historic importance, recommendations for statutory protection, management purposes, public presentation, a conservation campaign, and the threat of loss. A group of sites that English Heritage has recorded in this depth are four Cold War era research and development sites, two associated with atomic weapons and two with rocket-testing. At Spadeadam, Cumbria, between 1956 and 1960, resources were harnessed with a 'wartime' urgency to transform 3,000 hectares of desolate moorland into a technological landscape and one of the world's most up-to-date rocket research centres. Its role was to develop Britain's indigenous intermediate-range ballistic missile, Blue Streak. Before testing began, however, the missile programme was cancelled, although work on a joint European civil satellite launcher continued into the early 1970s, before the property passed to the RAF (Tuck and Cocroft 2004; Cocroft and Wilson 2006).

The local defence estate managers needed the documentation to help them understand the significance of the different features of the site, and to influence future development decisions. To create a baseline record, standard recording sheets were produced for each structure, providing at least a Level 1 record for each feature (*see above*). To accompany the record sheets, the main test areas were surveyed with GPS (Global Positioning System). Although some original plans survived, a large-scale point in time survey was required to document current survival and later alterations not recorded on the design drawings (*see* figure 1.23). Also missing from the earlier plans were the remnants of construction features connected with the building of the centre, such as the contractor's gravel sorting plant and the large temporary labour camps. A more significant discovery was the remains of a largely undocumented and abandoned test silo; technology that was later transferred to the United States for the Titan II programme (Cocroft 2006). In exceptional cases, plans and sections were drawn of the most significant structures.

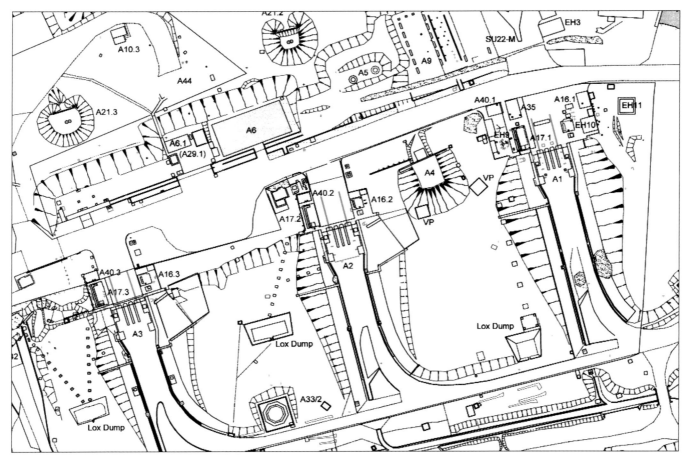

Fig 1.23 RAF Spadeadam, Cumbria: section of the Priorlancy Engine Test Area, surveyed with global positioning surveying equipment.
© English Heritage

Another important source of information is the memories of the personnel who served on these bases and of the people who lived around them. The integration of place and personal memory is a particularly potent form of record, one that is technically achievable, but often beyond the resources of most projects. At Spadeadam, English Heritage worked closely with an oral history project being run by the Tullie House Museum, Carlisle. This revealed the opportunities brought to the area through Rolls-Royce technical apprenticeships, and also the lasting impact on the character of the area through the engineering skills that were spread through the region.

At the Shoeburyness Range (an area on the south side of Foulness Island), Essex, to inform possible statutory protection a detailed documentary study was undertaken to locate sites of possible archaeological interest, which were correlated using a Geographic Information System (GIS). The development of the Atomic Weapons Research Establishment was our primary interest. Air photographic transcription was used to plot the inaccessible remains of earlier land reclamation, as well as agricultural and settlement features. The former Atomic Weapons Research Establishment was recorded using a similar system to the one used at Spadeadam.

Health and safety considerations limited access to areas of ground, building interiors or underground workings at the Shoeburyness project. Due to the highly classified nature of the work undertaken at Foulness, documentation on many of the trials is missing and so, unable to carry out extremely expensive tests, we had to assume that the land and buildings might be contaminated. This restricted our access to hardstanding areas and limited investigation of buildings to visual inspections of their exteriors.

Architectural surveys

Warfare in the 20th century gave rise to a huge variety of new building types, often making full use of products of the industrial age. During the Boer War (1899–1901) corrugated iron blockhouses and barbed-wire entanglements were constructed to dominate roads and railway lines. So too, during the First World War, the front-lines were relatively crude affairs of earth, wood, corrugated iron, barbed wire, and, to a lesser extent, reinforced concrete. This material, which came to the fore for military construction during the late 1930s, has great strength, and structures could be constructed by relatively unskilled labour in a short period of time.

Despite the carnage of the First World War, high architectural standards were maintained in the design of many wartime establishments. At Burton-on-Trent, Staffordshire, the National Machine Gun Factory was built in the style of a large neo-Georgian country house. Correspondingly, in Germany, the main buildings of the new 575-hectare Kirchmoser munitions factory, on the outskirts of Brandenburg, were finished in the ponderous neoclassical style favoured by Prussia. The use of architecture to reflect military pride continued into the interwar period. It is notable that the RAF and the Luftwaffe both chose traditional architectural forms for their administrative and accommodation buildings, while modernist styles predominated in the technical areas.

Grand buildings such as these, dominating their local landscapes, are susceptible to architectural investigations for which established guidance is available (English Heritage 2006). Often, especially where standardised building types are concerned, site plans and drawn records may survive in archives. To understand more specialised structures, an archaeological approach analysing the proportion of space allocated to different tasks and functions, information flow-lines, rank and gender divisions, may have much to offer.

Given the secretive nature of most defence establishments, detailed ground photography is invariably a high priority. This might include general views illustrating the relationship between structures and their setting, along with photographs of individual structures, significant architectural features and, if present, interior fittings. Recording should usually start at the earliest possible moment to inform discussions about possible designation or conservation strategies. Where it is not possible to keep a building, or at least not in its original state, it may be necessary to undertake a broad reconnaissance of a whole site, before identifying buildings or features for more detailed recording.

During the 20th century the internal combustion engine transformed conflict through the development of military aviation, armoured warfare and the mechanisation of military logistics. The armed forces also enthusiastically adopted wireless communication and radar detection. These new technologies created a demand for new building forms, such as aircraft hangars and wireless stations, while some, such as acoustic sound mirrors, represented technological dead ends.

During the Second World War, the rapid development of radar produced a large number of specialist buildings arranged in unique patterns according to the equipment's needs. The growth in the size of military aircraft and the complexity of their avionics was mirrored in the development of the airfield control towers. In the late 1930s these were simple watch offices, whereas a decade or so later, a typical military control tower had evolved into a complex information-processing structure of meteorological, telecommunications, radar and wireless rooms. To speed up internal communication, messages were carried around the building in pneumatic tubes. The growth in electrical airfield lighting demanded further space for control consoles.

This interplay between technology and architecture became most marked during the Cold War. Heavily protected structures, or bunkers, were designed to resist the blast from an atomic bomb and to operate in heavily contaminated environments. Bespoke infrastructure was also required for new weapons systems, such as surface-to-air or long-range missiles.

Characterising RAF Coltishall

An alternative method of approaching large defence sites is through characterisation. Most sites we encounter as archaeologists are empty and deserted places. Through our work we try to reconstruct their development phases, functional relationships between buildings, and their social history. In 2006, the closure of RAF Coltishall, Norfolk, provided a rare opportunity to document a modern airfield before and during closure (Figure 1.24). This project comprised a number of individual pieces of work, and included a photographic characterisation, which sought to portray the activities and use of space on the base, rather than a straightforward record of its architecture and buildings (Cocroft and Cole 2007). A novel feature of this project was the involvement of three visual artists, who, through their films and stills photography, brought a new dimension to our recording. In parallel, a cartographic characterisation project is planned to explore the chronological develop-

ment of the airfield, the relationships between its functional areas and the appearance of different sections of the airfield.

The common images we have of airfields are often restricted to pictures of aircraft being prepared for flight, either in the open or in hangars. If we analyse the activities on the airfield, many of the people who work on an airfield are engaged in light engineering or maintenance tasks, such as engine maintenance and testing, the servicing and repair of electronic equipment, and the maintenance of flight and safety equipment. Behind these people there are stores, catering personnel and laundry services, all of which are conducted on an industrial scale. On a typical airfield during the Second World War, around 17.5 per cent of the personnel were aircrew (Terraine 1985, 4–5). As a reflection of the increasing complexity and lethality of current combat aircraft, a modern fighter airfield might support around 30 fighters and a similar number of pilots. Behind this relatively small number of aircraft you would find a community, including dependants, of around 3,000.

An airfield is not just a place of work. It also provides a home for the personnel, who are arranged in an unusual community, organised and ordered by rank. Housing at Coltishall was strictly allocated according to rank and marital status, ranging from large detached houses for the senior officers to terraced houses for the airmen. Most of the social life of the base revolved around the messes. The officers' mess had the appearance of a gentleman's country club, with elegant reception areas for mess functions. The sergeants' mess was similarly

Fig 1.24 RAF Coltishall, Norfolk: before the base was closed photos were taken to show how the buildings were used.
© English Heritage DP029249

structured, although with subtle differences. These messes also provided accommodation for single personnel. In contrast, the airmen's institute was organised around large communal dining areas with accommodation in adjoining barracks. The interiors display evidence of different social expectations, as the original open barrack rooms have been subdivided to create single or double rooms.

Characterisation is of particular value where a site has the potential for continuing use or reuse. It allows negotiations to take place on how change might be accommodated, while preserving the essential essence of a site (Talbot and Bradley 2006, 43–48). This might include the mix of building materials, site layouts, ornamental planting, spacing and massing of structures. In a more developed form, characterisation might explore the values that different groups of people ascribe to a site: these may go beyond expert historical and technical assessments (Lake *et al* 2006, 49–57).

Murals and graffiti

The recording of military architecture, sites and technology might seem to be a detached and impersonal activity, divorced from human interaction. One almost universal trace we find of the ghosts of these places is through graffiti and murals (Figure 1.25). The prevalence, placing, use, subject matter and tolerance of wall art all provide evidence of distinct cultural traits that may offer many insights into the cultures of different armed forces and the units within them (Cocroft *et al* 2006). In the Soviet army, a force comprising many heterogeneous nationalities, murals were used extensively for training and compulsory political indoctrination.

Art, derived from popular culture, on the noses of aircraft, was a common feature of many wartime American aircraft, and similar images are found dotted across of many of their home bases. In peacetime, decorating aircraft and buildings was frowned upon, and during the Vietnam War it was even banned. After this conflict there were serious concerns about the effectiveness of the United States Air Force. To address these worries 'Project Warrior' was established, to restore pride and an esprit de corps (Glines 1993, 60–65). One simple method of reinforcing unit identity and a bond with aircraft was by promoting the return of painted mascots. This was quickly shown to lead to improved aircraft serviceability.

Murals painted in the semi-private work areas and accommodation blocks are often more revealing about the airmen's lives. They borrow themes from popular contemporary culture, including Superman, Garfield, album

Fig 1.25 Mural at RAF Upper Heyford, Oxfordshire: created in 1978–9 by Kenneth B Gore, this is a particularly elaborate example of artwork that can provide an insight into the cultures within various armed forces.
© English Heritage
AA051444

covers, and even the Simpsons. By careful study of their context, they also reveal how the buildings were used. Official emblems may be found in public areas, whereas others are only visible once a room or area had been entered. Wall art is far less common on RAF bases, although at Coltishall in 1971 a cellar was decorated as the Spitfire Club, and on return from the First Gulf War (1990–91) two hangar doors were painted with large murals.

Summary

One of the characteristics of 20th century military activity was its unprecedented appropriation of vast tracts of land for training areas, permanent installations, temporary camps and fortifications. In many cases the changes were so marked that they have over-written the earlier landscape characteristics of an area. To fully comprehend, and to present, the effect of 20th century total war on modern societies, archaeological methods of air photographic interpretation, field survey, and characterisation have been used to document and understand the impact of military activity. With these techniques there is, nevertheless, a risk that the study of warfare may be reduced to impersonal distribution maps, plans and drawings. While wider landscape studies represent the scale of activities; the built environment of these places reflects the day-to-day human experience of institutionalised life. This might be a munitions factory fronted by a grand, mansion-like administration building or a simple wooden accommodation hut. In rare instances, fragile traces of former occupants might remain in the form of graffiti. Even in a comparatively well-documented era archaeological excavations are able to create narratives for small events, perhaps on a battlefield or in an internment camp (see Brown, page 59). From these contexts mundane objects are able to provide a tangible, and indisputable, link to human suffering during the 20th century.

List of references

Anderton, M and Schofield, J 1999 'Anti-aircraft gunsites – then and now'. *Conservation Bulletin* **36**, 11–13

Bewley, R H and Raczkowski, W (eds) 2002 *Aerial archaeology: developing future practice*. Amsterdam: IOS Press

Bowden, M 1991 *Pitt Rivers: The life and archaeological work of Lieutenant-General Augustus Henry Lane Fox Pitt Rivers, DCL, FRS, FSA*. Cambridge: Cambridge University Press

Cocroft, W D 2006 'The Spadeadam Blue Streak underground launcher facility U1'. *Prospero* **3**, 7–14

Cocroft, W D, Devlin, D, Schofield, J, and Thomas, R J C 2006 *War Art murals and graffiti – military, life power and subversion*. York: Council for British Archaeology

Cocroft, W D and Wilson, L K 2006 'Archaeology and art at Spadeadam Rocket Establishment (Cumbria)' *in* Schofield, J, Klausmeier, A, Purbrick, L (eds) *Re-mapping the field: New approaches in conflict archaeology*. Berlin: Westkreuz-Verlag 15–21

Cocroft, W D and Cole, S 2007 RAF *Coltishall, Norfolk: a photographic characterisation*. English Heritage Research Department Report 2007/68

Childs, J 1995 'A very brief history of the use of land by the military' *in* Coulson, M and Baldwin, H (eds) 1995 *Pilot study on defence environmental expectations* NATO CCMS Report no.211 Swansea: University of Wales, 180-88

English Heritage 2003 Modernising English Heritage 2003/4: Coming of age. London: English Heritage

English Heritage 2006 *Understanding historic buildings: A guide to good recording practice*. Swindon: English Heritage

English Heritage 2007 *Understanding the archaeology of landscapes: A guide to good recording practice*. Swindon: English Heritage

Fletcher, M and Newman, P 2002 *RAF Perranporth, St Agnes, Cornwall: an archaeological survey*. Archaeological Investigation Report Series AI/44/2002. Exeter: English Heritage

Fowler, M J F 2008 'The application of declassified KH-7 GAMBIT satellite photographs to studies of the Cold War material culture from the former Soviet Union'. *Antiquity* **82**, 714–731

Glines, C V 1993 'The jacket that lives forever'. *Airforce* **76** (9), 60-65

Going, C J 2002 'A neglected asset: German aerial photography of the Second World War period' in Bewley, R H and Raczkowski, W (eds) *Aerial archaeology: developing future practice*. Amsterdam: IOS Press, 23–32

Harley, J B 1975 *Ordnance Survey Maps: a descriptive manual*. Southampton: Ordnance Survey

Hegarty, C and Newsome, S 2007 *Suffolk's defended shore: Coastal fortifications from the air*. Swindon: English Heritage

Lake, J, Monckton, L and Morrison, K 2006 'Interpreting Bletchley Park', *in* Schofield, J, Klausmeier, A and Purbrick, L (eds) *Re-mapping the field: New approaches in conflict archaeology*. Berlin: Westkreuz-Verlag 49–57

McOmish, D, Field, D and Brown, G 2002 *The field archaeology of the Salisbury Plain Training Area*. Swindon: English Heritage

Oswald, A, Ashbee, J, Porteous, K and Huntley, J 2006 *Dunstanburgh Castle, Northumberland:*

Archaeological, Architectural and Historical Investigations. English Heritage Research Department Report Series 26/2006

Roy, W 1793 *The Military Antiquities of the Romans in Britain*. London

Schofield, J 2002 'The role of aerial photographs in national strategic programmes: assessing recent military sites in England' in Bewley, R H and Raczkowski, W (eds), *Aerial archaeology: developing future practice*. Amsterdam: IOS Press, 269–282

Schofield, J, Klausmeier, A and Purbrick, L (eds) 2006 *Re-mapping the field: New approaches in conflict archaeology* Berlin: Westkreuz-Verlag

Talbot, G and Bradley, A 2006 'Characterising Scampton' *in* Schofield, J, Klausmeier, A and Purbrick, L (eds) *Re-mapping the field: New approaches in conflict archaeology* Berlin: Westkreuz-Verlag 43–48

Terraine, J 1985 *The Right of Line: The Royal Air Force in the European War, 1939–1945*. London: Hodder and Stoughton

Tuck, C and Cocroft, W D 2004 *Spadeadam Rocket Establishment, Cumbria*. English Heritage AI/20 2004

1. Methods of investigation: textual, visual, material

Seascapes of war: investigating with marine geophysics

ALESSANDRA SAVINI AND MONICA PETRILLO

Until a few decades ago, the scope of maritime archaeology was fairly limited, mainly by the limits of time during which scuba divers could remain immersed – underwater artefacts were often a long way beneath the surface. In the last 30 years scientific and technological progress has witnessed important breakthroughs in the exploration of seas and oceans (*see* Kunzig [2000], for an overview of the extraordinary history of ocean sciences).

This progress is essentially due to three factors:

- ability to calculate more precisely geographical position, thanks to the development of GPS – global positioning system
- continuous progress in research into underwater acoustics and its applications (materials used for the construction of the trans-ducer and the hydrophones)
- improvements in computer technology for recording, processing and disseminating the data obtained in digital format.

Although the origin of these technologies was driven by the need to find oil and natural gas deposits along the continental borders and in the ocean depths, their subsequent development and refinement has taken place as a consequence of their application in other sectors concerned with exploring or exploiting the oceans, such as deep sea fishing and off-shore engineering, as well as scientific and applied research. The continuous application of prototypes to a wide range of commercially available products has brought a steady improvement of such products, and a reduction in their prices. Therefore, it has become possible to explore an ever increasing area of the seabed, mapping even the smallest portions of the surface with great precision.

Specific research purposes require specific techniques of investigation of the submerged environment and vary accordingly. Generally all the investigations aiming at the reconstruction of the shape and nature of seabeds, looking at the geometry of sediments and underlying rocks, as well as observing the processes in the sea system, require instruments that use acoustic waves in water and look at how these are emitted and their behaviour. Most of these instruments are generally employed in floating workstations, in particular the oceanographic vessel (*see* Figure 1.26).

Fig 1.26 Acoustic survey instruments on an oceanographic vessel. © Conisma

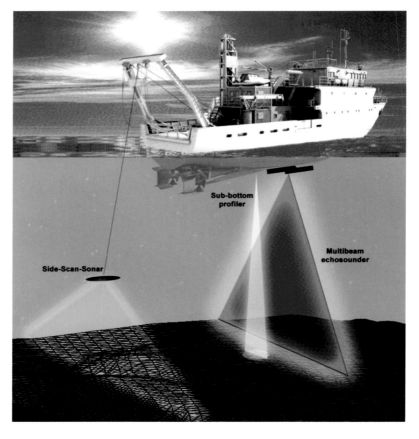

Side-Scan-Sonar

Sub-bottom profiler

Multibeam echosounder

Acoustic techniques for mapping the sea floor

The methods of underwater geophysical exploration that use acoustic principles are a form of remote sensing – of both the seabed's surface and its underlying layers (Morang *et al* 1997). On land, remote sensing investigations are mostly carried out with a range of techniques using satellites and aircraft, but at sea the electromagnetic waves, on which terrestrial survey is mostly based, are very much attenuated by water. Acoustic signals, however are not as badly affected underwater as optic and electromagnetic signals, especially at low frequencies (Jones 1999).

Acoustic geophysical methods are therefore a form of remote sensing that allows the researcher to obtain a remote image of the seabed and underlying layers. The result is a description of superficial geology: a model of the submerged site based on the variation of impediments to acoustic signals and the different coefficients of diffraction of air, water, sediment and rock (Morang *et al* 1997).

Accordingly, acoustic methods have been shown to be extremely useful where researchers need to 'visualise the submerged landscape', giving them a model that displays the principal morphometrical characteristics as well as important information about the nature of mapped materials.

Currently, the main research areas in which these methods are used are:

- determining depth (hydrographic surveys)
- investigating the surface sediments and creating visualisations of the features of the seabed
- measuring the thickness and examining the three-dimensional geometry of the layers that compose the sedimentary coverage on the seabed
- surveying gas sacs, rocky outcrops and geologic risks
- identifying benthic assemblages such as grasslands of phanerogam, colonies of corals and other sensitive biological areas
- identifying or inspecting wrecks and other submerged evidence of human activity.

Echo-sounders, side-scan sonar and sub-bottom profilers are the three main types of equipment used for collecting geophysical data in sea exploration programmes and thus in the production of the morphological and sedimentary models. All three are acoustic systems: they send sound impulses into water and measure the time between the emission of the impulse and the arrival of the reflected signal and/or defraction from above or under the seabed.

Single-beam echo-sounders are used for bathymetric surveys (of water depth). Multi-beam echo-sounders are an advance upon the traditional single-beam echo-sounder and enable the reconstruction of a very high-resolution 3D view of underwater structures and of the general topography.

The side-scan sonar provides an image (sonogram) from which the nature of materials can be identified.

The sub-bottom profilers provide high-resolution sismostratigraphy of the seabed that helps us understand the sedimentary processes acting on the seabed.

Each type of instrument records different aspects of the characteristics of the materials that constitute the seabed and the underlying layers. The best results come from synthesising data drawn from all the individual methods (Morang *et al* 1997; Savini 2004).

Applications in archaeology

Maritime archaeology is just one of the disciplines that has benefited in its operational abilities from marine geophysics (Quinn *et al* 1998; Quinn *et al* 2002; Ballard and McConnell, 2001). Such techniques are integrated by the use of magnetometers of various types that are still used to locate objects lying on the sea floor or partially buried. What the acoustic instruments can do is provide models of the submerged site that better describe the seascape.

The most cost-effective and efficient way of using acoustic technologies in maritime archaeology is by working in distinct phases and using different acoustic tools. The best way of exploring the sea floor, for example, is to use high-resolution multi-beam echo-sounders to pinpoint possible anomalies in the depths and obtain a detailed bathymetric map of the surrounding areas. Then, using high-resolution seismic techniques such as chirp sonar, these anomalies can be analysed and compared with the geometries of the sediments and rocky terrain naturally present on the seabed and under

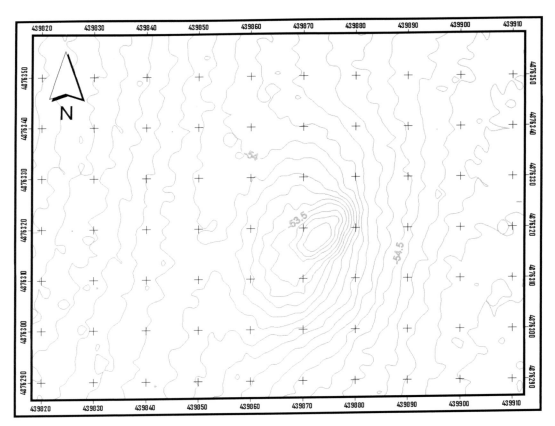

Fig 1.27 A bathymetric map obtained using multi-beam echo-sounders.
© Conisma

Fig 1.28 A remote operated vehicle (ROV) about to be lowered into the water prior to use.
© Conisma

it. Side-scan sonar provides detailed definition of the morphology of the anomalies for their dimensional characterisation.

Using multi-beam echo-sounders we can create a bathymetric map: Figure 1.27 shows an example. The quality of the results produced by the hydrographic investigation is determined by the frequencies of the transducers and how far away they are from the investigated items. Here, an average resolution multi-beam echo-sounder for medium water depth (that means with frequencies between 24 and 100kHz) has allowed a resolution equal to 10 _ 10m. While this gives us enough information to recognise an anomaly on the seabed – produced by a wreck, positioned at -53m of depth – it does not give any greater detail of representation. To find out more it would be necessary to use an echo-sounder at a frequency of at least 400kHz that, if used at more than 20m distance from the investigated object, could have allowed a sub-metric resolution.

Best of all at this point, with potentially spectacular results, would be the option of using ROV [remotely operated vehicle] technology (Figure 1.28), able to operate in depth with opportune transducers, but this requires not

*Fig 1.29 The Klein 3000
'fish' about to be used.
© Conisma*

*Fig 1.29 The Klein 3000
'fish' about to be used.
© Conisma*

*Fig 1.30 Detail of a
sonogram of an ancient
wreck.*
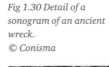
© Conisma

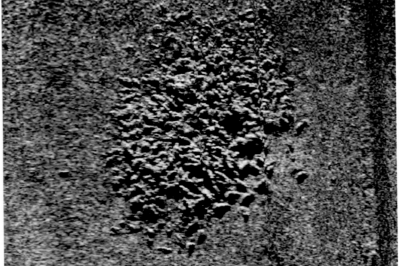

only the technology itself, but also a costly team of technicians. A cheaper option is to use a side-scan sonar.

The side-scan sonar, often called the 'fish', is dragged behind the ship near the seabed. The fish is connected to the ship with an electroconductive cable that hauls it along and transmits the data from the side-scan sonar to the onboard instrumentation .

The photograph (Figure 1.29) shows the Klein 3000 'fish' being pulled down in the water by the *Universitatis* ship. You can see along the side of the instrument the long dark window where the left transducer is lodged: there are two transducers, one on each side. As with other instruments that use the emission of sound, the side-scan sonar also emits acoustic signals, but the frequencies that the side-scan sonar uses are much higher and vary between 100 and 500kHz.

Practically flying above the seabed, the fish emits two fans of acoustic signals, perpendicular to the route followed by the ship, analysing a quite large zone of the seabed. The sonogram that results from the returned signals (diffracted signals, which therefore vary in intensity according to what materials they have encountered) furnishes a very detailed image of the seabed surface and of the objects present, delineating their form, according to the material that composes them and of their three-dimensional geometry.

With a detail of the sonogram (Figure 1.30) we can recognise the shape of some objects on the seabed surface. In this case they are amphorae, probably the cargo of an ancient sunken ship.

All the different phases of the underwater exploration are supported by an accurate positioning of the ship as well as from the side-scan sonar. Practically, it has been possible using this combination accurately to georeference every single portion of the seabed, enabling the feeding of this data into geographical information system or GIS. The accurate relief data, giving a plan of the site with sub-metrics resolutions, has enabled researchers to plan their underwater investigations more efficiently.

The chirp sonar (using reflection and refraction) enables researchers to characterise the investigation area by identifying its sismostratigraphy. This information can tell us about the nature of the first metres of sediment in the site and highlight possible buried structures. It can also give details of the main sedimentary processes. An emitted signal with specific characteristics of frequency, once it has reached the fund, is partly reflected toward the surface and slightly penetrates inside the seabed at a different angle in comparison to the initial angle of incidence. The part of the signal that travels inside the seabed, besides undergoing phenomena of reflection and refraction, is submitted to the phenomenon of absorption and therefore, once it has reached a certain depth, it is completely absorbed.

The frequency used by this technique of seismic high resolution is slightly inferior to the one used by echo-sounders, allowing the pene-

tration of the signal into the sediments present on the seabed. In the chirp sonar the frequency is not constant but is electronically modulated between 1 and 10 kHz. The transducer that emits the signal is positioned by the hull.

When the research vessel passes above an anomaly, the chirp sonar generates an image (Figure 1.31). This clearly shows that the bathymetric anomaly is not an apparent natural phenomenon on the sea floor, such as a rocky outcrop, but is caused by an emerging structure partly covered by sediment.

These techniques enable a precise pinpointing and partial characterisation of an underwater site that can then be visually explored using an underwater vehicle (ROV), which is wire guided and equipped with a video camera. Thanks to the georeference data the underwater vehicle can exactly identify the position and the state of preservation of an individual amphora. When the video images and relief side-scan sonar are put together (Figure 1.32) we can identify the discovered objects with a letter of the alphabet (preceded by the time of the image capture).

Fig 1.31 A bathymetric anomaly identified using chirp sonar from the research ship Universitatis. *© Conisma*

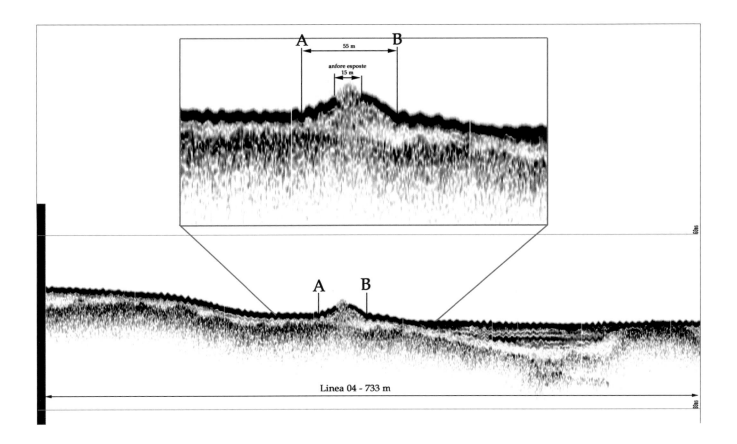

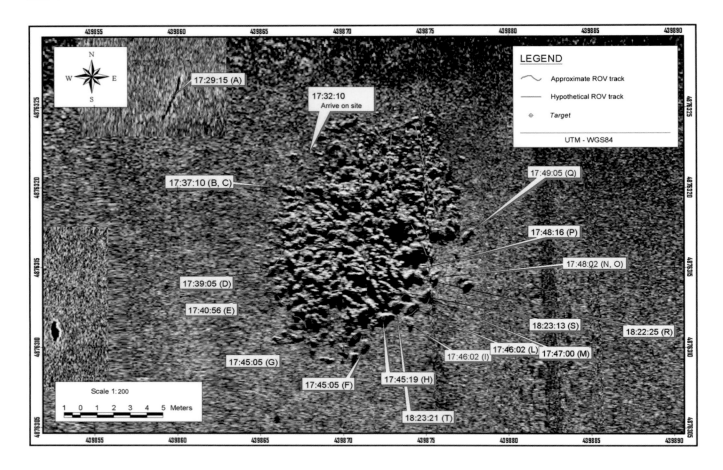

Fig 1.32 When the video images are paired with the results of the relief side-scan sonar, we can mark each individual object.
© *Conisma*

All these technologies can be used relatively affordably even in very deep waters. They are of enormous potential for the research and exploration of archaeological remains that are present in great abundance in the Mediterranean Sea as well as in other world oceans.

Wartime seascapes in the Gulf of Valona in southern Albania

This is an introduction to results obtained using the technologies discussed above by the technical support project for the production and management of an International Centre of Sciences of the Sea in Albania – CISM.

The research was carried out on board the oceanographic research ship *Universitatis* in the Bay of Valona, Albania in 2007 and 2008. The main aim of the research was the acoustic mapping of the seabed. As a result of the employment of side-scan sonar and high-resolution seismic profiling, we now have bathymetric data and sonograms from across the whole gulf. The work has not only identified the principal geomorphological, sismostratigraphical and sedimentological features of the Gulf, but has also revealed the presence of numerous wrecks of world wars I and II, underlining how much the submerged landscape of the Valona Gulf is linked to the hostilities of the 20th century.

Historically and still today the Gulf of Valona and particularly the bay, has been the site of intensive and varied human activity. We can see the results of this from the data and particularly from the side-scan sonar photo-mosaic. The mapped anomalies can be divided in two basic groups:

- anomalies linked to the presence of artefacts on the seabed
- anomalies arising from changes to the morphology of the seabed as a result of human activity

The seabed of the bay is studded with objects of unknown origin and typology. Bearing in mind that, during wartime, the Adriatic Sea was mined, some of them may well be unexploded devices.

Some anomalies, however, are shipwrecks. The research has identified first, the wreck of the hospital ship, *Po*, the largest and the most important wreck recorded during the survey, situated in the south-east area of the bay. The hull is lying on the sea floor, at around 35m deep, where it is possible to observe an abrupt bathymetric rise. This is important for planning further exploration: it might pose a threat to carrying out some types of survey for example. Because marine animals and plants colonise wrecks, the *Po* might nevertheless be worth further exploration for the specialists who work in the naturalistic and biological field (*see* Figures 1.33 and 1.34).

The research has also plotted the wreck of the *Daisy Queen*, also a large and important ship, just off Cape Linguetta and other wrecks, as yet unidentified, both within the bay and off Cape Linguetta.

The seabed of the bay shows morphological evidence that can clearly be ascribed to human activities, such as:

- Linear morphologies resembling tracks on the sea floor: some are caused by trawling nets used in the intense exploitation of fish stocks in the Gulf. More marked traces are the result of minesweeping.
- In the southern part of the bay near the Albanian navy base there are morphologies with a circular form. It has been suggested that they are caused by mines, exploded on the sea floor, but this is not certain.

Further direct investigations (sampling, visual exploration, and so on) are necessary in order to better identify the nature of the different individual anomalies on the Gulf of Valona seabed. Nevertheless, the acoustic mapping carried out so far has yielded a model of the submerged landscape and has revealed not only the presence of important wrecks, but also underlined how much human interaction there has been over the years with the maritime environment. The wars alone left a huge impact, with both the wrecks and the following mine-clearing operations, and Albania's later economic upturn also left its mark.

The Gulf of Valona illustrates how much these sophisticated instruments are essential to investigate the temporal evolution of a submerged landscape and to obtain contemporary, historical information about important human stories such as wars and the following phases of development.

Fig 1.33. The wreck of the Po.
© *Conisma*

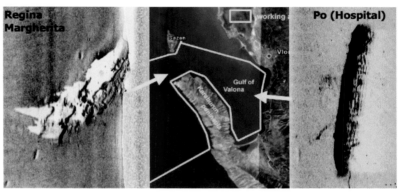
Fig 1.34 Scan Sonar Klein 3000 image: heavy cruiser Regina Margherita (WWI) and hospital ship Po (WWII) found in the Gulf of Valona, Albania (CISM project).
© *Conisma*

Riassunto

Negli ultimi trenta anni il progresso scientifico e tecnologico ha agevolato l'esplorazione dei mari e degli oceani. In particolare l'archeologia sottomarina ha usufruito di queste innovazioni che hanno consentito di aumentare i tempi d'immersione, di raggiungere profondità maggiori e di restituire modelli della realtà sommersa che, in modo non invasivo, apportano informazioni sulla natura dei materiali mappati.

Tutte le indagini volte alla ricostruzione della morfometria, della natura dei fondali marini, della geometria dei sedimenti e delle rocce sottostanti, nonché all'osservazione dei processi in atto nel sistema marino, utilizzano strumenti che sfruttano i principi di propagazione delle onde acustiche in acqua.

Gli ecoscandagli (Echo-sounders), i sonar a scansione laterale (Side-Scan Sonar) ed i Sub-bottom Profilers sono le tre principali classi d'equipaggiamento per raccogliere dati geofisici e per costruire i modelli morfologico e sedimentologico delle aree investigate; tutti e tre si basano sulla propagazione di impulsi sonori nell'acqua e misurano il tempo trascorso tra l'emissione dell'impulso e il segnale di ritorno riflesso e/o diffratto da sopra o sotto il fondale. Gli ecoscandagli a singolo fascio (Single-beam) servono ai rilevamenti (surveys) batimetrici. Gli ecoscandagli a fascio multiplo (Multi-beam), perfezionamento dei tradizionali Single-beam, permettono la restituzione di un'immagine ad alta risoluzione delle strutture sottomarine e della topografia. Il Side-Scan Sonar fornisce un'immagine (sonogramma) da cui si può ricavare la natura dei materiali esaminati. I Sub-bottom Profilers servono a rilevare ad alta risoluzione la stratigrafia del fondale marino.

Queste tecniche sono state determinanti durante le indagini per la localizzazione di un sito archeologico al largo delle coste liguri, a largo di Albenga, nell'ambito di un progetto di ricerca in collaborazione tra la Soprintendenza per i Beni Archeologici e le università italiane attraverso l'impiego della N/O Universitatis (di proprietà del CoNISMa – Consorzio Nazionale Interuniversitario per le Scienze del Mare).

Le fasi della ricerca sono state: l'esplorazione del fondale tramite ecoscandagli multi fascio ad alta risoluzione, per evidenziare eventuali anomalie ed ottenere una carta batimetrica di dettaglio; il confronto di tali anomalie con le geometrie dei sedimenti e degli affioramenti rocciosi presenti sul fondo marino e al disotto di esso, utilizzando tecniche di sismica ad alta risoluzione; la definizione dettagliata della morfologia delle anomalie per la loro caratterizzazione dimensionale, utilizzando il Side-Scan Sonar.

In tal modo è stato possibile identificare un accumulo di anfore, probabilmente il carico di una nave affondata, determinandone l'esatta posizione e lo stato di conservazione.

Le stesse tecniche sono state adottate nell'ambito del "Progetto di assistenza tecnica alla realizzazione ed alla gestione di un Centro Internazionale di Scienze del Mare in Albania – CISM" e hanno consentito di evidenziare nel Golfo di Valona alcune anomalie facilmente riconducibili alla presenza di relitti di imbarcazioni sul fondo, identificati, infatti, nel relitto della nave Ospedaliera Po e della nave Regina Margherita.

Quest'ultimo esempio evidenzia quanto queste sofisticate strumentazioni siano essenziali per indagare l'evoluzione di un paesaggio sommerso e quindi scoprire informazioni storiche su importanti vicende umane quali le guerre e le successive fasi di ripresa.

List of references

Ballard, R D and McConnell, M, 2001 'Adventures in ocean exploration'. *National Geographic*

Jones, E J W, 1999 *Marine Geophysics*. Wiley

Kunzig, R 2000 *Mapping the deep*. Norton

Martino, G, Pandolfi, O, Caleo, C, 2005 *The Albenga B shipwreck: a case study*. 9th International Symposium on Ship Construction in Antiquity: TROPIS 2005 (25–30 August 2005, Agia Napa, Cyprus)

Morang, A, Larson, R and Gorman, L, 1997 'Monitoring the coastal environment: Part III: Geophysical and research methods'. *Journal of Coastal Research* **13**(4), 1064–1085

Quinn, R, Adams, J R, Dix, J K, and Bull, J M, 1998 'The *Invincible* (1758) site – an integrated geophysical assessment'. *The International Journal of Nautical Archaeology* **27** (2), 126–138

Quinn, R, Breen, C, Forsythe, W, Barton, K, Rooney, S and O'Hara, D, 2002 'Integrated geophysical surveys of the French frigate *La Surveillante* (1797)', Bantry Bay, Co. Cork, Ireland. *Journal of Archaeological Science* 29, 413–422

Savini, A 2004 *Metodologie di analisi di prospezioni geofisiche in ambiente marino e loro implementazione in applicazioni S I T* PhD Thesis: Department of Geological Sciences and Geotechnologies. University of Milano-Bicocca

1. Methods of investigation: textual, visual, material

Landscapes of occupation: a case study from the Channel Islands

GILLIAN CARR

To an archaeologist a landscape is more than just its physical features. The artefacts in a landscape are equally important and sometimes help to define the terrain in which they are situated. This is especially true of conflict landscapes, which can reveal a great deal about the individual experiences of living in such an environment.

Landscapes that have been occupied are types of conflict landscapes. It is, however, civilians who mainly experience, live in and own such landscapes, although the military often inhabit the territory or take it by force. It is the civilians – the occupied – from whose perspective the study of such landscapes is usually undertaken, rather than that of the occupiers, although the latter also have their place: without the occupiers there can be no occupation.

Using the new field of occupation archaeology, developed by the author (Carr unpublished [a]), this paper will outline its application to the study of the landscapes of war, detailing the physical characteristics of such landscapes and the objects in them, and taking the Channel Islands as a case study.

Landscapes of occupation

The Channel Islands were the only British territory to be occupied by the Germans during WWII. Between 1940 and 1945, they endured a difficult occupation, made more difficult because they were islands, cut off from the rest of the UK. After the Germans arrived, all trade between the UK and the islands ceased and new trading partners in France had to be established. After the Allies invaded France in the summer of 1944, the islands were cut off from their only source of food and fuel and the inhabitants – civilians and soldiers alike – slowly starved.

They were saved only by the arrival in December 1944 of the Red Cross ship, the *Vega*, which came at monthly intervals until the islands were eventually liberated in May 1945.

The occupation was such a traumatic period for the entire population that it has become an integral part of the islands' identity and heritage. For people in the Channel Islands, the Occupation (for them always with a capital O) *matters*. It is talked about daily, features in the local newspapers regularly, and the annual Liberation Day celebrations are still tremendously popular.

Although the islands are small, they have many private museums dedicated to the occupation, which are packed full of wartime memorabilia. From Nazi daggers and 'souvenired' autograph books from *Soldatenheim* members *(a Soldatenheim* was a rest and recreation centre for German troops) to home-made make-do-and-mend items, many island attics – and trophy cabinets – boast a modest collection of trinkets dating back to this period (Carr, unpublished [b]). Each artefact is a repository of family history or linked to an occupation story. The items' owners enjoy reciting their stories. They also enjoy writing them down, and every local bookshop has a sizable collection of occupation memoirs and diaries, which continue to sell well.

The two main islands of Jersey and Guernsey also both have occupation societies, which make it their business to collect and record every scrap of data relating to this period. There is no escaping the immediacy of the occupation and no chance to forget about it and let it lie, as the islands are bristling with German fortifications, which are no longer seen as blots on the landscape but instead as important historic monuments (Carr 2007a).

Shaping the landscape

No landscape, physical or artefactual, can make itself. Before outlining the characteristics of the occupation landscape, it is important to introduce the many 'players' who shaped it, who made the occupation landscape a multi-faceted concept, and who willingly or unwillingly constructed, manipulated and recycled it. Importantly, the occupation landscape of today is different to, or – perhaps one should say – more than it was at the time of liberation in 1945. For example, memorials have been erected to commemorate the occupation. Also the contribution of those who were evacuated or deported and who later returned must be taken into account, and the objects that they may have made during their absence must be included. Memorials have also been erected to commemorate events of the years of occupation, and they, too, play their part.

In the Channel Islands, the landscape of occupation first comprises the contribution of the islanders, including those who spent the war years elsewhere. When it comes to objects of the time, the people who were evacuated contributed the least to what survives today of the wartime landscape. The people who were deported, however, often contributed the most, as many of them had made things while they were interned and brought these back with them after the war. People who stayed in the islands also made a range of items that speak of the experience of occupation.

The second group who inhabited the occupation landscape were, of course, the soldiers of occupation, who left behind many of their weapons and tools of war, some of which were kept as souvenirs by local people after liberation. Sometimes the soldiers made and gave gifts to local inhabitants, for example to the families with whom they were billeted, to children, and to women with whom they had relationships, although gifts between soldiers and women are *very* much in the minority. They are not willingly brought out and shown by their owners because of potential accusations of collaboration, still a sensitive subject for many. The line between items that were given, and those that were left behind and subsequently became memorabilia, is blurred, and acquisition of the latter group was and is not perceived as theft.

The third category of people who contributed to the landscape of occupation visible today is the slave or forced workers: These unfortunate people, many hundreds of whom died on the islands due to the harsh conditions in which they were kept, were the most dispossessed of all in the Channel Islands during the occupation years. They were brought to build Hitler's Atlantic Wall, working for the Organisation Todt (the Nazi German paramilitary construction organisation named after its founder). They were virtually destitute and that is reflected in the scarcity of items that they were able to make during the occupation. Yet they were responsible (unwillingly) for the imposing concrete bunkers and fortifications that so typify the occupation landscape today .

Occupation artefacts

How does an 'occupation landscape' differ from other conflict landscapes? And to what extent are the Channel Islands typical? Some of the occupation landscape characteristics of the Channel Islands listed below overlap, but their combination together is unique. In this, the Channel Islands are atypical because the characteristics all occur within a small, geographically bounded area, something that would not necessarily be the case elsewhere in occupied Europe, where such features would be more dispersed.

The islands also escaped some aspects seen in other occupied countries, such as ghettoisation – parts of towns and cities where Jews were confined. This was not only because the Channel Islands had very few Jews – although there were some (Cohen 2000) – or Jewish quarters, but also because St Peter Port and St Helier, the islands' largest towns and the capitals of Guernsey and Jersey respectively, were arguably too small for ghettoes.

Powerful memory objects

An occupation landscape produces specific types of material culture, monuments and urban structures. The items of interest are specifically those that were handmade, recycled, reworked or otherwise personalised and not anonymous machine-made or mass-produced items. It is the trench art (any object made by any person from any material, as long as it and they are associated in time or space with armed conflict or its consequences; Saunders 2003, 11) and items of 'make-do-and-mend' that most often speak of the individual experiences and emotions of military occupation, rather than the 'souvenired' pistols, helmets and other items of militaria that are so favoured by collectors.

The circumstances in which an item is made, by whom, and why, make the creation of hand-made items meaningful. They can show us the hunger and desperation of civilian populations during food shortages, the boredom and home-sickness of prisoners of war, the suffering of forced workers, and the attitudes of the occupying army: raw, powerful and often still tangible emotions that are otherwise not so easily accessible.

These handmade items are powerful memory objects. Not only can they be used to unlock their owners' long-hidden memories, but they are also, in a very real way, carriers or receptacles of cultural memory for Channel Islanders. Although the stories and references of a few occupation artefacts are well known throughout the islands by the older generation, and these stories have often been passed down to children or have been taught in schools, so that today people still know what they symbolise or what they were (such as the V-for-victory sign, both visual and oral), many such stories and memories are on the cusp of disappearing as the occupation generation also die out.

The collection of oral histories, memories, and a digital archive of the islands and islanders' wartime artefacts, has been central to my research. The recollections can provide the context for items that, through the passage of time, as memories have faded, have lost their meaning. Such items are often now inherited, or thrown out in house clearances and bought in jumble sales or junk shops, 'rescued' by collectors and even museum owners for financial gain or to enhance their collections, and the accompanying memories have often not been written down, or have been forgotten or disregarded. Making an archive of the meanings and memories of these objects will not only preserve them but will also make an important contribution to the heritage, and thus a key aspect of the identity, of the Channel Islands and islanders today.

Characteristics of landscapes of occupation in the Channel Islands

Although every occupation by German forces during WWII was unique in its circumstances and degree of violence and destruction, there are clearly certain common features that link all of them. Not all of these are necessarily to be seen in the Channel Islands, because they are islands, are rural, are small, and have few people living there, most of whom were not an ethnic target of Nazism. Nevertheless, while the islands escaped systematic bombing, destruction and clearing of urban areas, such as was seen in the Warsaw ghetto, the built environment was attacked.

Just before the occupation began the Germans bombed the harbours of St Peter Port and St Helier. However, the damage was soon repaired and the ports brought back into their original use. The Channel Islands therefore lack the kinds of bombed landscapes, common in other countries that were involved in the war. Similarly, while there are no communal mass (or massacre) grave pits filled with the bodies of people who starved to death or were murdered by the Germans, a graveyard of 329 forced workers was found in May 1945 by liberating forces on Longis Common in Alderney, with a further 64 graves found in the parish graveyard (Pantcheff 1981, 64–74). After the occupation there were rumours of mass graves and these rumours persist in Alderney today but they have never been substantiated. There were certainly deaths from malnutrition among the civilian and military population (Knowles Smith 2007, 138–9), especially in the last year of occupation, and among the forced worker population such deaths were commonplace.

Below 12 characteristics of the landscape of occupation of the Channel Islands are listed. While several aspects of heritage relate to the occupation, both tangible and intangible, as discussed here, this latter area lies largely outside the scope of this paper.

1) *Artefacts that are evidence of the shortages of raw materials, food and fuel caused by the disruption in trade and food production, and the additional burden of feeding and generally providing for the army of occupation.*

Food shortages in the islands were such that, even before the D-Day landing of June 1944, people were living on semi-starvation rations (Knowles-Smith 2007, 125–139). After the Allied invasion of Europe, all trade with France was cut and the islanders and occupying garrison alike had to survive on what was already in the islands. Even before the Allied invasion, people collected and dried carrageen seaweed and used it for blancmange. After flour had run out, potatoes were grated and the gratings washed and dried and used as a flour substitute to make bread. People also began to grow their own tobacco plants, which resulted in a number of home-made guillotine-style tobacco cutters. New kitchen instruments were invented or cobbled together out of a variety of scraps of wood and metal in order to make the tools to process these new food substitutes. Examples include the potato flour grater and the sugar beet press, in which chopped and boiled beets were pressed to make a syrup that served as a sugar substitute.

Fig 1.35 Detonator box carved by a German soldier: in 1945 the carrot and swede were the only food still available.
© Gillian Carr

Fig 1.36 (right) Wooden bowl with crest carved by German soldier.
© Gillian Carr, courtesy of the German Occupation Museum, Guernsey

The ordinary German soldiers also suffered from the food shortage and unlike the civilian population, they did not receive Red Cross parcels with the coming of the *Vega*. The most poignant object made by a soldier from this period is a recycled detonator box that was engraved with a map of Jersey and the date '1945' (Figure 1.35). Flanking the map is an engraved carrot and a swede: the only food still available by that date.

Some objects demonstrate how people coped with the fuel shortages, such as the 'oven' made out of a biscuit tin, devised either while gas and electricity supplies were rationed or totally unavailable, and designed to be used in the fireplace. People also cooked with hay-boxes, made from wooden boxes stuffed with straw;

saucepans, after being brought to the boil, were put inside the box, packed tightly all around with insulating straw, and the lid pushed on. The food in the pan simmered away in the box with no additional fuel consumption.

One of the most common occupation items is the re-soled shoe. Many Channel Island families own a treasured pair of shoes from the occupation years, when the shortage of raw materials required that worn-out shoes were re-soled time and again with what was to hand – the many layers of poor quality leather, worn car tyre rubber or wood still visible.

2) *Artefacts that represent a power relationship between the occupier and the occupied. These sometimes involve the appropriation of symbols of identity.*

The most interesting, yet until now unrecorded, metaphor of the unequal power relationship between the islanders and their occupiers revolves around the ultimate symbol of identity: the islands' shields or crests. Those of Jersey and Guernsey are very similar, showing three leopards passant guardant [looking outwards]. Both islands issued coins bearing the crest, and these portable images proved to be very useful to both occupiers and occupied in the silent battle for its ownership (Carr 2008; Carr unpublished [c]).

When the Germans arrived, they appropriated the crest, claiming it as theirs to use now that they had 'conquered' the islands. They generated a range of trench art, almost all of which bore the crest. Most popular of all was the carved wooden bowl with the crest in the centre (Figure 1.36);

there are many of these in Guernsey especially. There are other German-made artefacts engraved with an island crest, such as wooden tobacco boxes or candle sticks. Coins with the crest were especially prized and local newspapers complained about the shortage of coins (Guernsey *Evening Press* 1941) because of Germans appropriating them as souvenirs. Coins bearing the crest were turned into medals (Lumsden 2001, 83–4), and soldiers used the crested coins in their trench art, most frequently as cigarette rests in ashtrays, or as a decoration on cigarette lighters. While this appropriation of such a potent symbol was going on, the islanders began to use the crest themselves, turning coins into jewellery in their own trench art, to reclaim their identity in a defiant manner. At the end of the occupation, when many German soldiers stayed behind on the Islands as POWs to help clean up the minefields, some of them fashioned further items, often given in exchange for kindnesses. Several of these artefacts also bore the crest, and should be seen in this context as a symbolic acknowledgement of the return of the islands to their rightful owners.

3) *Artefacts that evoke the experience of being watched, whether by the occupying army or by friends and neighbours who might report or denounce forbidden activities.*

The most typical of these items, which were often hidden and deliberately disguised as something else, is the crystal radio set, though other objects also fit into this category. People began to make these disguised radios after the Germans confiscated radios in June 1942, after which listening to the news represented an act of great defiance and being caught carried severe penalties (Sanders 2004, 21–27, 104––121). Those caught were fined heavily, often sent to prisons on the continent, from where they drifted into concentration camps. Crystal radio sets were often cleverly hidden – inside light switches or fittings, biscuit tins, battery packs and even inside books (Figure 1.37).

4) *Artefacts that express resistance or defiance against the occupying authorities.*

Artefacts of this kind of popular subversion are often deliberately ambiguous in form, or even sometimes encoded, but they tend not

to be entirely hidden. They are, after all, intended to be seen and understood by a specific audience: sometimes the occupier and sometimes the occupied, although it would be overly simplistic to reduce the complexities of the occupation situation into just two opposing audiences.

The most enduring symbol of this category, reproduced in many media and in many other artefacts, is the V-for-victory sign (Carr unpublished [d]). In 1941, the BBC started the V-for-victory campaign to be broadcast to the occupied countries of Europe, encouraging people to chalk up the V-sign and make the rhythm of the letter V in Morse code wherever possible (Blades 1977, 177). Although the broadcasts were not specifically aimed at the Channel Islands, people there nonetheless heard them and painted V-signs on the roads and street signs and walls of St Helier and St Peter Port (Cruikshanks 2004, 168–169). These painted symbols were soon seen as sabotage, although they were later appropriated by the Germans and modified with a laurel wreath painted underneath, which was taken to denote German victory, but which did not entirely stop the campaign.

After reprisals against the islanders, the V-signs went underground. A number of V-sign badges were carved out of shillings by two Guernsey men (Figure 1.38), and worn beneath the lapels of suits. People

Fig 1.37 Crystal radio set hidden inside a book.
© *Gillian Carr*

Fig 1.38 V-sign badge, carved out of a one shilling coin.
© *Gillian Carr, courtesy of the Valette Military Museum, Guernsey*

would flash them at trusted friends in the street as a way of boosting morale (Carr and Heaume 2004). Hidden V-signs were also incorporated into the stamps and the sixpenny bank note designed by Jersey artist Edmund Blampied, much to the delight of islanders (Syvret 1986, 126). Later on, when 2,200 islanders were deported to German internment camps in 1942 and 1943, the V-sign continued to be incorporated into many examples of trench art made in the camps as a way of expressing solidarity with their fellow islanders (Carr 2009 forthcoming; Carr unpublished [e]). After the occupation, the V-sign flourished openly once more and is still used and understood by all islanders, most particularly during Liberation Day celebrations.

5) *Artefacts of oppression – typically truncheons, whips or other weapons designed to inflict injury, usually used on forced foreign workers.*

Among artefacts surviving from the three forced worker camps and one concentration camp in Alderney is a cosh, now on display in the island museum, and made from the wooden handle of a tennis racquet, one end of which is heavily weighted with lead and wrapped.

In the German Occupation Museum in Guernsey, alongside the leather whips, coshes and manacles, all of which were used in the Organisation Todt prison, Paradis, in Guernsey, a small rubber policeman doll sits in the display case. The doll policeman hung over the doorway of the prison and the inmates had to bow to it when passing. Without survivor testimony, no one would have guessed what humiliation such a small rubber doll represented, showing how context and oral testimonies can be key to interpretation.

6) *Artefacts that evoke liberation.*

Objects associated with the islands' liberation are not entirely confined to those made in May 1945. Some have been made since, over the years, as part of the annual celebration of liberation, as the cultural memory of the occupation is played out and passed down to the next generation.

Not only did the V-sign see a resurgence in 1945, as it does on Liberation Day in the islands today, but there are also a few home-made flags and patriotically-coloured ribbons and rosettes dating from this period, made from scraps of material.

Further liberation-related artwork and trench art was made in the civilian POW camps of Germany by interned Channel Islanders. Recently, an excellent example of liberation trench art from the islands came to light in the shape of two painted German helmets. The artwork is taken from two locally well-known pictures drawn by wartime Guernsey newspaper cartoonist Bert Hill.

The first helmet depicts Churchill looking on as a lion, wearing British army uniform, slashing a sword through the shackles that are restraining a Guernsey donkey chained to a swastika, The dates shown on the helmet are those of the start of the Occupation and VE (Victory in Europe) day. The word 'Freedom' is painted above the images.

The second helmet shows a Guernsey donkey kicking a German soldier out of the island (Figure 1.39). A large V-sign is painted on one side of the helmet and the date of (and word) 'liberation' is shown on the other. What makes these items precious to local eyes is that the ultimate symbols of liberation adorn the ultimate symbol of oppression: the German helmet.

7) *Civilian landscapes studded with defensive military buildings such as forts or bunkers, in areas that provide a good view over the land*

Fig 1.39 Painted German 'liberation' helmet © Mark Lamerton

or coast to keep an eye on any potential invaders.

The Channel Islands of Guernsey, Jersey and Alderney still contain hundreds of concrete bunkers, fortifications and gun emplacements (Figure 1.40). For a long time after the occupation, people hated these structures. After the war, many were stripped of their contents, covered over with soil, and buried from view once it was found that blowing up thick reinforced concrete was virtually impossible and very expensive. As time has passed, many have been brought back into use, as fishermen's stores and workshops, mushroom farms and wine cellars. A few have been converted into house extensions or tourist accommodation.

In recent years, several bunkers have been turned into museums, such as Jersey Military museum and Guernsey La Valette Military museum and others have been restored and refitted to how they looked when still used by the Germans. On the whole, the fortifications today are seen as important historic monuments and part of the islands' heritage.

8) *Civilian buildings that were converted to military use or taken over by military personnel.*

During the occupation some civilian buildings in the Channel Islands, such as hotels or private houses, were turned into military HQs, soldiers' social clubs, or had soldiers billeted in them alongside the original occupants. Identifying these buildings mostly depends on local memory and old photographs, although local publications exist (Forty 1999). However, a very few houses still show a V-sign with a laurel wreath underneath, which was often painted by Germans on the houses where they were billeted. With civilian re-occupation, association of certain buildings with their wartime past has mostly faded with time.

9) *Occupation landscapes often include places of internment, terror and cruelty. This category includes prisons, slave or forced worker camps, and concentration camps.*

The Channel Islands has several sites, ranging from the local prison in Gloucester Street in Jersey, where many 'political

prisoners' (as they are called locally) were held, to the site of Paradis, the Organisation Todt prison in Guernsey. The Gloucester Street prison no longer exists, but the site is commemorated. *Paradis* is not marked by any plaque.

There are also the sites of the forced worker camps and concentration camp in Alderney – the latter was finally commemorated with a plaque in September 2008. The sites of two of the forced worker camps are heavily overgrown and extremely difficult to find, while a third is now the island's camping site, and the fourth has bungalows built on top of it (Carr 2007b). Because most of the associated paperwork was destroyed, our information about what happened at these places comes either from survivor testimonies or from those who helped to hide escaped workers; no excavation has yet been carried out.

10) *Parts of occupation landscapes are also appropriated landscapes. These are typically no-go areas that were mined or covered with barbed wire to prevent civilian access.*

Many coastal areas in the Channel Islands were mined and the public were forbidden from visiting many of the beaches, either for their own safety or in case they escaped by boat. The sea was also forbidden, the areas where fishermen could fish were greatly restricted and much of their catch had to be surrendered to the Germans. For a population whose diet was, and still is,

Fig 1.40 Pleinmont Tower, a German naval observation tower, Guernsey.
© Gillian Carr

greatly supplemented by all kinds of seafood, this fishing restriction exacerbated the food shortage, but boosted wartime recipes for items such as limpet or ormer, collected from beaches that were still accessible, and casseroled.

11) *Graveyards relating to deaths that occurred because of the occupation*

There are three types of graves

- those of people who died of starvation or diseases associated with malnutrition
- those of people murdered by the Germans
- military graves of German soldiers who died or were killed during the occupation.

The slave worker cemetery on Longis common in Alderney contains graves of people in the first two categories and was found by the liberating troops. The War Cemetery in Howard Davis Park, Jersey is similar and includes the grave of Maurice Gould.

Maurice was a teenage boy who with two friends tried to escape by boat from Jersey, but they were caught and sent to various 'nacht und nebel' prison camps on the continent. Nacht und nebel – literally, night and fog – was a German directive that resulted in the capturing and disappearance without trace of people in German-occupied territories who had been accused, specifically, of being resistance workers. These people usually ended up in penal prisons and concentration camps or were murdered, often both. Maurice died of TB in Wittlich prison, in Germany, and his body stayed in the prison cemetery until 1997, when his friend and fellow escapee, Peter Hassall, brought his body back to Jersey.

There are also military graveyards of German soldiers on several of the islands. The graves are kept in an exemplary state and have not, to my knowledge, been vandalised.

12) *Monuments, memorials and plaques dedicated to those who suffered during the occupation.*

Memorials and plaques are principally in St Helier and St Peter Port. Almost all the older ones consist of a simple plaque on a wall, such as the one marking the spot in St Helier from which many British-born islanders were deported to internment camps in Germany, or that in St Peter Port, marking the place where, immediately before occupation, bombs were dropped onto tomato trucks and many people were killed.

More recently, from the 50th anniversary of liberation in 1995 onwards, new forms of memorial have been unveiled. They include the Liberation Monument in St Peter Port, an obelisk that acts as a sun dial, its shadow falling on marked hours of the day when various events took place on the day of liberation (and which are also marked on the memorial). In the 1990s, the islanders finally began to research and commemorate their own 'political prisoners', people who had offended against the German regime. Perhaps because their acts of defiance had been perceived as somehow less spectacular than those of the armed resistance groups on the continent (not a feasible proposition in a small island with one occupying soldier for every three civilians), these people had remained unsung heroes (Sanders 2004, 122).

The Lighthouse Memorial was erected in St Helier in memory of all Jersey 'offenders' and unveiled in 1996. In 2003, an additional plaque was added, dedicated to those islanders who died in Nazi prisons and camps during the occupation. There are many interesting issues – outside the scope of this paper – surrounding the period of time that elapses or has to elapse before people are ready to commemorate or acknowledge certain events.

The archaeological characteristics of the occupied landscape can clearly be found, with additions, elsewhere in parts of Europe occupied by Germany during WWII. The challenge, and indeed the value, of this sort of study will be to see to what extent these hallmarks of occupation apply to occupations longer ago, or in the future, even. How many of these features can be seen in the current occupation of Iraq, or in the archaeological record of Roman-occupied Britain, for example? Many will no longer survive, or perhaps did not exist in the first place. Many of the artefacts of occupation are, by their very nature, transient and ephemeral. So far back in time the fine archaeological detail of an occupation can easily be lost. Were, for example, certain items relating to food and its preparation made in such a way because of grave shortages or because everyday life was like that anyway?

Sometimes an occupation lasts so long that the difference between the occupiers and occupied can become blurred (Carr 2006); who then celebrates when the occupiers leave? Often the greatest (and most telling) changes are to be seen in the first generation of occupation, as people react to and negotiate with the changed conditions of their daily lives. The occupations of WWII lasted four or five years, yet that period was long enough to influence and affect those that experienced it – and often the next generation – for the rest of their lives.

This paper and case study aims to point the way forward for, and demarcate, a new area of study; an innovative and potentially rich aspect of conflict archaeology that has the potential to contribute greatly to the lived heritage and identity of formerly-occupied countries today and their inhabitants, who live with both the shared and individually experienced legacy of that occupation.

Acknowledgements

I would like to thank the people of the Channel Islands for showing me their artefacts, and also the various museum curators and owners who let me photograph their collections. This research was carried out with funding from the British Academy, the McDonald Institute for archaeological research, and St Catharine's College, Cambridge. I would also like to thank Nick Saunders for his encouragement.

Bibliography

Blades, J 1977 *Drum Roll: A professional adventure from the circus to the concert hall*. Faber and Faber: London

Carr, G unpublished (a) 'Occupation archaeology'

Carr, G unpublished (b) 'Occupation artefacts: a guide'

Carr. G unpublished (c) 'Of coins, kings and V-signs: appropriated identities in the Channel Islands'

Carr, G unpublished (d) 'The Archaeology of occupation and the V-sign campaign in the Channel Islands during WWII'

Carr, G unpublished (e) 'Silent resistance and the V-sign campaign in Channel Islander WWII German internment camps', in Symonds, J, Badcock, A, and Oliver J, (eds), *Historical Archaeologies of Cognition*. London: Equinox Publishing Ltd

Carr, G 2006 *Creolised Bodies and Hybrid Identities: examining the early Roman period in Essex and Hertfordshire*. Oxford: British Archaeological Reports (British Series) 418

Carr, G 2007a. 'Manipulating time and changing perceptions: WWII fortifications in Guernsey and Jersey'. Paper presented at the Theoretical Archaeology Group conference, University of York, December (unpublished)

Carr, G 2007b 'The politics of forgetting on the island of Alderney', *Archaeological Review from Cambridge* **22**, 2, 89–112

Carr, G 2008. 'Of coins, crests and kings: contested symbols of identity in the Occupied Channel Islands'. Paper presented to the 5th Biennial Fields of Conflict conference, Ghent, October (unpublished)

Carr, G 2009 *Occupation: Behind the Wire*, (museum catalogue) Jersey: Jersey Heritage Trust

Carr, G and Heaume, R 2004 'Silent resistance in Guernsey: the V-sign badges of Alf Williams and Roy Machon', *Channel Islands Occupation Review* **32**, 51-55

Cohen, F 2000 *The Jews in the Channel Islands during the German Occupation 1940-1945*. Jersey: Jersey Heritage Trust (in association with the Institute of Contemporary History and Weiner Library, London)

Cruikshank, C 2004 [1975] *The German Occupation of the Channel Islands*. Stroud: Sutton Publishing

Forty, G 1999 *Channel Islands at War: a German perspective*. Hinkley, Leicestershire: Ian Allen Publishing

Guernsey Evening Press 1941 25 July, p 2 and 27 December, p 3

Knowles-Smith, H R 2007 *The changing face of the Channel Islands Occupation: record, memory and myth*. Basingstoke and New York: Palgrave Macmillan

Lumsden, R 2001 *Medals and decorations of Hitler's Germany*. Shrewsbury: Airlife

Money, J 1993 *Aspects of war: the German Occupation of the Channel Islands 1940–1945. Entertainment and pastimes*. Guernsey: June P Money

Pantcheff, T X H 1981 *Alderney Fortress Island: The Germans in Alderney 1940-1945*. Chichester: Phillimore

Sanders, P 2004 *The ultimate sacrifice: the Jersey islanders who died in German prisons and concentration camps during the Occupation 1940–1945*. Jersey: Jersey Heritage Trust

Saunders, N 2003 *Trench Art: materialities and memories of war*. Oxford and New York: Berg

Syvret, M 1986 *Edmund Blampied: a biography of the artist 1886-1966*. London: Robin Garton Ltd for the Société Jersiaise

Recovery of Spanish Civil War sites in the Valencia Region: From methodological research to the creation of tourist routes

JOSÉ RAMÓN VALERO ESCANDELL

Despite the enormous amount of literature on the Spanish Civil War (1936–39) there are still a great many gaps in the record, even where there is relatively abundant information and in the most thoroughly studied fields, such as the political and military aspects of the conflict. There is still considerable ignorance about everyday wartime life, the civilian work carried out by the defeated side, the repression during and after the war. Little has been recorded about most of the sites that played a major role throughout the war and immediately after. In some parts of Spain there were so many sites that they could be said to make up real warfare backdrops. This does not necessarily mean that battles were fought on those sites.

The concept of war sites: memory and evocation of times of warfare

We class as 'war sites' all places significantly involved in the conflict, not just those with political and military associations, but production sites and sites of cultural and social relevance. To be included as a 'war site' a place of cultural and social relevance must however have undergone significant changes as a result of the war. This means, for instance, that a factory that was manufacturing soap in the years before, during and after the war could hardly be considered a war site, unless there had been relevant and exceptional changes in its operative, structural or complementary uses.

War sites are therefore classified into the following four types:

1 Sites built for wartime purposes, namely, shelters, trenches and bunkers

Many of these disappeared shortly after being built, due to the unusual and temporary nature of their construction. Some shelters and similar structures were sealed up once the Second World War ended, though many can easily be recovered. As a rule, only those sites located away from urban areas still show evidence of their original use.

2 Sites whose use was changed during the war to meet new requirements

Examples include recreation centres and schools that were turned into military clinics or field dressing stations, or country estates near urban areas that became school camps for evacuated children.

3 Sites that experienced important events during the war, both military and political

These include sites of battles, bombardments or strategic positions – for example the location where the Nationalists broke through to the Mediterranean via Vinarós. Sites of political importance include the site of El Fondó de Monòver airport from where the defeated Spanish government left the country.

4 Structures built or altered after the conflict in memory of the war

Many memorials were erected to remember the victorious side. These include numerous war memorials and the commemoration of buildings, such as the Alicante prison where José Antonio Primo de Rivera – founder of the

Spanish fascist party, the *Falange Española* [Spanish Phalanx] – was jailed until he was finally executed in 1936 by a firing squad. The prison became a place of pilgrimage for Falangist organisations.[1]

What has happened to the sites

In all the types of sites mentioned above, both the/their remembrance of the wartime period and their re-use for cultural purposes differ quite considerably. This depends on whether:

- the site essentially is evocative of that time
- the site is properly preserved (regardless of the fact that the activities currently carried out are different from those undertaken in times of war)
- the site has been transformed, to a greater or lesser extent
- memorials have been built at the site

Sites that are evocative could include some defensive fortifications in the interior of the Valencian region, and almost all types of shelters, including municipal, factory and military shelters. Occasionally such sites have been preserved almost untouched after so many decades. They were almost always closed to the public, shrouded in mystery. This is what happened to the last seat of the Spanish Republican government, also the residence of the Republican prime minister of Spain, Juan Negrín, who held office during the last two years of the war, 1936 to 1939. The estate is in the province of Alicante; it is known as Finca El Poblet, in the town of Petrer – or *the Yuste Position* – in the military jargon of the time. It has hardly been altered since the war and was hidden away from prying eyes by a dense thicket (Valero 2004).

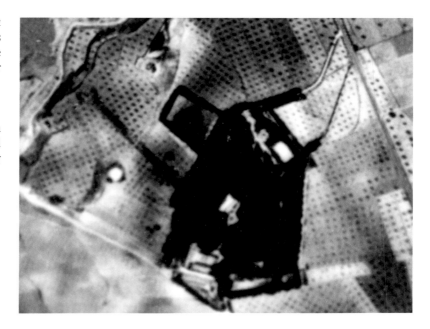

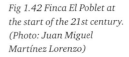

Fig 1.41 Finca El Poblet in Petrer was the last residence of the Spanish Republican government. The photo was taken in 1956 when a US military aircraft flew over Spain taking the first ever aerial photogrammetric picture of the country. (Reproduced by permission of SIGUA at Alicante University)

Fig 1.42 Finca El Poblet at the start of the 21st century. (Photo: Juan Miguel Martínez Lorenzo)

Valencia's City Hall is an example of a site that has been properly preserved, although the activities currently carried out in it today are different from those undertaken in times of war. The building was used during the war as seat of government, parliament or venue for the Anti-Fascist Intellectuals Congress (Aznar 2007).

Sites that have been transformed, sometimes radically, include the port of Alicante, which witnessed a massive exodus of Republicans, and the Campo de los Almendros, an unirrigated grove, also in Alicante, where those who were unable to flee the country by sea gathered.[2] Neither of these two places recall these tragic episodes, as the port is now a recreation area while the grove has become a suburb.

At some sites memorials have been built. Examples include the numerous crosses scattered around all towns and villages in memory of the fallen on the victorious side. Recently, the memory of the defeated side is being recovered, and memorials and commemorative stone plaques in their honour are now more common.

Whatever the type of site, preserving, or where appropriate promoting, such sites in memory of the Civil War requires highlighting identifiable traits connected with that point in time, disseminating available information on the sites, explaining their connection with the conflict, and – if necessary – researching fundamental or complementary aspects that may foster knowledge of those places. Depending on their intended use, further data and learning materials will be needed to add to their didactic appeal as well as to promote their cultural potential (even for touristic purposes if integrated in clearly defined projects). Awareness of war sites can be boosted, and a good example to follow is that of Alcoi. There, a visit to a shelter has been complemented by the restoration of an infirmary, with photographs on the walls of bombardments on the town and testimonials of those who survived the attacks.

Factors affecting current public knowledge

Although many structures and places are still today linked to the Civil War in some way, public knowledge of these depends (to a greater or lesser extent) on a number of factors.

First and foremost, the extent of public knowledge depends on how the site is connected to the conflict. People usually know significantly more about sites where notable military and political events occurred rather than about those used for financial, social or cultural purposes. A battlefield is much more likely to be associated with war than a building that was adapted to house refugees.

People are more aware of a site's connection with the conflict and its original role in cases where its use has been maintained ever since. Some places were used for several different purposes during the war. For example, the Salon La Mundial in Elda, was originally a shoe factory but was used during this period (simultaneously or successively) as a social club run by the Spanish socialist party, a company store, a field dressing station, the improvised premises of the local leisure centre, the main welfare service canteen and a billet for Moroccan occupation troops.

The public may have little awareness of a site if its current use or appearance is very different today from what it was during the war. Unless one is a connoisseur of the Spanish Civil War, it is quite difficult to evoke the events that took place in the old docks in the port of Alicante, which has now been developed into a recreation area, or in the vineyard which in the past used to be the airfield from which Negrín's Republican government and Dolores Ibarruri, known as La Pasionaria – the most renowned female member of the Spanish Communist Party, member of the parliament and icon of the popular and military resistance against the fascists – took flight in 1939.

Another factor determining the extent of public awareness is whether the powers that be show any wish to commemorate the war. That is something that General Franco's regime was highly aware of during its first decades in power. Gradually, however, interest in remembering the conflict – which had a role in the foundation, recognition and even justification of the dictatorial regime – waned. With the transition to democracy after Franco's death, efforts were made to try to forget something that divided a society in which a number of known participants remained alive. Attempts were made to overcome past events, fostering obscurity and removing many symbols without replacing them with others that might evoke the defeated side.

Following on from this factor affecting public awareness, is the issue of whether the site or structure stresses values defended by the powers that triumphed, which in Spain was the armed forces who won the war. The latter sought to keep the memory alive of both what they considered to be heroic deeds in battle, and the pain suffered by their supporters. In doing so a great number of symbols and gravestones – anything that brought the defeated side to mind – were utterly obliterated.

Levels of public awareness also depend on the extent to which a site or its history is part of what people know about their environment. The role played by emblematic buildings of their city or of places that support their identity is generally remembered. More inconspicuous war sites that are less at the heart of people's everyday lives are for the most part condemned to oblivion.

If a large group of protagonists or direct witnesses in the events connected with a particular site are still alive memory of the connection between historical facts and places is higher.

This memory decreases significantly among the public if witnesses have disappeared, are few in number, had tangential involvement, or are relatives who evoke those episodes. Today there are hardly any direct political participants in the Spanish Civil War still alive. There are also fewer and fewer people who were militarily engaged, and – after seven decades – only the young of the time can bear witness to this. Hence, it is no longer possible to interview important figures – compare this to more recent conflicts such as in Bosnia, Algeria or the Cuban revolution.

The number and quality of documents connected with a site helps inform the public and make them aware of the significance of a particular spot. Archives and collections represent a superb wealth of material and include a great variety of sources, such as press articles, literature, personal writings, photographs, souvenirs and recordings. On the other hand, as one comes down to the daily routine of specific sites – especially in small towns – the number and quality of documents notably decreases. Sometimes, it is simply impossible to learn with any certainty what happened there during the conflict.

Finally, personal memories, hazy or clear, endure when past episodes become legends. This is the case for great battles, important political events or violent incidents. Connections are barely made between major events and daily routines such as work, supply management and culture.

Researching an issue that remains controversial

Some features peculiar to the Spanish Civil War prevent much detached objectivity on events and places. One must not forget that the clash was characterised by its ideological nature and conflicting conceptions of the world. It was a civil conflict, although there was a significant foreign intervention: Nazis and fascists supported the ultra-conservatives, while internationalist volunteers and Soviet advisers backed the Republicans. The conflict was a confrontation more between national concepts and understanding of concepts of state role and organisation. This is proved by the great involvement of Catalonia in defending Madrid. The Civil War constituted an internal conflict at the core of each particular territory and society, where supporters of both sides coexisted.

Subsequent generations took on the legacy of the dispute. On 25 May 2006, 68 years after the bombing of Alicante's market that killed more than 300 people, a commemorative stone plaque was placed on one of the building's entrance doors. A few days later the plaque was vandalised and has been replaced with another one with a glass shelter. The conflict still generates a lot of attention: it is virtually the main *Spanish* issue of the 20th century.

In view of all this, one can easily imagine how much reluctance is encountered when attempting to undertake research on the Civil War. In recalling specific events, people express concern about who might benefit or be damaged. There is sometimes distrust because disclosed information could reveal a relative or friend's guilt. Some people believe that throwing light on these matters only hampers the reconciliation that began following the Amnesty Act, which was actually a piece of legislation intended to bring closure.[3] Crucial subjects remain taboo. Any in-depth study would furthermore touch on the role played by institutions that held effective control, such as the army, the Catholic Church, financial corporations large and small – ranging from main banks to local farming cooperatives, and the most influential families in each area. It is therefore not uncommon to find those who seek totally or partially, legally or to all intents and purposes, to hinder access to archives.

All this obviously has an effect on any museum project or on promoting and bestowing greater status to war sites. Curiously enough, places where military action took place can be approached with more neutrality. There is especially extensive data about both landscapes where battles were fought and the regional capitals that were controlled by the conflicting sides, including Valencia (Aragó *et al* 2007), Salamanca (Robledo 2007) and Barcelona. Barcelona's city archive has not only collected a great many publications, but also allows for online access to a well-stocked photographic collection. When it comes to more day-to-day matters, however, connected with life in small towns and villages, factory environments and social relationships, the coverage of information is nevertheless insufficient, patchy and fragmentary.

In approaching the recovery and preservation of sites linked to the Civil War in specific geographical areas it is first necessary to determine what is meant by war sites, to assess all available resources on the subject matter, as well as to ascertain the basic role played by those places during the conflict. Doing this involves using often uneven data from all sources connected with library collections, newspapers, traditional archives, photographs, cartography and oral testimonies.

In the case of Valencia, sources available include:

- local histories
- local journals
- literary works
- biographies and memoirs
- periodicals and newspapers
- archives
- photographs
- maps
- oral histories

Local histories

Local histories give a general picture of the development of the war in particular territories and studies on specific issues.

Local journals

Several of these – often published annually – are preserved, often featuring festivities focusing on historical events or local customs.

Literary works

Novels, plays and poems enjoyed more or less widespread dissemination, some of which pay special attention to the period's best remembered episodes (yet often not explicitly).

Biographies

Biographies and memoirs – usually hand-written – are only recently being published, as those who previously feared to express how much repression and hardship they had suffered have now reached old age, and either they or their families have decided to publish their memoirs.

Magazines and newspapers

Various periodicals and newspaper sources with local scope were frequently published by workers' parties or trade unions, and even though they were prone to an ideological bias, they contain extremely rich information on events and places. Regional papers were published right until the end of the conflict, almost always following the seizure of existing newspapers. The national press enjoyed much greater dissemination – very rarely did it offer data on small towns but it has nonetheless contributed by depicting key events.

Archives

A considerable amount of documents contained in archives are yet to be explored. People studying them usually focus on political and military aspects, at different levels. Local archives confer special importance to town council minutes, which reflect local vicissitudes. These collections, however, also contain a wide range of documents, including plans, lists, inventories and public health-related files. Such information is sometimes extraordinarily valuable to discover how estates and buildings were altered to meet the needs of war.

National collections, such as the section on the Civil War in the Salamanca AHN (*National History Archive*) or those managed by the army, such as those in Ávila and Segovia, keep military records, maps and information on local political organisations throughout the country. A large number of files on political parties and trade unions are preserved, though not very uniformly. There are also many private archives which are certainly disparate but nonetheless indispensable at local level.

Photographs

Photographs can teach us a great deal about landscapes of war and sudden turning points in people's lives and environment.

Photographic archives – or specific sections within broader archives, specialised websites (*Memoria republicana, guerracivil.org* or *Alicante vivo*, to name a few) and extraordinary collections owned by photographers – portray the conflict. The few aerial photographs that exist arouse particular interest. A recently published book about the air attacks on the town of Alcoi is a good example (Beneito 2007). There are also thousands of private photographs taken by families, some better than others, but all of which contribute something. They are zealously kept as private heritage, however, their owners often make them available to researchers.

Maps

Cartography is extremely helpful for researchers. The pages contained in the Spanish National Topographic Map have proven to be especially useful: more so when combined with modern mapping and aerial photographs using Geographical Information Systems and other computer applications to overlay layers of information. An example of the latter is the so-called 1956 *American Flight*.[4]

Pictures show that many towns have remained almost unchanged since 1939 as regards urban planning. There are also numerous military maps. Studies on key issues that had an effect on people's daily lives can be made thanks to simple notes in the margin of a map or thematic plans. For instance, some maps have survived featuring the places attacked during the bombardment of Alicante and showing how flour was distributed throughout the province.

Oral histories

Finally, although compilations of written transcriptions and tape recordings are available, though often disparate, gathering oral sources is equally imperative and urgent. First-hand witnesses of the conflict can contribute valuable information that may shed light on conventional data or enable us to understand the past better. Since almost all major protagonists have died, ordinary people – usually they were teenagers or young men and women at the time of the Civil War – who have little connection with the conflict but in-depth knowledge of specific sites can provide clarification, anecdotes and clues to continue researching, despite memory lapses and continuing silences due to fear. When approaching interviewees whose rela-

tives were involved in the war, one frequently observes mythologisation and biased information and they tend to be afraid to convey the horror suffered by those closest to them. It is possible, however, to recover typical family histories and gain access to important material, including letters, photographs and objects. Increasing the number of participants produces a snowball effect that allows many more than expected to be contacted.

Recovering the memory of war sites becomes a simpler task if a conscious synthesis of sources is undertaken. The following case shows what I mean. A book published in New York during the war (SCWAA 1938) contains drawings by evacuated children who had been admitted to school camps around the country. Many portray both disasters of war and the quiet life they were leading in their new homes. A few of those drawings include the stamp of a school camp located in Beneixama (Alicante).

When I visited this town an old man gave me directions unhesitatingly it seemed. He pointed out the farmland where the school camp had been established. He told me about events that had taken place there and came with me to visit the site, which surprisingly preserved features depicted in the children's drawings. A history of the camp's evolution was achieved thanks to complementary testimonials.

The school camp was moved from its original location to a beautiful stately home in the centre. Later it was permanently established in a convent located in the nearby Villa de Biar. Cartography, archive documents, new personal testimonials and photography will undoubtedly enable us to reveal more about the history of that school camp.

Fig 1.43 Title page of They still draw pictures, published in New York in 1938 by the Spanish Child Welfare Association of America.

Fig 1.44 An evacuee boy made this drawing of Beneixama School Camp in Alicante province.

Fig 1.45 The building that housed Beneixama School Camp as it looks today. (Photo: José Ramón Valero Escandell)

Fig 1.46 (right) The stately home in the centre of Beneixama, to which the school camp was moved, as it looks today. (Photo: José Ramón Valero Escandell)

Fig 1.47 (far right) Eventually the Beneixama School Camp occupied this convent in the nearby Villa de Biar. (Photo: José Ramón Valero Escandell)

PROJECT...	
DATASHEET FOR THE BUILDING OR SITE	
Order Nº:	
Name	
Other name	
Municipality	
Location	
Geographical coordinates	
Location map and photograph	Location map / Current photograph
Period	
Original use	
Use during the Civil War	
Present use	
Description	
Historical interest:	
Source of information:	
Notes or complementary items:	

1. IDENTIFICATION: | | Nº

TYPE: **CIVIL** | SUBTYPE 1: **EVERYDAY LIFE**
| SUBTYPE 2: **COUNTRY HOUSE**

LOCATION:

Coordinates:

2. CHARACTERISTICS OF THE RESOURCE

DESCRIPTION:

BODY RESPONSIBLE:

PUBLIC ☐   PRIVATE X

Specify: Private house

ASSESSMENT OF THE RESOURCE:

Great appeal ☐

Of tourist interest ☐

Complementary resource ☐

Has no present tourist interest X

DEGREE OF PRESERVATION:

Excellent ☐ Good X Average ☐ Poor ☐ Non-existent ☐

FRAGILITY (possibility of deterioration through public use)

Very high ☐ High ☐ Average ☐ Low X Non-existent ☐

Specify : Exterior visit to the resource

Cultural and/or tourist use of war sites

The research presented here has been undertaken in a systematic way. Information from different sources has been synthesised, thus enabling an in-depth study of Civil War sites and suggesting cultural uses for them. Furthermore a team from the Universidad de Alicante conducted a detailed analysis on four villages in the region of Valle Medio del Vinalopó (Valero 2007). The first step was to produce an individual record for each village, including: its accurate location, using maps, photographs and even geographical coordinates to facilitate access by GPS (global positioning system); land uses before, during and after the war; a detailed description of the site; its possible historical interest to further understand the evolution of the conflict in the site's zone of influence; and information sources to confirm the village's connection with the war.

The aim is to achieve a more detailed picture of life there and to formally add interesting additional comments (see data sheet Figure 1.48). Similarly, a number of supplementary resources – including documentary archives, museum collections, audio recordings, interesting objects and photographs – will need a systematic, detailed inventory to be produced. This will facilitate access to the resources in order to promote the architectural heritage's appeal and understanding.

In those places where the rich cultural heritage is suitable for public interpretation – and even tourist potential, if it evokes general interest – further research should cover potential new uses. The assessment needs to address the value of the resources at hand; the degree of preservation and fragility; accessibility; information signs; available equipment and services both on-site and nearby; the kind of potential use; and closeness to other similar sites which may add to its value. As an example, see datasheet 2 (Figure 1.49), including one such proposal designed by Professor Rosario Navalón who works at the University Institute for Geographic Research at Alicante University. She is a co-director of the study on the region of Medio del Vinalopó. Professor Navalón produced the section on potential tourist interest and creation of cultural routes.

Dissemination of the key role played by these sites during the Civil War inevitably requires strengthening the levels of planning legislation or policies to protect the sites from redevelopment, especially should no such preservation policy be currently in place, or if major construction works are being carried out nearby. It would be even more convenient if

Fig 1.48 (above left)One of the data sheets used by the Universidad de Alicante team to survey four villages in the region of Valle Medio del Vinalopó.
© José Ramón Valero Escandell

Fig 1.49 (above) Data sheet used by the Universidad de Alicante team in its survey of four villages in the region of Valle Medio del Vinalopó, assessing the value of the resources, preservation and fragility, accessibility, information signs, available equipment and services both on-site and nearby, the kind of potential use, and closeness to other similar sites which may add to its significance.
© Rosario Navalón

relevant war sites were officially declared 'assets of cultural interest'. Interest is undoubtedly fostered by publication, both in the form of specialised academic analysis and articles written in the local media. Further promotion is ensured by holding temporary exhibitions on the most interesting issues connected with the site, more so if rich and appealing period material is available. There are areas that bore witness to major war episodes, including Valencia (capital of the Republic for a number of months) and Vinarós and Maestrazgo (in the province of Castellón), where Nationalist troops chose to drive a wedge between Catalonia and the other Republican territories. The Elda Valley is another significant war site, since it was there that Negrín's Republican government finally fell. The prime minister's residence was located in the nearby town of Petrer, close to Monòver airfield, from which his government left the country.

Some very important landscapes of war – where the final defeat actually occurred – are scattered around the province of Alicante. One such site is the harbour area or Campo de los Almendros. Permanent exhibitions or heritage visitor centres may introduce the public to this period of the country's history and to resources that help to understand this better.

Creating more or less permanent cultural routes on suitably preserved war sites with historical relevance, and various interesting characteristics is anything but nonsensical. People's interest in these is unquestionable if they are displayed to new generations as a path for reflection upon past mistakes which no country should ever repeat: a clear commitment to peace, tolerance and peaceful coexistence.

Resumen

La recuperación de los lugares de la guerra civil en la comunidad valenciana: de la investigación metodológica a la creación de rutas turísticas

Los lugares que protagonizaron la Guerra Civil Española son tan abundantes en algunos espacios geográficos concretos que podríamos hablar de auténticos paisajes de guerra, no sólo en los ámbitos políticos o militares, sino también en los productivos, culturales y sociales. Básicamente son cuatro tipos de lugares: los construidos por razones bélicas – refugios, trincheras, casamatas...–; los que se adaptaron a la situación excepcional generada por la guerra – hospitales de sangre o fincas de recreo reconvertidas en colonias escolares–; los escenarios de batallas o actos políticos relevantes; y los monumentos conmemorativos de aquella tragedia.

El recuerdo del tiempo bélico y su reutilización cultural depende del grado de conservación del lugar: continúan usos y apariencia de entonces, mantiene sólo la vieja imagen del lugar, ha sufrido cambios radicales o es conmemorativo. Conservar los lugares como memoria del conflicto requiere resaltar los rasgos identificativos del momento, divulgar la información destacable vinculada al tema o investigarla en profundidad, elaborar materiales complementarios que potencien su atractivo didáctico y expositivo.

Su grado de conocimiento público depende de factores como el tipo de vinculación con el conflicto (atrae más lo militar), la pervivencia de funciones, la conservación de la imagen histórica, la divulgación o silencio de la vinculación por parte de los poderes públicos, su carácter de lugares socialmente identitarios o significativos, la supervivencia de testigos, la abundancia de documentación o la mitificación de los hechos a ellos asociados.

Abordar la recuperación implica conceptualizar tales lugares, analizar los recursos disponibles, precisar las funciones desempeñadas. La información es fragmentaria, pero rica y variada. En Valencia las fuentes bibliográficas predominantes son historias y revistas locales, obras literarias, biografías a veces manuscritas. Disponemos de prensa republicana desde la escala local a la estatal y de archivos – locales, nacionales...– parcialmente inexplorados. La fotografía de época, imprescindible, conservada en fondos públicos o colecciones particulares, es accesible en algunas páginas web; además, existen fotografías aéreas, como las de los bombardeos italianos. La cartografía facilita el estudio con mapas temáticos de época –frentes, abastecimiento, siniestralidad...– y su comparación con otros actuales. Finalmente, los testimonios directos, de urgente recuperación. Interrelacionar convenientemente estas fuentes – oralidad, archivos locales, mapas, fotos, biografías...– facilita la recuperación de la memoria de los lugares.

La investigación sistemática profundiza en ellos y permite su utilización cultural. Se requieren fichas detalladas de lugares y edificios – uso, localización, conservación...–, a partir de fuentes informativas diversas, ampliadas con material complementario que potencie el atractivo y su comprensión histórica. Cuando la riqueza patrimonial permita el aprovechamiento cultural, deberemos reforzar la protección urbanística y realizar estudios paralelos valorativos sobre fragilidad, accesibilidad, equipamiento, servicios disponibles... Publicaciones, científicas o divulgativas, y exposiciones temporales potenciarán el interés. Sobre territorios ligados a momentos esenciales – Valencia capital, Negrín y el Vinalopó, el puerto de Alicante...– caben exposiciones permanentes y centros de interpretación; incluso rutas culturales, ligadas al fomento de la convivencia pacífica.

List of references

Aragó, L et al 2007 *Valencia 1931–1939: Guía Urbana: La ciudad en la 2ª República*. Valencia: PUV

Aznar Soler, M (ed) 2007 *Valencia capital cultural de la República, 1936–1937*. Valencia: Consell Valencià de Cultura

Beneito, L A 2007 *Alcoi, objetivo de guerra*. Alcoy: Producciones Kronos

Robledo, R (ed) 2007 *Esta salvaje pesadilla: Salamanca en la guerra civil española*. Barcelona: Crítica

Spanish Child Welfare Association of America 1938 *They still draw pictures*. New York: Spanish Child Welfare Association of America

Valero Escandell, J R 2004 *El territorio de la derrota, Los últimos días del Gobierno de la II República en el Vinalopó*. Petrer: CEL

Valero Escandell, J R (ed) 2007 *Inventario de lugares y recursos de los municipios de la Mancomunidad del Vinalopó vinculados a la Guerra Civil y posibilidades de utilización turística de los mismos*. Unpublished survey from a contract for advisory work and technical assistance between the University of Alicante and Mancomunidad Intermunicipal del Valle del Vinalopó

Footnotes

1   Members of the fascist group *Falange Española*, were known as Falangists

2   During the civil war, Republicans were supporters of the democratically elected government, fighting against Nationalist rebels

3   Translator's note: an amnesty act was passed in Spain on 14 October 1977 awarding immunity to those responsible for repression under Franco's regime with a view to stabilising the country and ensuring democracy

4   Translator's note: On 17 June 1956 a US military aircraft flew over Spain, taking the first ever aerial photogrammetric picture of the country, including the photo of Finca El Poblet. The operation was known as the 1956 *American Flight*

1. Methods of investigation: textual, visual, material

The archaeology of the Battle of the Atlantic

DAVID PARHAM

One of the most important conflicts of both world wars was the Battle of the Atlantic fought between Germany and the Allies for control of the seaways.

Relatively unknown at the time, the remains of this conflict are largely limited to detritus littering the seabed between North America and Europe. In both world wars the 'Battle' continued from the first day of the conflict until the last and was fought across the world's oceans from the Arctic to the Southern Ocean, although the main focus was upon the western approaches (an area of the Atlantic lying to the west of the British Isles) and Britain's coastal waters. Close study has revealed a wealth of archaeological remains on the seabed and this paper aims to present these findings and offer a tested methodical approach for the investigation of these sites.

Britain's coastal waters contain the greatest density of shipwreck losses, and some of the oldest and most spectacular shipwreck sites in the world (Roberts and Trow 2002). Many of these sites contain remains from 20th century conflict. During both world wars, the German forces deliberately sought to sabotage Britain's seaborne trade. Much damage was inflicted and, arguably, it was it through this strategy of slow strangulation rather than the artillery of land, air or sea battles, that Germany came closest to victory. Given that Britain was so dependent upon seaborne trade to feed its people, supply its industry and export its goods (Terraine 1989), the seas that defended the nation against invasion, also made its navies vulnerable.

Before the First World War Britain's overwhelming superiority over its only serious competitor at sea, imperial Germany, had led both nations to believe that Britain was more than capable of protecting its seaborne life-line. The advances of naval technology brought on by the industrial revolution, however, were to call this assumption into question.

In the 1914–1918 conflict, the biggest threat to British shipping was the German Unterseeboot (literally undersea boat – or U-boat for short). Germany's first submarine, U 1, was commissioned in 1905 but the U-boat did not become a fully efficient weapon until 1912 (Jackson 2000).

At the outbreak of the First World War U-boats were something of a nautical curiosity. Early spectacular success against British warships in September 1914, however, forced the Royal Navy to take them seriously. Before the end of the year a number of merchant ships had been sunk without warning by submerged U-boats. Early in 1915, Germany declared the waters around Britain to be a war zone, in which all allied ships would be sunk without warning. For political reasons this declaration was withdrawn in September 1915, only to be reimposed in the autumn of 1916, initially with restrictions which were withdrawn in early 1917. Even with restrictions the situation had become desperate and Admiral Jellicoe, commander of Britain's Grand Fleet, considered that if things got worse then Britain would have to sue for peace by the summer of 1917. Without restriction it became even worse: 455 merchants were sunk within three months of the German declaration of unrestricted submarine warfare.

In the end the situation was saved by a simple, tried and tested 18th century technique: convoy. Merchant ships were gathered together so that they could sail together. This worked in two simple ways: first, it brought all the ships to be protected in one place. This created a concentrated larger target, but one that was harder to find than a wider spread of single ships. Secondly, it allowed warships to escort the convoy. This way, instead of searching for U-boats, the warships were on station if they chanced upon U-boats. Almost overnight losses dropped from 25 per cent to less than 2 per cent (Terraine 1989).

In 1939, faced with the onset of another war, Britain adopted the convoy as the primary means of protection for its merchant fleet. Initially casualties were heavy in British coastal waters but the German occupation of the European coastline from Norway to Spain meant that for much of the war shipping movements were limited to coastal trade. The battle for Britain's survival took place in the North Atlantic away from the British Isles. Following the invasion of Europe in June 1944 international shipping was once more routed into the British coastal waters as convoys carrying supplies direct from both the UK and the USA entered the English Channel. Here they were subject to both submarine and air attack, but at this stage of the war the initiative was with the allied anti-submarine forces, and merchant ships were not sunk in any substantial number, while casualties among U-boats were high (Terraine 1989).

The project

These seaborne conflicts have largely passed out of popular knowledge and, on the few occasions when the media has dealt with the subject, it has been as a backdrop to other issues. What remains of this conflict therefore is on the seabed and around the coast of the United Kingdom. Between 1984 and 1992 the author and a group of diving colleagues undertook a diving survey of a number of previously unknown wrecks off south Cornwall between Dodman Point and Polperro, and later undertook historical research about the area between the Lizard Point and Plymouth.

The project, which was undertaken jointly with the United Kingdom Hydrographic Office, discovered 12 previously unknown shipwreck sites and briefly investigated a further 200. Within the area of investigation we found the remains of ships or aircraft of every type deployed and from every phase of the battles of both world wars. These included merchant ships such as the SS Carolus, anti-submarine warships such as HMCS Trentonian and U-boats themselves, such as the UB 118.

The remains of relatively recent wrecks provide a range of types of information. First we can determine an exact position for what was probably a rather inexact loss position recorded at the time of sinking. The wreck also provides an answer to an outstanding historical question about ships that 'disappeared'. Secondly, the wreck may also (depending on its condition and accessibility) tell us about the effectiveness of the weapons that sank it, and the strength, or otherwise, of the ship's structure or design. The sites also have great potential to tell us about the social conditions on board, although this work would involve a larger landscape characterisation, which was outside the scope of our project. This work has given us an idea, however, of the wealth and breadth of remains present on the seabed and starting points for focused historical research.

Historical accounts of the conflicts in the Atlantic deal with losses as a statistical fact, for example telling us how many hundreds of thousand tons of shipping were lost. What this project has done is look at this historical data at the level of individual losses, which allows access to data on the composition of the crew, vessel particulars and how individuals reacted. The project has also developed a field-tested methodology for rapidly assessing and evaluating iron or steel shipwreck sites. This was developed over a period of 10 years and enhanced in the course of examining more than 200 sites covering the entire range of industrial shipwrecks.

Fig 1.50 Shipping losses from the Lizard Point to Plymouth.

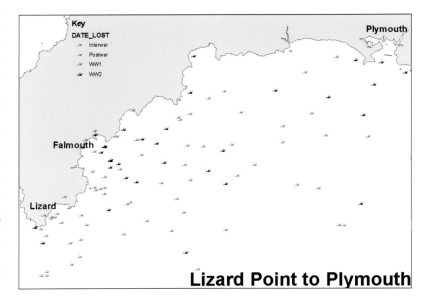

Broad methodological approach

It is important that underwater survey work be conducted by individuals that have the knowledge and experience to recognise and interpret what they see. Anyone investigating wrecks from the two world wars should be aware that not all wrecks of the correct type and period found in areas affected by the main conflicts in the Atlantic were involved in battle when they were lost. The wreck of the coastal steamer SS *Orchis*, built rapidly in 1917 during the First World War to replenish shipping losses from earlier in the war sank in 1935, as a result of an accident, a loss completely separate from her war service.

There are two methods of identifying 20th-century shipwreck sites. One uses the known losses for the area, while the other uses information available from the site to establish identity. The former is the easiest, but is not always possible. Although the collection of shipping casualty intelligence during the world wars was generally well developed, especially near major ports, in more remote areas it is not as extensive. In every instance, for a casualty to be recorded, someone had to either survive or witness the wrecking or its aftermath. This did not always happen and even relatively modern wrecks can be found significant distances from their assumed position of loss. Even where confirmed sinking positions are recorded, the wreck can lie a considerable distance away.

Method 1: using known losses

Historic data required

Historically, details of shipping casualties were recorded not by geographical location but by their date of loss. This made the compilation of inventories for specific areas very difficult. Recent collation exercises have, however, produced a number of national or local collated databases. These include the United Kingdom Hydrographic Office database of wrecks; the maritime records of the various heritage agencies, such as English Heritage's National Monuments Record, Royal Commission for Ancient and Historical Monuments in Scotland, Royal Commission for Ancient and Historical Monuments in Wales and Department of the Environment, Northern Ireland.

Other sources include Richard and Bridget Larn's *Shipwreck Index of the British Isles*; sites and monuments records in county records; and local wreck guides. These will not be exhaustive and sometimes other primary sources will need to be consulted.

Information required from historic data

The aim of looking at various historic sources is to understanding the characteristics of each loss. At the very least you need to know:

1 name (and former names)
2 builder
3 yard number
4 engine builders (if any)
5 owner(and former owners)
6 length
7 breadth
8 tonnage (note which calculation)
9 layout
10 armament (if any)
11 type and details of method of propulsion (in its broadest sense)
12 cargo
13 cause of loss
14 seabed inspection

Close examination of a wreck on the seabed will often provide enough information to connect it with one of the candidates provided from the historical sources. Inspection should be aimed at providing information about the wreck's form and function, cause of loss and period of loss. It is essential to make at the very least a scaled sketch, showing:

1 broad layout
2 height above seabed (at various locations)
3 size and position of cargo hatches (if any)
4 areas of major constructional damage
5 position and type of its power-plant
6 details of its armament (if any)
7 cargo (if any)
8 general condition (*see below*)

It is easy to confuse apparent items of cargo with ships' fittings, equipment or armament, so investigators need to take care here. When the sinking ship hits the seabed, the impact often causes damage, and this needs to be distinguished from damage that is evidence of the possible original cause of the ship's going down. Later activity, perhaps from attempted salvage or fishing, can also cause damage and it is vital not to draw hasty conclusions.

Wherever possible there should be should be visual inspections, using divers or ROVs (remotely operated vehicles). Remote acoustic survey can provide an indication of layout, height above seabed and size and this mapping can be enhanced by close physical inspection. Nevertheless in order to identify a wreck you will almost always need a level of detail beyond what these techniques can achieve.

Method 2: using information from the site

Additional work required

If it is not possible to match the wreck with any known losses in the area using the techniques above, there will have to be a more detailed inspection, aimed at identifying the period of construction. This will record key details, such as:

1   constructional form of the wreck's shell plating (outer hull)

2   the constructional form of the wreck's hull base and the framing that supports the shell plating (in broken up sites)

3   the type of engine and screw/paddles (if any)

4   lifeboat davits (if any)

5   anchors (if any, they are often deployed during sinking)

6   cargo-handling equipment (if any)

You may find useful individualised markings, such as:

1   any lettering or markings located on bow or stern

2   bell (hard to find as it is often displaced during the ship's loss or subsequent decay)

3   shipbuilder's plate (usually bolted to the front of the bridge)

4   engine maker's plate, (attached to the machinery)

5   domestic utensils that often carry the ship owners' logo, but not always that of the final owner

At important sites where a more extensive record is required, it is a good idea to construct a base plan from published material, available photographs or engineering drawings. This can then be enhanced and corrected during the survey rather than starting to record what are extremely complicated structures from scratch.

Condition

Traditionally the condition of wrecks was recorded not in drawn form but in a written description reported to the United Kingdom Hydrographic Office. However this does not readily allow direct comparison. The tabulated condition survey with a standard formula allows direct comparison between individual sites.

Structural damage	Salvage that has already occurred	Lying	Condition
None	None	Upright	Complete
Minor	Minor	On side	Swept
Heavy	Major	Upside down	'Wracked'
Major	Structural	Broken up	Dispersed

Diving survey

A diving survey can be conducted relatively rapidly if the structure itself is used for base navigation. Divers need to have a broad understanding of 20th-century shipping, contemporary maritime material culture and the impact upon these of long term submergence. Historical sources provide the former two, but you need to have had experience to be able to recognise in a wreck the effects that being submerged for a long time can have on a structure.

Ethics

Until recently, post-industrial shipwrecks were treated as mere scrap metal by their owners, the government (Larn 1997) and sea users. However, in more enlightened times the social standing of these structures has altered and they are now both seen as important elements of our national heritage, and often as the last resting place of those who died in the service of their country. There are both ethical and safety issues to consider.

Any work should aim to be sympathetic and informative to those affected by the casualties' loss. Most known British wrecks are from the Merchant Navy, a service that suffered casualty rates many times that of the armed services. Only if taking things from a wreck and bringing them to the surface will play a key part in identifying that ship and its story can such a process be justified.

Investigators should aim to have as little impact upon the site as possible. Objects to be recovered should be clearly identified before they are brought to the surface (see below) and should be returned to the site or a suitable location once they are no longer needed. Investigators must immediately inform the Receiver of Wrecks that things have been taken, and pass on what they have learned to the relevant national monuments record as well as to the United Kingdom Hydrographic Office wrecks officer.

Safety

All of these structures have undergone an unimaginably violent event and have lain in an extremely corrosive environment for a very long time. They often house heavy machinery in structures that have been weakened, by both the sinking and the corrosion; many are now in a state of imminent collapse. They may contain weapons or other hazardous material that should be left well alone. Anyone working on wrecks should be aware of this and should not go into a wreck or try to recover any potentially hazardous materials.

Britain's coastal waters contain a wealth of maritime archaeological riches from the largest naval campaigns of the 20th century's two major conflicts. These wrecks stands as memorials to the great losses suffered by all those involved; in the years since their loss they have also become important economic resources for fishing and tourism. They offer great research potential for providing a much more personal and detailed view of modern war at sea from a resource that is often dismissed as nothing more than scrap iron.

Bibliography

Bevan, J 1996 *The infernal diver: The Lives of John and Charles Deane, their invention of the diving helmet and its first application.* Gosport: Submex

Churchill, W S 1950 *The Second World War Vol. II.* London: Cassell & Co

Jackson, R 2000 *Submarines of the World.* Hoo, Kent: Grange Books Ltd

Larn, R and B 1997 *Shipwreck Index of the British Isles: Vol 1* London: Lloyds Register of Shipping

London, P 1999 *U-Boat Hunters – Cornwall's Air War 1916-19.* Truro: Truran

Ministry of Defence (Navy) 1964 *Royal Navy BR 155 Diving Manual.* HMSO

Roberts, P and Trow, S 2002 *Taking to the water: English Heritage's initial policy for the management of maritime archaeology in England.* Swindon: English Heritage

Teague, D C 1982 *Strike First – They shall not pass unseen.* Plymouth: Baron Jay Ltd Publishers

Terraine, J 1989 *Business in Great Waters: The U-Boat Wars, 1916–1945.* London: Leo Cooper

1. Methods of investigation: textual, visual, material

Strange meetings: archaeology on the Western Front

MARTIN BROWN

'The pity of war, the pity of war distilled'
from Strange Meeting *by Wilfred Owen 1918*

When the First World War ended it left behind extensive archaeological remains affecting whole landscapes. These are scattered from the battlefields of Gallipoli and Salonika to the training grounds in the combatant nations. Nowhere, however, is this more pronounced than on the Western Front, where the battlefields stretched from the Belgian coast to the Swiss border.

Remains are sometimes on the surface or deep underground in the shape of shelters, dugouts and tunnel systems. In some places the ground remains riven by massive earthworks, dug by soldiers or cast up by the power of explosives. As the war passes out of living memory and archaeology has extended to consider the more modern and contemporary era, the conflict has become the subject of archaeological research. This paper explores some of the new directions in this branch of archaeology and considers some of the issues surrounding it that do indeed make for strange meetings. It considers the archaeological scale and potential of the conflict, how it differs to other, more traditional archaeology and the strong resonances it has for the wider public.

A contested landscape

The visitor to the Western Front can still discern that this has been a contested landscape. To the casual traveller's eye the landscape is littered with cemeteries and monuments that reveal the human cost of the war, be it the humble cemetery with a handful of graves or the Thiepval Memorial to the Missing with its many thousands of names. If one stands, for example, beside the Commonwealth War Graves Commission's Serre Number Two cemetery, in France, near the Somme, and looks back north, the view includes two further cemeteries, a memorial chapel and three personal memorials to individuals.

Fig 1.51 Contested ground – farmer's field, historic landscape, burial ground, heritage site or sacred site – part of the Somme Front in 2006
© Martin Brown

To the archaeologist, however, the view also includes the gentle hollows of two German mine craters and, when the ground is newly ploughed, the chalky smears indicating the lines of trenches dug by French, German and British soldiers. Ploughing also still unearths unexploded munitions, which the farmers pile beside the road, ready for collection by the authorities. Anyone can see the presence of the war.

A more reflective look, however, reveals this to be a landscape of victory: the defeated Germans are absent in the memorials, save for two names on a small memorial close to where the individuals were found in 2003 and paradoxically, as such, remains contested. The rural calm may be seen as a thin bandage lain on the deep scars of war.

Perhaps today this is where the contested nature of the landscape begins afresh: now that the war is passing out of living memory some may see the land as an historic battlefield but to others it represents a livelihood, either as productive farmland or as prime development land. As recent arguments over the A19 motorway extension in Belgium have shown, these views may be utterly incompatible (Saunders 2007, 154–161).

Such debates are further complicated where different interest groups come from a range of nations. One of the more telling moments in an episode of BBC TV's archaeological drama series *Bonekickers* (2008) featured a number of characters from UK, France and Germany arguing about the wreck of a tank while another character muses that he thought the war had ended in 1918; one small scene encapsulated the international interests inherent in this field of study. It is also significant that the series included such a story in its plotlines, underlining the fact that archaeologists' presence is now established in the militarised landscapes of the First World War.

Digging trenches?

Early archaeological work on the Front, which was largely undertaken by amateurs, tended to concentrate on the iconic. The First World War is defined by trench warfare: schoolchildren learn about the trenches and tours visit surviving trenches, such as Newfoundland Park at Beaumont Hamel, so it is no surprise that such monuments attracted early attention by groups working near Ieper (Ypres) in Belgium and on the Somme (Saunders 2007, 116–118, 139–144) and indeed the author's fieldwork in this area began in the same way.

However the iconic could range from the world's first tanks (Desfosses, Jacques and Prilaux 2008 106–107) to named individuals enshrined in the national memory, such as author Alain Fournier in France (Saunders 2007, 101) or poet Wilfred Owen in the English-speaking world (Brown and Fraser, 2008, 147–172). As such these projects served a useful purpose in drawing attention to the developing phenomenon of First World War archaeology, not only in academic circles but also among the wider public and in the media. The work prompted the development of several television programmes on the subject and triggered further research, including the Wilfred Owen project cited above.

Media attention has funded some of this, but it has the effect of perpetuating the image of the war as solely one of trenches that seem divorced from the wider landscape in which they were located (Price 2007, 175–184). This initial concentration on the exploration of trenches did, however, allow a body of expertise to develop and permitted practitioners to work on easily identifiable sites. The focus of much research on the trenches has allowed rapid advances in theory and methodology of the archaeological study of the First World War and has helped to inform this paper (Saunders 2007, 104–126).

The trenches themselves have offered a wide range of evidence of *materiel* – military materials and equipment – and of the culture of the trenches, as well as telling us more about both particular actions and the men who occupied the trenches. The landscape context of these trenches has also developed from such work, as the immediate location in terrain prompted a wider consideration, often based on map and aerial photo evidence of how sites fitted into a wider whole. As First World War archaeology has developed it has begun to consider the world in which the war was fought and to consider its wider landscape setting (De Wilde 2006 137–142; De Meyer 2006 143–146)

Looking over the parapet

To soldiers in the trenches the view was almost unremittingly of the mud or chalk into which their positions were dug, punctuated by the timber or corrugated iron used in their construction. They could, of course, look up towards the sky, important for the weather it brought but a glance into no-man's-land could be fatal as snipers waited to kill the unwary. However, despite the fact that looking at the land surrounding their particular trench was taboo, every soldier knew that he sat in a wider landscape of conflict. Soldiers spent time in training camps, hospitals and reserve areas, while their officers, as well as engineers and artillerymen studied maps and aerial photographs to identify threats and targets and to select objectives for operations. For the archaeologist studying the fields of conflict tools such as the original maps and contemporary aerial photographs remain essential, alongside new techniques, such as geophysical survey and GIS (Geographical Information Systems), which allows terrain modelling, enabling researchers to both pinpoint targets for intervention and to set them in wider contexts.

For example at St Yvon, in Wallonia, Belgium, at the southern end of the Ieper Salient, the group No Man's Land [full title: No Man's Land – The European Group for Great War Archaeology and the Comines-Warneton Historical Society] has employed a multi-disciplinary approach. This includes work by Birger Stichelbaut, from the University of Ghent on the rectification (annotation/transcription of photographs to emphasise features of interest) of aerial photographs and the creation of GIS overlays of modern and historic mapping and images. Stichelbaut's work has been complemented by a geophysical survey carried out by Peter Masters of Cranfield University that has studied some 20 hectares so far (Plugstreet 2008) and in turn been added to the composite mapping of the site. Historical geographer Peter Chasseaud has also done a phenomenological study (the marrying up of observable physical phenomena with theory by means of experiments; Brown and Osgood forthcoming [a]).

While geophysical survey, particularly magnetometry, with its ability to cover large areas relatively quickly has long been an archaeological tool there had been doubts about its value on the battlefields with their heavy concentrations of military debris in the soil. Despite such doubts, work on the UK Army's training area on Salisbury Plain, in Britain and on former battlefields in Belgium has shown the value of this technique (Masters 2007). Nonetheless it is important to see time depth in the landscape, as well as spatial context because the landscape in

which the war was fought was not the same as it is today. Of course this may be an obvious point to anyone looking today at these landscapes of conflict, where no building in the former combat zone pre-dates 1920, but this perspective does not entirely explore the world known by and lost to the civilian population of 1914.

The pre-war population of the battlefields

The introduction of the civilian population who lived in the battlefields into the narratives opens a new avenue in the archaeological study of the western front, as it broadens the research and recognises the scope of the tragedy and the war's impact beyond its effect on the men in uniform. In West Flanders pre-war maps have been used to explore the countryside that the armies entered and shows it to have largely been a later medieval landscape of small fields, scattered woodlands and moated farmsteads (Stubbe 2006, 147–152).

One such farm was at St Yvon, known as Factory Farm by British military cartographers and fortified by the German invaders before its destruction by an Allied mine in 1917 (Barton, Doyle and Vandewalle 2004, 173). Here ongoing archaeological work has revealed not only traces of the German efforts at defence but also the shattered remains of the farmhouse, as well as domestic objects that bear witness to the life of the family who were forced from their home by war (Osgood, Brown and Hawkins 2006, 34, 58–61; Brown and Osgood, forthcoming [b]). Elsewhere on this farm research has uncovered evidence of the post-war attempts to domesticate the shattered landscape that must have been all but unrecognisable to the returning refugees (Brown and Osgood, forthcoming [b]). Thus the archaeology initially demonstrates the warfare and the process of reconstruction but from the remains one may extrapolate experiences of dislocation, trauma and loss on a communal scale across whole landscapes.

Further away from the scenes of fighting archaeologists are also beginning to consider the wider landscape impact of the war. On Salisbury Plain, Wiltshire, UK, a project has been running since 2005 looking at the training landscape there; in Staffordshire, UK, a further project has begun on the two major divisional training camps of the First World War and will soon begin work on part of the site that housed German prisoners of war (Brown and Nichol 2006).

Objects evoking the conflict

If a single broken wine glass can be an indicator of trauma, other objects may also symbolise the conflict and the actions of individuals within the wider conflict. Finding a bottle of savoury sauce, such as the HP brand, or a mustard jar at St Yvon can tell us how boring at least one man found his rations, such as the corned beef and hard biscuits that were issued to British and Commonwealth troops. A bottle of Eno's Fruit Salts, also found at St Yvon, along with the sauce bottles conveys the negative effects the diet could have on the digestion! A tin – for chocolate or cigarettes – can show the importance of comforts to boost morale when in extreme situations. However these items, such as the chocolate tin and the sauce bottle may also evoke the clash of empires that characterised the First World War: a tin excavated in Thiepval Wood on the Somme records that it was a gift from British Caribbean colonies sent to troops in theatre. That the tin was found in the front-line trenches is, in fact, a story in itself since to reach its destination it had to cross oceans patrolled by enemy submarines and then move through the rear echelons to the infantry in the trenches. There were numerous opportunities for loss, theft or consumption on the journey but this small comfort seems to have been enjoyed by soldiers actually in the combat zone and within sound of their enemies.

Food and tobacco are not the only things that sustained the men who found themselves in such dire circumstances. We also find evidence of more intangible comforts, including those denoting belief, folklore and ritual among the soldiers. A pipe from the site of a First World War training camp on Cannock Chase in Staffordshire, UK bears the symbols of the quasi-masonic Royal Antediluvian Order of Buffaloes (Brown and Nichol 2006, 4); these pipes are said to be broken over the head of an initiate into the Buffalo's' Lodges (Louis Brown, pers comm). Talismans, formed from bullets and shrapnel balls seen in the class of transformed military materials known as 'trench art' have been interpreted as having been made in order to ward off harm from any further bullets or mortars (Saunders 2003, 99–100).

Despite the joke current amongst archaeologists that 'ritual' is the preserve of the mystified prehistorian, it is clear that folk magic and unorthodox ceremonial can be discerned in the archaeological record of the First World War. Focusing on the most personal of artefacts – those carried by the individual – it is also possible to see something of an individual personality. In the bread bag of Albert Thielecke, a German *Unteroffizier* excavated on the Somme in 2003 we found not only a pipe, but also a harmonica and even a prehistoric flint (Brown and Fraser 2008, 167–168).

Landscapes in conflict

The sites of the First World War are more than simply their physical context. They belong in a cultural landscape, one that is fraught with emotion and can stir up strong passions. The war has always been a contested cultural event and remains so, as debates over the necessity, purpose and significance of the conflict continue to rage (Todman 2005, 120–152).

The fact that the events under investigation are relatively recent means that many people, including those engaged in fieldwork, have personal connections to individuals involved, such as Jon Price at Serre in 2003 (Brown 2007, 56–57). There are also many people who, because of the popularity of family history or of family or other connection, feel connected in a very direct and personal way to the First World War and its sites. This can create interest and

Fig 1.52 The body of a German soldier identified as Jakob Hones, excavated at Serre 2003. Courtesy of Walter Rapp

support for research but may also hinder it if archaeologists are seen as intruding on what is considered almost sacred ground.

Other connections, such as national history, can also influence views of the war, whether for archaeologists or for the wider public. Archaeologists need to be aware that in contrast to many other sites in European archaeology, save perhaps for the major megalithic monuments (Bender 1998, 133–145), there are wider public debates, discourses and contestations to negotiate! The wider engagement with the historic landscape was clearly illustrated by opposition from people in Britain to the extension of the A19 motorway around the city of Ieper in Flanders (Saunders 2007; 18, 161). The need to take into account the feelings and views of the wider public is nowhere more pronounced than in the excavation of human remains, quite literally the man in the landscape. Archaeologists not only excavate the casualties of the war and identify them, but having done so may find themselves contacting and even meeting the individual's descendants (Brown 2007, 57 and Fig 1). This may entail the use of techniques more akin to forensic archaeology in order to extract the maximum information from the skeleton and its associated artefacts, since the evidence is valued not only for archaeological interpretation but also to identify and perhaps give 'closure' to a family (Brown and Fraser 2008, 169).

Strange meetings

Great War archaeology is different. On one level First World War archaeological research is like any other archaeological research, employing various techniques to investigate sites and to set them in context. Archaeology can use its normal range of techniques to explore not only individual sites of conflict but also the wider cultural landscapes within which they are set and on which the conflict had such a dramatic effect. This context may be international, as soldiers come across the globe to the battlefield or the civilians flee to another country.

The study of sites and the artefacts associated with them can also help to repopulate the battlefield itself with soldiers and with the civilians displaced by the conflict who then had to return and rebuild both the land and their lives. The collected objects can also serve to recreate a more rounded picture of the people involved by presenting pictures of humans who ate,

drank, smoked and engaged in war, work and social activities. Furthermore, the human dimension extends beyond the direct participants in and victims of the war. First most of the investigators have connections to the war and indeed some can remember aged relatives who fought. Secondly, the descendants of those involved in the war may still feel a close connection to their ancestors and can have definite opinions on their treatment and study, especially where human remains are involved.

In contrast, looking beyond the sites of battle, a researcher quickly becomes aware that the scale of the war was vast and that so far little work has been conducted on training sites and no one has investigated medical or logistics sites, such as stores and depots, which are equally little studied in the military histories. As such it is clear that there is still much scope for further investigation of the impact of the conflict across the landscape and on the individuals caught up in it.

Archaeological study of the First World War explores new ground, quite literally, and seeks not to follow military history but rather to complement it in exploring both terrain and the human experience. As such it leads to strange yet fulfilling and fruitful meetings.

List of references

Barton, P, Doyle, P, Vandewalle, J 2004 *Beneath Flanders Fields*. Stapleford: Spellmount

Bonekickers, BBCTV, Broadcast date 01/08/2008

Bender, B 1998 *Stonehenge: Making space*, Oxford: Berg

Brown, M 2007 'The Fallen, The Front and The Finding: Archaeology, Human Remains and the Great War', *Archaeological Review from Cambridge*, **22**, 2, 53–68

Brown, M and Fraser, A 2008 'Mud, blood and missing men: Excavations at Serre, Somme, France' *in* Pollard, T and Banks, I, (eds) *Scorched Earth: Studies in the archaeology of conflict*. Leiden: Brill, 147–172

Brown M and Osgood R forthcoming (a), 'Unearthing Plugstreet'. Sparkford: Haynes

Brown M and Osgood R forthcoming (b), 'Comines/Warneton : d'Australie et Angleterre à la Wallonie, fouilles archéologiques sur les sites de la Grande Guerre 1914-1918 à Saint-Yvon' in Remy, H (ed) Chronique de l'archéologie wallonne, 16 Namur: Service public de Wallonie et Institut du patrimoine wallon

Brown, M and Nichol, K 2006 'Excavations at Brocton Camp, Cannock Chase, Staffordshire'.Unpublished archive report for Staffordshire County Council Historic Environment Record

Defosses Y, Jacques A and Prilaux G, 2008 L'Archéologie de la Grande Guerre, Rennes: Editions Ouest France

De Wilde, M 2006 'De Erste Wereldoorlog en Archaeologie' in Chielens P, Dendooven, D and Hannelore, D, (eds) De Laatste Getuige. Tielt: Uitgeverij Lannoo nv, 137–142

De Meyer, M 2006 'Luchtfotos uit de Eerste Wereldoorlog: Vroeger en Nu', in Chielens P, Dendooven, D and Hannelore, D, (eds) De Laatste Getuige. Tielt: Uitgeverij Lannoo nv, 143–146

Masters, P 2007 Geophysical Survey of the Great War Practice Trenches on Perham Down, Shipton Bellinger, Salisbury Plain, Wiltshire, Cranfield Forensic Institute Report No. 006 Cranfield

Osgood, R, Brown M, Hawkins, L 2006 'Before the Storm', Wartime, **34**, 58–60

Owen W 1918 'Strange Meeting' in Stallworthy J 2002 Wilfred Owen: The War Poems. London: Chatto & Windus

Plugstreet 2008 http://plugstreet.blogspot.com, accessed 20/08/08

Price, J 2007 'Great War, Great Story' in Clack, T and Brittain, M, (eds) Archaeology and the Media. Walnut Creek: Left Coast, 175–184

Saunders N J 2003 Trench Art: Materialities and memories of war. Oxford: Berg

Saunders, N J 2007 Killing Time, Archaeology and the First World War. Stroud: Sutton

Stubbe, L 2006 'Een lappendeken met groenen naden: Het landschap van de Ieperboog' in Chielens P, Dendooven, D and Hannelore, D, (eds) De Laatste Getuige. Tielt: Uitgeverij Lannoo nv, 147–152

Todman, D 2005 The Great War, Myth and Memory. London: Hambledon and London

2. Defining values and significance: memory, commemoration and contested landscapes

Topography of terror or cultural heritage? The monuments of Franco's Spain

ALFREDO GONZÁLEZ-RUIBAL

On history and monuments

The Spanish Civil War (1936–1939) had an important impact on the landscape of Spain. The armed conflict and the subsequent dictatorship changed the face of the country, leaving deep scars in the shape of trenches, bombed out cities and villages, redundant fortifications, concentration camps and fascist monuments. Many features of this war landscape had remained forgotten and untouched until the building rush of the last ten years and the general upsurge in interest about the Civil War (González-Ruibal 2007).

During the last decade, there has been a growing debate in Spain over the management of the material legacy of the Franco dictatorship, which lasted from 1936 to the dictator's death in 1975. The policies developed by the socialist government from 2004 onwards have fuelled this debate. The Historical Memory Law (ley de la memoria histórica) was passed in 2007 by the Spanish government. It recognises the victims of political, religious and ideological violence on both sides of the Spanish Civil War and of the dictatorship of General Franco and promotes the moral restitution and recovery of their personal and family memory. Although these policies are not significantly different to those implemented in Germany, France or South Africa in relation to civil conflicts, they are creating a great social stir and are often portrayed as a biased attempt by a political party wilfully to rewrite history. It seems that active remembrance and commemoration is considered all very well in other countries and for other periods, but for the recent history of Spain it is expected that we must espouse oblivion (Tremlett 2006). This attitude is mostly a local phenomenon, but in recent years some foreign observers have adopted the conservative Spanish perspective, most notably *The New York Times* (Rothstein 2007; Kimmelman 2008), one of whose correspondents asserted that the new law (BOE 2007), passed to commemorate the victims of the Civil War and manage the monumental remains of the dictatorship, 'doesn't make much sense' (Kimmelman 2008).

According to Michael Kimmelman, 'over the years most of these [Francoist] monuments have already been carted off, making the law largely toothless and symbolic'. Even if it were true that the monuments have already been carted off, and it is far from true, would that justify letting the Francoist legacy stand as if it were simply another element of Spain's rich cultural heritage? Should we not at least qualify its message in some way? Kimmelman does not suggest anything of this sort. And neither do many Spaniards. The keyword is 'history': Franco's monuments are 'history' and, therefore, have to be preserved for posterity untouched.

But, what is and what is not history? Is history not also the ruins of concentration camps, battlefields and prisons, which can be found in many parts of the country? Many would accept that they are history, but a history that has to remain forgotten: 'let us not recall the things that divided us in the past and may still divide us in the present', they say. The idea is that we have to preserve things as they have come to us – buried if buried, alive if alive. What this way of thinking amounts to is that we ought to remember what the dictator wanted us to remember: his mausoleum, statues and triumphal arches, and to forget what the dictator wanted us to forget (or not to look at): prisons, mass graves, and battlefields. After all, what people usually identify with as cultural heritage is the bright side of history: monuments, works of art and places of heroic deeds. Franco's buildings fit much better in this category than his repressive institutions.

A monumental silence?

Michael Kimmelman says that we have to ignore Franco's monuments and leave them to their own devices, because nobody talks about them anymore and nobody cares: they have been displaced from Spanish collective memory. As the enormous recent national interest in the Civil War proves, however, the remains of Francoism are anything but forgotten (Gálvez Biesca 2006; Richards 2006). Yet at the same time, it is true that there is 'a monumental silence', or at least a monumental uneasiness, regarding the remains of the war and Franco's past.

We should ask ourselves about this silence, instead of accepting it as something natural. As it is well known, silence belongs with dictatorship and is the product of fear and trauma – see Byrne (2007, 81–98) for a good example of an archaeological reading of a silenced landscape. Silence is enforced by physical and symbolic violence and contributes to protract and worsen trauma (Lister 1982; Herman 1997). When an individual goes through a terrible emotional shock, he or she often becomes mute. The same occurs with societies: usually, a generation has to pass after traumatic events, before they can be properly addressed.

Fig 2.1 The façade of the basilica of the Valley of the Fallen.
© Alfredo González-Ruibal

In Spain, those who want to know about the past are the grandchildren of those who killed or were killed in the war – the generation that has no personal experience of dictatorship. Silence has dominated Spain until very recently due to the effectiveness of General Franco's repressive policies. Therefore, if we ignore and take for granted the material legacy of the dictatorship, we are complicit with its policies. In fact, by choosing the past that we want to remember, we decide the future that we wish to have. As massive landmarks, the sites of the Civil War and Francoism force us to take them into account and to rethink fundamental political values.

Here we will try to show how the material remains of Franco's dictatorship are (mis)managed and how a different approach could produce not only a different interpretation of the past, but also foster more democratic values. For this, two of the most important building projects of the immediate post-war period are examined: the Valley of the Fallen and Carabanchel Prison.

From the Valley of the Fallen to the Fallen in the Valley

The Valley of the Fallen [*El Valle de los Caídos*] is a large mausoleum, built by order of General Francisco Franco near Madrid for those who died in the Civil War, for the founder of the Falange, the Spanish fascist party (José Antonio Primo de Rivera), and for the general himself (Figure 2.1). Although the project started immediately after the war, using forced labour, the construction ended only in 1959, after several requests by the dictator to increase the size of the main building, a huge underground basilica larger than St Peter's in the Vatican (Monumento Nacional 1962; Sueiro 2006; Smith 2007). Around 40,000 individuals are buried in the basilica that constitutes the central architectural feature of the site.

Current defendants of the Valley, drawing on Franco's own statements, argue that the monument was meant to preserve the memory of those who died in the conflict, irrespective of their political affiliation. The reality is far from bipartisan: apart from the obvious fact that Franco is the most conspicuous individual buried at the site and that the representation of Republicans is negligible, everything about this memorial was conceived to exalt Franco's rule and the national-catholic principles on which the regime was based.

The architects resorted to a revival of Spanish Renaissance architecture, the style of the golden age of the Spanish empire, and this became fashionable all over the country. They drew inspiration from the nearby monastery of El Escorial, built by Philip II in the 16th century: the vision was to build Franco's memorial into part of the 'royal route' in the mountains near Madrid where El Escorial and the 18th century palace of La Granja are also located. It was a not very subtle way of trying to make the Francoist regime blend in, presenting it as a logical sequel to the reign of Spanish kings. Imperial emblems and religious references abound. Although the monument is mainly built in a neo-traditionalist style, there are also a number of modernist elements: they include the colossal scale of the buildings and sculptures and the style of the statues. Both show close connections with fascist aesthetics and ideology.

Today, the Valley of the Fallen site is part of what is called 'national heritage', a series of historical sites that used to belong to the kings of Spain. Important historical buildings are included, such as Madrid's 18th century Royal Palace. As part of the national heritage and due to its strategic location (the site commands wonderful views of Madrid), the Valley receives hundreds of thousands of visitors every year, both national and international.

There is not, however, a single sign that contextualises the place. A visit to the Valley today is no different to one that could have taken place in the 1960s (Smith 2007). It is not surprising therefore to find that extreme-right activists, nostalgists and members of the Falange gather at the site. For them it is a perfect, unchanged place that still fulfils its function of praising totalitarianism to perfection. One of the things that is brushed aside is the fact that the edifices were built by 6,000 political prisoners (Sueiro 1976).

With the Spanish government's new law about commemorating the victims of the Civil War and the dictatorship (BOE 2007), the Valley of the Fallen can no longer be kept as a monument to Francoism. According to the law, 'The foundation in charge of managing the Valley of the Fallen will include among its objectives to honour and rehabilitate the memory of all those who died as a consequence of the Civil War of 1936–1939 and the political repression that followed, with the purpose of increasing our knowledge of this historical period and the constitutional values. Besides, it will promote the aspirations of reconciliation and coexistence that exist in our society' (BOE 2007: 53414). Because the legislators were aiming to avoid confrontation, the law is very vague and does not help in finding solutions to issues such as the management of the Valley of the Fallen. How is one to promote 'aspirations of reconciliation and coexistence' in a fascist memorial?

In the view of the author the place has to be transformed drastically but intelligently and for that it is not necessary to alter its fabric. As has already been proposed, a museum should be installed inside the basilica (after removing Franco's remains), that tells the story of the monument and the terrible conditions in which it was erected.

Another crucial step for deconstructing the valley is undermining its monumentality. For this, the author proposes a twofold archaeological move: firstly, the monument has to be redefined in the landscape, detaching from being linked to the long-term royal and imperial history of Spain to the short-term history of war and dictatorship. Secondly, the history of the site itself has to be made clear, disclosing its real nature through the presentation of the archaeological remains associated with its construction.

With regard to the first point, the area of El Escorial was part of the front-line during the whole conflict. This has left an impressive amount of archaeological remains everywhere. In one of the municipalities around El Escorial, for example, 107 sites with evidence of war use have been recently recorded (Colectivo

Fig 2.2 Concrete-reinforced trenches from the Civil War in Fresnedillas de la Oliva, 16 km away from the Valley of the Fallen.
© Alfredo González-Ruibal

Guadarrama 2008) (Figure 2.2). Other municipalities have similar amounts of remains and several routes for visiting war sites in the area have been recently proposed (Arévalo 2007). War ruins allow us to challenge the epic image of the 'crusade' celebrated by Franco's monument, as they show the sordid and violent side of the conflict. The idea, then, is to remove the Valley from the national heritage list and include it in a topography of terror composed of war and post-war sites in Madrid.

In the Valley of the Fallen itself, the sites related to forced labour have to be identified, excavated and displayed, giving pre-eminence to those sites of suffering over the monument itself. With a group of colleagues, the author has been investigating a forced labour camp north of Madrid and we have discovered over 40 huts where the families of the inmates lived while their relatives served their sentences (Falquina *et al* forthcoming). Since women and children depended on men for their survival, they joined them in the camps and shared their fate. The archaeology evokes the terrible living conditions: people lived packed in tiny, unhealthy shacks, made with dry stone and covered with thatch. They slept on the floor, were malnourished, and suffered from extremely low temperatures during the winter. There is plenty of evidence for the existence of similar camps in the Valley of the Fallen (Lafuente 2002, 125-

–130; Sueiro 2006). The remains of those camps need to be located, excavated and displayed.

With this double strategy – excavating the labour camps and inserting the Valley into the war routes – the genealogy of the monument can be disentangled and the ideological constructions that distort its true nature can be thoroughly counteracted, thus preventing revisionist interpretations based on oblivion and the concealment of evidence.

From prison to agora

The other site that I would like to discuss is not, strictly speaking, a Francoist monument. It is rather an anti-monument: the prison of Carabanchel.

The prison was one of the biggest of its kind in Europe. It was built between 1940 and 1944 by 1,000 political prisoners, most of them members of the defeated Republican army or political parties (Díaz Cardiel 2007, 13). Like most other prisons built in Spain at that time, the structure followed the old-fashioned panopticon model (Johnston 1961, 319–320), which had mostly fallen into disuse elsewhere.

The immense cupola at the heart of the space was a powerful metaphor of the new totalitarian regime of surveillance that would characterise the post-war period (Figure 2.3). The site was an important place of political repression for the whole period of Franco's dictatorship. It was a temporary detention centre for people that awaited other destinations torture was routinely carried out on the premises and people were executed by garrotte and firing squad there until the end of the Franco regime.

After the dictatorship, it became an ordinary prison until its closure in 1998, when the building was abandoned, without any plans for future use. The place is now degrading very fast, due to vandalism and systematic looting. Part of it has been occupied by illegal immigrants and drug addicts, and its walls have become a museum of graffiti.

The area where the prison was built was a former battlefield, associated with the Battle of Madrid (Reverte 2004). Carabanchel and Aluche were working-class neighbourhoods (or, rather, villages), south of the city, whose inhabitants were active politically in unions and leftist parties. It was precisely there where Franco's army was halted, after two months of crushing offensives in 1937. The stubborn defence put up by the militias, who fought house-to-house against Franco's well-trained colonial army, prevented the future dictator from entering Madrid for the remainder of the war. Instead, Carabanchel became a front-line for two and a half years and, as a result, almost half the buildings in the neighbourhood were destroyed (Sánchez Molledo 1998, 140).

Building the colossal prison in Carabanchel was undoubtedly a deliberate decision, a reprisal against the working classes and a permanent reminder of the dangers that awaited those who dared resist General Franco. The whole neighbourhood was rebuilt as a segregated working-class township, according to the totalitarian ideology of the time (Moreno 1983, 155–157). The streets were given the names of the generals that participated in the war against the Republic (Millán Astray, Romero Basart, Fanjul, Saliquet).

For the residents of Aluche and Carabanchel, the prison became an essential part of their lives and their history. It is perceived in this way today: many of those who live in the surrounding areas were imprisoned there, or have relatives and friends who were. Nowadays, Carabanchel Prison is a significant landmark in the collective memory of Spaniards.

The future of Carabanchel

Despite the historical and architectural relevance of the building, there are no plans for preserving it. The authorities want to reassess the use of the land where the prison stands and sell it to developers. The residents' associations reject this proposal and are asking for the land to be kept for public use; they want part of the prison to be preserved as a memorial to democracy. The residents' groups claim that the neighbourhoods have been traditionally marginalised and lack any place for socialising or public facilities. As one of the activists put it, 'this is a city without an agora'. The 17 hectares of land on which the prison stands and the institution's role in the cultural memory of the neighbourhood provide a great opportunity to create this commemorative space.

The authorities' abandonment of the building for a decade, however, has been deliberate. They want people to get tired of trying to preserve the building and simply approve any plan that will rid them of an increasingly dangerous ruin. The strategy, though, has not worked so far. On the contrary, the decaying of the building has been instrumental in mobilising the residents even more. They have organised demonstrations, public lectures, guided tours to the prison and exhibitions. They have recently proposed a comprehensive plan for redeveloping the area, which includes a hospital, a centre for senior citizens, an institution of higher education, a park and a democratic memorial in the prison's panopticon[1]. Although both the Spanish socialist government and the local right-wing authorities are ready to accept a hospital, they still insist in building private housing and tearing down the prison. As this text is revised for publication, in October 2008, the demolition of the prison seems imminent[2].

The author has been working with a research team from the Spanish Higher Council of Scientific Research (CSIC)[3], which is trying to assess the social relevance of the monument and to understand its place in the cultural memory of the neighbourhood – something akin to what British experts call 'characterisation' (Schofield 2005, 128–130). The author would like to elaborate a little on the possibilities offered by the prison as part of a topography of terror in Madrid. In the first place, as the residents suggest, it would be a good idea to protect the panopticon. Following similar projects elsewhere (for example, Strange and Kempa 2003; Corsane 2006), this structure could be transformed into a museum, where the history of the prison and, more generally, incarceration and political repression during Francoism are properly appraised.

Fig 2.4 Map of the Carabanchel Prison neighbourhood, with important war sites. © Alfredo González-Ruibal

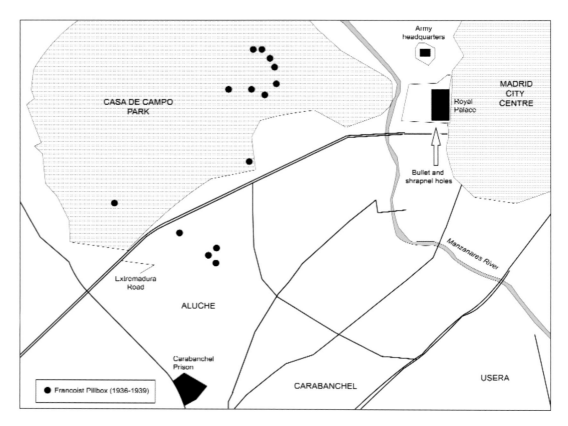

The museum, although focusing on the Francoist period, should also describe the terrible revolutionary violence in Madrid during the Civil War, that claimed the lives of thousands of people, many of them innocent civilians. After all, Carabanchel Prison is the successor to the Model Prison, which stood near the centre of Madrid. That institution, of which nothing remains, became infamous for the mass execution of its inmates by communists and anarchists in November and December 1936 (Reverte 2004, 241–244, 350–351).

As in the case of the Valley of the Fallen, the building should be understood as part of a particular landscape of conflict. Whereas Franco tried to insert the Valley of the Fallen into a historically-legitimised imperial route, Carabanchel Prison has fallen victim to an abolition of history. The prison was imposed, like a monster into the midst of a shattered neighbourhood – as a sort of divine punishment. Until recently, and still for many people today, the relationship between Francoism, the Civil War, and the prison is far from obvious. Mapping the specific connections between the prison and its surroundings enables us to grasp history in a direct, physical way.

The area surrounding the building bears the testimony of the Spanish Civil War in the guise of trenches and bunkers preserved in the nearby park of Casa de Campo (Castellano Ruiz de la Torre 2004, 230–238) (Figure 2.4). They belonged to the 16th and 18th divisions of the Francoist army, which besieged Madrid during the conflict, but were unable to conquer the city. From their positions in Casa de Campo, the Francoists shelled Madrid throughout the war killing and wounding hundreds of civilians. So far, no steps have been taken by the public authorities to preserve or display the remains of the war and they lie abandoned and ruined, just like the prison itself.

By linking together the prison, the battlefield and other local sites associated with war and repression in Madrid, a more critical understanding of the city's recent history can be achieved. This topography of terror should serve to foster a democratic counter-memory that overcomes oblivion and replaces the fascist history that the dictator bequeathed to us – a history that is still inscribed in the street names of Aluche and Carabanchel.

In a sense, what has been proposed here is to transform a monument into a ruin and a ruin into a monument, in order to produce a critical, democratic reading of Spain's recent past. That is, the epic qualities of the Valley of the Fallen have to be deconstructed, by counteracting its monumentality with the ruins of the forced labour camps and the battlefields of the Civil War. On the contrary, the epic qualities of Carabanchel, as a centre where democracy was forged during the dictatorship, have to be enhanced and remembered through the construction of a memorial in the prison. In both cases, the sites have to be inserted into the wider context of the Civil War and Francoism, as part of a topography of terror (Braun 2002).

This, of course, is a proposal that will be disliked by some. Fredric Jameson said that 'history is what hurts' (Jameson 1981, 102). It seems that we are not fully aware of it and insist on producing sanitised, apolitical visions of the past. Yet there are historical experiences – especially recent ones – that cannot be reconciled. It is not possible to construct a narrative that pleases both the victim and the torturer. It is neither advisable nor ethically sound.

The problem of monuments that try too hard to conciliate has been pointed out by Koshar (2000, 258), in relation to the rhetoric of victimisation that emerged in Germany in the 1980s, which intended to honour all Germans as victims. A narrative that presents everybody as a victim or everybody as a perpetrator is politically irresponsible. As Hannah Arendt (2005, 87) wrote: 'Where everybody is guilty, nobody is; public confessions of collective guilt are the best defence against the discovery of culprits, and the magnitude of a crime is the best excuse to not do anything'.

A political attitude toward the past does not mean that we have to produce simplistic historical accounts in black and white. It actually means three things: first, extremely conciliatory memorials and historical displays have to be avoided because they are inherently unjust and promote a dangerous levelling of values; second, priority has to be given to truly democratic values, discourses and memories over all others; third, conflict cannot be crossed out from the remains of the recent past. As Dolff-Bonekämper (2002) remarks, 'there is no societal therapist who can help avoid unjust attacks while questioning the collective attributions of innocence, guilt, and responsibility'.

As time goes by, Spanish society will be able to face its negative past unhindered by Franco's shadow. Hopefully, at some point history and politics will no longer be regarded as things to be feared and shunned, but as an open field for endless discussion, based on widely shared democratic values. Historians, anthropologists and archaeologists have an important role to play in bringing forward a different past, one in which no justification is allowed for dictatorships of any kind.

Acknowledgements

The author would like to thank the organisers of the 2008 Landscapes of War Workshop held in Rostock for their invitation and also colleagues at the workshop for their insightful comments, which have improved this article.

Resumen

Durante la última década, ha habido un creciente debate en España sobre la gestión del legado material de la Guerra Civil y la dictadura (1936–1975). Este debate se ha generalizado a partir de las políticas desarro-lladas por el gobierno socialista a partir de marzo de 2004. Aunque estas políticas no son en esencia diferentes de las existentes en Alemania, Francia, Sudáfrica y otros países, están creando una gran controversia y se critican, sobre todo en España, pero también internacionalmente, como un intento sesgado de reescribir la historia por parte del gobierno. Mientras se defiende el recuerdo activo para otros países y períodos, se aboga por el olvido en el caso de España. En este trabajo se explora la naturaleza problemática del patrimonio franquista a través de dos ejemplos paradigmáticos y controvertidos, directamente relacionados con la guerra civil: el Valle de los Caídos y la prisión de Carabanchel, ambos en Madrid. El primero es un lugar de memoria fascista; el segundo, de lucha por la democracia. Sin embargo, el Valle es un monumento bien cuidado que recibe cientos de miles de visi-tas al año y el segundo una ruina en riesgo de desaparición. Trataré de demostrar aquí cómo se puede cambiar esta situación mediante la arqueología y producir una memoria diferente de la guerra y de la represión dictatorial.

Footnotes

[1] http://www.avaluche. com/spip.php?article415

[2] http://salvemoscarabanchel.blogspot.com/
Since the initial writing of this paper, despite protests from academics and local residents, the prison has been demolished

[3] Led by Dr Carmen Ortiz and funded by the FECYT

Bibliography

Arendt, H 2005 *Sobre la violencia*. Madrid: Alianza. First published 1970 *On Violence*, New York, Harcourt

Arévalo, JM 2007 *Senderos de guerra. 20 rutas históricas por la sierra de Guadarrama*. Madrid: La Librería

BOE 2007 'Ley 52/2007, de 26 de diciembre, por la que se reconocen y amplían derechos y se establecen medidas en favor de quienes padecieron persecución o violencia durante la guerra civil y la dictadura'. *Boletín Oficial del Estado* 310: 53410–53416

Braun, M S (ed) 2002 *Spuren des Terrors. Traces of Terror. Stätten national-sozialistischer Gewaltherrschaft in Berlin*. Berlin: Braun

Byrne, D 2007 *Surface collection. Archaeological travels in Southeast Asia*. Lanham, MD: Alta Mira Press

Casanova, J 2004 [2002] 'Una dictadura de cuarenta años' in Casanova J (ed) *Morir, matar, sobrevivir. La violencia en la dictadura de Franco*. Barcelona: Crítica, 3–50

Castellano Ruiz de la Torre, R 2004 *Los restos del asedio. Fortificaciones de la Guerra Civil en el frente de Madrid. Ejército nacional*. Madrid: Almena

Colectivo Guadarrama 2008 'Navalagamella. Catálogo de vestigios de la Guerra Civil Española en su término municipal'. Colectivo Guadarrama – Grupo de Preservación Histórica, Madrid, unpublished document

Corsane, G 2006 'Robben Island: facing the challenges of creating a National Museum in a World Heritage Site'. in Schofield, J, Klausmeier, A, Purbrick, L (eds) *Re-mapping the field: new approaches in conflict archeology*. Berlin; Bonn: Westkreuz-Verlag, 64–71

Díaz Cardiel, V 2007 'Algunos recuerdos de mis cuatro estancias en la cárcel de Carabanchel', *El Rapto de Europa* 11: 13–19

Dolff-Bonekämper, G 2002 'Sites of hurtful memory'. *Conservation: The Getty Conservation Institute Newsletter* 17, 2, 4–10

Falquina Aparicio, A, Fermín Maguire, P, González Ruibal, A, Marín Suarez, C, Quintero Maqua, A, Rolland Calvo, J, 2008 'Arqueología de los destacamentos penales franquistas en el ferrocarril Madrid-Burgos: el caso de Bustarviejo', in González-Ruibal, A (ed), *Arqueología de la Guerra Civil Española, Complutum*, 19(2), pp. 175–95.

Fundación Francisco Franco 2005 *El Valle de los Caídos. Lugar de reconciliación y de paz.* <http://www.generalisimofranco.com/valle_caidos/07.htm> accessed 8 April 2008

Gálvez Biesca, S 2006 'El proceso de recuperación de la "memoria histórica" en España: una aproximación a los movimientos sociales por la memoria'. *International Journal of Iberian Studies* 19,1, 25–51

González-Ruibal, A 2007 'Making things public: archaeologies of the Spanish Civil War', *Public Archaeology* 6,4, 203–226

González-Ruibal, A forthcoming 'Contra la pospolítica. Arqueología de la Guerra Civil Española' in Angelo,

D (ed) *Arqueología y política*. World Archaeological Congress

Herman, J L 1997 *Trauma and recovery*. New York: Basic Books

Jameson, F 1981 *The political unconscious: Narrative as a socially symbolic act*. Ithaca, NY: Cornell University Press; London: Methuen

Johnston, N 1961 'Recent trends in correctional architecture' *British Journal of Criminology* 1,4, 317–338

Kimmelman, M 2008 'In Spain, a monumental silence'. *The New York Times* 13 January 2008 <http://www.nytimes.com/2008/01/13/arts/design/13kimm.html> accessed 7 April 2008

Koshar, R 2000 *From monuments to traces: Artefacts of the German memory, 1870–1990*. Berkeley: California University Press

Lafuente, I 2002 *Esclavos por la patria. La explotación de los presos en el franquismo*. Madrid: Temas de Hoy

Lister, E D 1982 'Forced silence: a neglected dimension of trauma'. *American Journal of Psychiatry* 139, 7, 872–876

Monumento Nacional 1962 *Monumento Nacional de Santa Cruz del Valle de los Caídos. Guía Turística*. Madrid: Patrimonio Nacional

Moreno Jiménez, A 1983 *Carabanchel. Recuperar el espacio vivido*. Madrid: Junta Municipal del Distrito de Carabanchel

Reverte, J M 2004 *La Batalla de Madrid*. Madrid: Crítica

Richards, M 2006 'Between memory and history: Social relationships and ways of remembering the Spanish Civil War'. *International Journal of Iberian Studies* 19,1, 85–94

Rothstein, E 2007 'The Spanish Civil War: Black and White in a Murky, Ambiguous World'. *The New York Times* 24 March 2007 <http://www.nytimes.com/2007/03/24/arts/design/24fasc.html> accessed 7 April 2008

Sánchez Molledo, J Mª 1998 *Carabanchel. Un distrito con historia*. Madrid: La Librería/Ayuntamiento de Madrid

Schofield, J 2005 *Combat archaeology. Material culture and modern conflict*. London: Duckworth

Segovia, C 2004 'Un veterano republicano y otro de la División Azul portarán la ofrenda del Rey el día 12'. *El Mundo*, 9 October 2004

Smith, H 2007 'Seventy years of waiting: A turning point for interpreting the Spanish Civil War? in Ryan, C (ed) *Battlefield tourism: History, place and interpretation*. New York: Elsevier, 99–110

Strange, C and Kempa, M 2003 'Shades of dark tourism – Alcatraz and Robben Island' *Annals of Tourism Research* 30, 2, 386–405

Sueiro, D 1976 *La verdadera historia del Valle de los Caídos*. Madrid: Sedmay

Sueiro, D 2006 *El Valle de los Caídos. Los secretos de la cripta franquista*. Madrid: La Esfera de los Libros

Tremlett, G 2006 *Ghosts of Spain: Travels through a country's hidden past*. London: Faber and Faber

2. Defining values and significance: memory, commemoration and contested landscapes

Contested pasts and community archaeologies: public engagement in the archaeology of modern conflict

The last ten years have seen the transformation of the archaeology of modern conflict from a minority interest into a radical and lively sub-discipline. This development has been based in no small part on work that has arisen out of managing resources of cultural heritage, with a strong emphasis on the social contexts of conflict, memorialisation and contestation (dispute). From these foundations a range of research projects, conferences and publications have grown. One of the great strengths of this emerging field of study is the willingness of many scholars to get involved with people and organisations from other academic disciplines and even outside the academic world, collaborating, for example with the media, the military, amateur enthusiasts, artists and others.

Throughout research and fieldwork on the archaeology of the Second World War in Britain we have been interested in and committed to public participation and education. We have come to understand both the academic value of having the public involved in modern conflict archaeology, and the social significance of such projects. The power of this relationship moves beyond the basics of education, outreach and public archaeology. It has led the author to hypothesise that:

- archaeology of modern conflict is most effective when conducted as community archaeology

and conversely

- the most effective form of community archaeology is the archaeology of modern conflict.

In this paper a theoretical and methodological approach to community archaeologies of modern conflict is outlined that assesses the value and validity of these hypotheses. This approach is based on a model of conflict archaeology as an interdisciplinary practice studying the material culture and archaeological remains of the conflict together with historical sources and memory work, based on oral history (for example, Schofield 2004; Schofield *et al* 1998). While such approaches are commonly practised in conflict archaeology there has not been very much discussion about them at a theoretical level, particularly in their historic and mnemonic (memory evoking) elements. This paper addresses these weaknesses.

The use of discrete sites and their locales as focuses for conflict archaeology fieldwork lies at the core of the author's approach, as it naturally brings together elements of the local community, as well as other stakeholders, such as schools and museums. It also provides a clearly defined dataset to work with. Most of the case studies mentioned in this paper are British, but the principles discussed are universal, and are probably of even greater value in places where the memory of conflict is more violently contested than it tends to be in Britain.

A model for public and community archaeology

To begin, we will explain what we mean by public or community archaeology. The 'public' element of public archaeology seldom originates with 'the public' themselves. It is more commonly embodied by governmental as opposed to private interests. The concept of the 'public sphere', as a forum in which individuals engage in public debate and collective negotiation with the authorities, bridges this gap with openness and inclusivity as its most fundamental characteristics (Matsuda 2004).

Recent studies of archaeological subjectivity and public perceptions of the past have highlighted a trend in contemporary archaeological research that aims to make archaeology more meaningful and accessible to the general public. This supposedly manifests itself in a shift away from disseminating accounts that are dominated by just one perspective towards the production of multiple histories, recognising that 'different people in different places will have very different ideas about which aspects of the past matter' (Grima 2002, 85).

For this to become a genuinely democratising process within archaeology it must include a dialogue between the archaeologists and the wider public. Meaningful and empowering pasts cannot be created for a marginalised audi-

ence; we must recognise that 'the distinction between archaeological research and public engagement with the past is organisational rather than intrinsic' (Grima 2002, 87). This optimistic perspective on public engagement with the past underpins my explorations of public archaeologies of modern conflict. It is worth at this point briefly discussing some examples of, and precedents for, public and community involvement in conflict archaeology.

Dialogue with the public

The Shoreditch Park Community Archaeology Project in 2005 excavated a row of houses in London's East End that were destroyed by bombing. Hundreds of people from local community groups and schools were involved in the excavation over three weeks (Figure 2.5), in which a large quantity of material was recovered, illuminating life on the British 'home front' during the Second World War (Simpson and Williams 2008). The author's role was to carry out an oral history survey of local people who had lived on or near the site at the time of

Fig 2.5 Community archaeology on a Second World War site: teaching and learning archaeological fieldwork skills at Shoreditch Park, London. © Gabriel Moshenska

the bombing. Many testimonies were collected and have since been used in museum displays and educational materials that the project has triggered (Moshenska 2007).

Some communities are not defined geographically; interest groups of various kinds can and should also be considered as a source. The Defence of Britain Project, which ran from 1995 to 2002, involved more than 600 amateur archaeologists volunteering their time to survey and record Second World War anti-invasion defences around Britain (CBA 2002; Schofield 2005). As one of the coordinators noted: 'From the outset it was recognised that wide public involvement was needed, both to identify and record surviving remains, to draw on the memories of those who built or manned these defences, or who simply remembered where they were' (Saunders 1998, 7).

In the course of the Defence of Britain Project nearly 20,000 sites were added to the database, which now forms a valuable tool for heritage management and research (CBA 2002). The involvement of interested members of the public was key to the success of this project, and shows the high levels of public interest and support for modern conflict archaeology.

Arguments for an interdisciplinary public archaeology of modern conflict

The types of project that most interest the author are small-scale, local research projects focused on a specific site or historic event, that combine historical, archaeological sources as well as things people remember, with public involvement at every stage, all combining to create a narrative around the site. Most archaeological research into modern conflict takes place on this modest scale, often carried out by local amateur groups and archaeology societies. A significant number are sponsored by television production companies. In the last few years an increasing number of independent and university-based researchers have focused on conflict sites in America, western Europe and the Middle East as a form of empowerment (for example, Faulkner 2005; Saitta *et al* 2006).

The form of most of these projects is straightforward: background research is carried out in local and national archives, and often including oral history in the preliminary work. Excavation follows, most often with the aim of highlighting or restoring a site of significance.

The combination of history, memory and archaeology is key to such projects, and provides both its academic and social value. As Schofield (2004) and others have argued, such straightforward interdisciplinary projects on a small scale are ideal for student or school projects. However, the broader theoretical and methodological significance of these little surveys is often neglected.

Arguments from historiography

In the author's view public archaeologies of modern conflict can serve a very valuable purpose in bridging the gap between local and national history. Recently historians have begun to compare local histories of the home front in Britain, the so-called 'X at War' phenomenon, with national and international histories of the conflict, revealing that local studies showed less engagement with current theory than national ones. In the 1970s historians such as Angus Calder reacted against the dominant mythologies of the 'Blitz spirit', while more recently the rapidly evolving theories of memory have highlighted the distortion of individuals' memories by the collective popular consciousness (Calder 1991; 1992; Popular Memory Group 1982). These developments have largely been bypassed in local studies: 'the history which queries the war experience as a positive national, social, and industrial experience has not melded with local history' (Sokoloff 2002, 36).

Having highlighted this problem, namely the gap between local and national history, how can the interdisciplinary, site-based approach outlined above help to move beyond it? Sokoloff suggests that detailed studies of small distinct areas and their diverse and often transient populations can offer a view of life in wartime that transcends the 'conservatism of community' (Sokoloff 2002, 38). Thus studies of temporary housing, air-raid shelters or other similar sites can expose the complex dynamics of these communities within communities. Bringing documentary sources and first-hand memories together means that differing views of the past can be challenged and debated, while the presence of the archaeological remains tends to focus the narratives on the immediately local area, and on personal experiences rather than the bigger picture (Moshenska 2007). Archaeology of modern conflict very often focuses on objects such as defensive structures, aircraft and munitions, many of which were highly standardised industrial products. These objects can bridge the gap between the local experience of war and the wider, national or international perspectives, raising controversial issues such as the economics of warfare that are most often neglected or considered irrelevant in local histories.

Arguments from memory studies

From the perspective of memory studies, public archaeology projects that use people's recollections as primary source material are doubly interesting: memory is both an aspect of the research, and part of the social environment in which the research takes place.

Oral history on conflict archaeology sites can be extraordinarily useful. Informants have helped me to trace the location of buried defensive structures, filling in the gaps in geophysical surveys. Elderly informants have often been able to identify artefacts and features that were mysterious to most people, and to provide a startling level of detail to reconstructions and interpretations.

Scholars of memory in oral history and cultural theory are, however, increasingly questioning the utility and reliability of firsthand memories as historical sources (Green 2004). This is a challenge: is it possible to usefully work with oral histories in an interdisciplinary project, taking into account the distortions of memory, deliberate or otherwise, by social, political, neurological, biochemical and personal factors?

One response to this challenge is to explore the unique potential of the archaeological site to act as a mnemonic – that is to help people remember. Interviewing an informant about their childhood in the ruins of their old home, or in an air-raid shelter, will have very different results to the same interview carried out in their current home. Similarly, the use of excavated or collected material culture can also act as useful reminders in interviews (Moshenska 2007).

The mnemonic value of material traces of the past is enormous: the modern conflict archaeological site can be an extraordinarily aesthetic bombardment of textures, sights and smells, all infused with memories for someone who was there at the time. The emotional impact of this experience can be very powerful,

and therefore has ethical implications; when planning an interview of this kind it is important to discuss the emotional aspects with the informant beforehand.

The archaeological site is not just a mnemonic for individuals. It can be a reminder to the local community of what has gone before. There are very different processes of memory taking place on the archaeological site. For informants, older members of the community who remember the War, a site is a *milieu de mémoire*, or memory environment, in which the artefacts, historical sources and memories of others constitute part of a shared process of remembering. For younger members of the community who take part in the project it is a *lieu de mémoire* or site of memory encounter, a way of commemorating and paying tribute to older generations, and providing material for the process of collective remembering or memorialisation that is the broader, community-wide mnemonic effect of the project.

Why public archaeology?

Returning to the hypotheses outlined earlier: first, why does modern conflict archaeology lend itself so readily to public involvement and engagement? Part of the reason is that the material remains of modern conflict are so readily available, plentiful and widely distributed. What is more, they usually lack legal protection or scheduling, so they are accessible. The structures and remains themselves – many built from brick or reinforced concrete – are built to withstand more serious violence than an inexperienced fieldworker is capable of inflicting. Amateur archaeologists whom we would be reluctant to unleash upon a fragile prehistoric site can hone their skills in the safe and unchallenging environment of a pillbox or bomb-shelter excavation. For school students it offers a rare chance to link archaeology to school history courses (Moshenska forthcoming [a]). Most importantly, general familiarity with many of the structures and artefacts, as well as with the historical background, makes the sites more broadly comprehensible to budding amateur archaeologists than a prehistoric one might be.

Secondly, aside from the historical and mnemonic factors already mentioned, why is community archaeology the best way to do archaeology of modern conflict? The material remains of the Second World War are seldom the subject of rescue or research excavations, so it is often left to local historians and museums to preserve and study them. In Britain for example, apart from a few sites of national significance very few remains of the civil defence infrastructure have been studied or recorded in an organised manner: any work that has taken place tends to be locally based.

Archaeology in public

Nevertheless, the interest and involvement of the local community in local history studies cannot be taken for granted. This is another area where archaeologists have an advantage: our work has the potential to be open, accessible, disruptive and spectacular, compared to that of the local historian, stuck in a dusty archive. In many of the projects worked on, members of the public have stood and watched the team work for hours, returning day after day to check progress, ask questions, and engage in discussion. It is this that makes the project a memory space, and that draws in older local people who remember the site in the past. So effective is this attraction that it has rarely been necessary to advertise these site-based oral history projects: the archaeologists have usually been inundated with informants who heard about the archaeology first and wanted to be involved (Moshenska 2007).

The combination of historical knowledge, archaeological data and memories becomes more than the sum of its parts when it is opened to discussion within a community, and centred around a site. The value of this experience is in what people learn and share, taking a new perspective on their local area with a greater sense of knowledge, empowerment and curiosity.

Arenas of memory contestation?

Thus far, this discussion has been based on the assumption that the sites under investigation are not historically controversial or contested. This is, perhaps, a privileged British perspective on modern conflicts, and particularly the Second World War – the focus of the author's research.

Very often, however, around the world, archaeological work on sites of modern conflict is a politically laden activity, which different interest groups try to use or manipulate for their own ends. Examples of this include the

excavation of murdered Republicans from Spanish Civil War mass graves (González-Ruibal 2007), and the archaeology of the anti-fascist resistance in northern Italy. Even in Britain sites of violent heritage such as the Long Kesh/Maze Prison in Northern Ireland remain politically controversial (McAtackney 2007).

How are we to assess the practice of archaeology and the role of the archaeological site in these contexts?

To better understand the archaeological site as a site of memory, we need to consider it as an arena, into which individuals, interested parties, the media, and others are projecting a range of contested memory narratives – their different memories tell different stories, depending on their perspective and they may even challenge each other's recollections – hence 'contested memory'. Telling these different stories within the arena of a public archaeology project may be an attempt, albeit on a small scale, to overcome prevailing or even oppressive versions of 'how it was'. It is important to note that the archaeologists' own social or political agenda will be just one of many viewpoints competing in the arena.

On an aviation archaeology project, this process of contesting memories in a public archaeology arena involved attempts by local people to appropriate the intensive media coverage to promote their personal memories of a wartime air crash. The television producers in turn were trying to evoke a positive viewpoint on wartime London that was strongly at odds with the local version of events. Due to the fact that much of the television coverage was broadcast live, this made for an occasionally amusing and confusing mess. However, the most interesting conclusion from the perspective of the researcher is that elements of the local community recognised the archaeological site as a good arena in which to vigorously promote their perspective on the past (Moshenska 2006).

What makes an archaeological site such a good 'memory arena'? There are several factors. Historic conflict sites tend to promote dominant narratives through memorials, parades, and other events. Archaeological interventions are, in comparison, temporary, disruptive, public spaces. They are often visually impressive, attracting a crowd eager to discuss the events under investigation. The act of digging is linked in the popular imagination with remembering, particularly remembering pasts that have been buried or suppressed, both literally and metaphorically. Themes of this kind resonate in the excavations of the former Gestapo headquarters in Berlin in the 1980s, and the slogans of the diggers: 'grass must not be allowed to grow over it' and 'the wound must stay open' (Bernbeck and Pollock 2007; Till 2005). Public archaeology on contested sites of conflict such as this, like forensic excavations on sites of genocide, can be acts of defiant remembering against dominant narratives of amnesia.

Another important element in archaeological arenas of memory is the types of materials uncovered on conflict sites. These tend to be the remains of ordinary people, individual possessions, ordinary dwellings, the commonplace but fascinating remains of everyday life. Even on battlefields the viewpoint is a tiny, high-resolution one. This viewpoint lends itself to a traditionally radical history-from-below perspective, which emphasises the experience of conflict from the bottom up, rather than the top down view presented in mainstream military history, memorials, and the dominant memory narratives (Moshenska forthcoming [b]). Whichever memory narrative predominates in the arena of public archaeology will be strongly impressed upon those people taking part in the excavation, those watching it, and to a lesser extent those who follow it through the media. This places an enormous ethical burden on the researchers to work alongside the local communities with caution, consideration, respect and humility.

Applying the model

The approaches that the author has developed and the analyses that underlie them are not restricted to the British examples that have been used to develop them. They are internationally applicable, and will be of particular value in areas where the memory of conflict is still socially or politically divisive. The sites about which people remember past events in differing and even contradictory ways are almost always closely controlled spaces and events such as cemeteries, memorials, battlefields or killing fields, camps, museums or commemorative ceremonies. It is difficult for the alternative memory narratives to be heard within these environments, or for disparate viewpoints to be pushed into the public sphere and debated.

Public archaeological site projects are remarkable spaces that can evoke memories for a number of reasons. Unlike many other archaeological methods, it integrates the community into the processes of producing knowledge, rather than treating it merely as a source of data. This has considerable radical potential. In post-conflict environments the archaeological site can be a place for reconciliation and exchange of views between members of hitherto estranged communities. The archaeology of modern conflict is well suited to reconciliation work in another way. Divorced from the rhetoric, the ideology, and the broader historical context, the chaotic remains of shattered towns, homes, bodies and lives are a stark reminder of the pitiless results of violence.

There are any number of environments in which the model outlined in this paper could be usefully applied, and some good work is already taking place. Public archaeology work on First World War battlefields has been used to bring together former loyalist and nationalist paramilitaries from Northern Ireland, working on sites where their grandfathers' generation fought and died together (M Brown pers comm). In Spain the campaigns to exhume murdered Republicans, often in areas where only the fascist dead are officially commemorated, is allowing people to learn the stories of their relatives' deaths for the first time (González-Ruibal 2007). In many cases a silence had been maintained by families and loved ones beyond the fascist period into the present day. In towns and villages where the relatives of the dead still live alongside the relatives of the killers, these processes are not uncontroversial, yet they continue, and the local and personal historical narratives must be rewritten.

An approach to the archaeology of modern conflicts has been outlined, based on the interdisciplinary investigation of sites within their local areas, as well as in their broader national and international contexts. The importance of public or amateur involvement in these processes has been highlighted, as a social imperative, a practical utility and an educational opportunity. The author has emphasised above all the social and political power of what people recall about the sites and their context, and the ways in which memories can be manipulated and used for a variety of ends. By putting community involvement at the core of research methodology, proponents can strengthen and enrich our archaeology of bombsites, battlefields, defences, and divided cities.

List of references

Ashplant, T G, Dawson, G, Roper, M 2002 'The politics of war memory and commemoration: contexts, structures and dynamics' in Ashplant, T G, Dawson, G, Roper M (eds) *The politics of war memory and commemoration*. London: Routledge, 3–85

Bernbeck, R and Pollock, S 2007 'Grabe, Wo Du Stehst!' An archaeology of perpetrators. *in* Hamilakis Y and Duke P (eds) *Archaeology and capitalism*. Walnut Creek, CA: Left Coast Press, 217–33

Calder, A 1991 *The Myth of the Blitz*. London: Pimlico

Calder, A 1992 *The People's War: Britain 1939–1945*. London: Pimlico

CBA 2002 *A Review of the Defence of Britain Project*. <http://www.britarch.ac.uk/projects/dob/review/index.html> accessed October 2008

Faulkner, N 2005 'Great War Archaeology Group mission statement'. *Newsletter of the London Socialist Historians Group* **23**, 1–3

González-Ruibal, A 2007 'Making things public: archaeologies of the Spanish Civil War'. *Public Archaeology* **6**, 4, 203–226

Green, A 2004 'Individual remembering and "collective memory": theoretical presuppositions and contemporary debates'. *Oral History* **35**, 35–44

Grima, R 2002 'Archaeology as encounter'. *Archaeological Dialogues* 9, 2, 83–9

Matsuda, A 2004 'The concept of "the Public" and the aims of public archaeology'. *Papers from the Institute of Archaeology* **15**, 66–76

McAtackney, L 2007 'The contemporary politics of landscape at the Long Kesh/Maze Prison site, Northern Ireland' *in* Hicks, D, McAtackney, L, Fairclough, G (eds) *Envisioning Landscape: situations and standpoints in archaeology and heritage*. Walnut Creek, CA: Left Coast Press, 30–54

Moshenska, G 2006 'Scales of memory in the archaeology of the Second World War'. *Papers from the Institute of Archaeology* **17**, 58–68

Moshenska, G 2007 'Oral history in historical archaeology: excavating sites of memory'. *Oral History* 35, 1, 91–7

Moshenska, G forthcoming (a) 'Second World War archaeology in schools: a backdoor to the history curriculum?' *Papers from the Institute of Archaeology* **19**

Moshenska, G forthcoming (b) 'Resonant materiality and violent remembering: archaeology, memory and bombing'. *International Journal of Heritage Studies* **15**

Popular Memory Group 1982 'Popular memory: theory, politics, method' in Johnson, R, McLellan, G, Schwartz, B, Sutton, D, (eds) *Making histories: Studies in history-writing and politics*. London: Hutchinson, 205–52

Saitta, D, Walker, M, Reckner, P 2006 'Battlefields of class conflict: Ludlow then and now'. *in* Pollard, T, and Banks, I (eds) *Past Tense: studies in the archaeology of conflict*. Brill, Leiden

Saunders, A 1998 'The Defence of Britain Project' in English Heritage *Monuments of War: the evaluation, recording and management of twentieth-century military sites*. London: English Heritage, 7–9

Schofield, J 2004 *Modern Military Matters: studying and managing the twentieth-century defence heritage in Britain: a discussion document*. York: Council for British Archaeology

Schofield, J 2005 *Combat Archaeology: material culture and modern conflict*. London: Duckworth

Schofield, J, Webster, C J, Anderton, M J 1998 'Second World War remains on Black Down: a reinterpretation'. *Somerset Archaeology and Natural History* **142**, 271–86

Simpson, F, and Williams, H 2008 'Evaluating community archaeology in the UK'. *Public Archaeology* 7, 2, 69–90

Sokoloff, S 2002 'The Home Front in the Second World War and local history'. *The Local Historian* **32**, 1, 22–40

Till, K 2005 The New Berlin: memory, politics, place. Minneapolis, MN: University of Minnesota Press

Winter, J 2006 *Remembering war: The Great War between memory and history in the twentieth century*. London: Yale University Press

2. Defining values and significance: memory, commemoration and contested landscapes

Memorialising war: the narratives of two European cities, Coventry and Dresden

ANDREW RIGBY

Edmund Jacobitti (2000) has reminded us that 'history ... is always and necessarily a selective interpretation of events, an interpretation that arises only because of some pressing question in the present'. Historical narratives do not just happen, they are created. This is particularly so in the case of those interpretations of the past that become part of what might be called collective (or public) memory, where a particular version of the past becomes part of the common stock of knowledge held by the community or perhaps a section of the community. Such 'memories' emerge as a result of a drive by particular opinion-leaders who engage in various types of memorial activity in order to project their perspective of 'how it was' into the public domain (Wood 1999, 2–3).

Collective memories (like personal ones) require renewal and reproduction, otherwise they fade. As Hirsch (1999, 32) has pointed out, there is a need for 'reminders' that embody particular representations of the past. One particular form of reminding involves the creation of public monuments and other sites of memory, intended to symbolise particular narratives. Other reminding activity involves commemorative events and rituals that serve as history lessons in the formal and informal education of community members.

Of course such memorial locations and activities can also become sites of 'contestation' – dispute. Conflicting groups seek to define and reproduce them as symbols of their particular interpretation of what they recall happening in the past. The Cenotaph in London's Whitehall, for example, is seen by many as a powerful memorial to the fallen, those who made the ultimate sacrifice on behalf of their country in war. Others see it as a monument to the UK's imperial past and the warmongering of the British state (Edkins 2003, 16–18). What is more, the symbolism of a particular memorial site or activity, the history lesson that it is said to communicate, can be changed over time. Jay Winter (1998, 98) has recorded how the war memorials of the First World War were originally places where communities united in commemorating the dead, who were symbolically reunited with their community in the ceremonies that took place at the memorials. Nowadays they are to many people simply artefacts of a vanished age.

A recent example of such a process of redefinition being undertaken deliberately, not just as a result of passing of time, has been the attempt to rebrand the Orange Day Parades that take place in Northern Ireland on 12 July and which by tradition have represented a self-consciously provocative symbol of Protestant supremacy. As reported in The Independent (8 July 2007) there has been a not altogether successful effort to alter the day's image and to present its associated activities as a celebration of a society at peace with itself and an occasion for family fun.

The Northern Ireland example reminds us that public or collective memories of whatever sort cannot persist over time without the active agency of those seeking to reproduce them. Which memory, and the history lesson encapsulated within it, is reproduced will reflect the balance of power between different agencies at different phases during the process of memorialisation (Barsalou and Baxter 2007, 1). This short paper will review the different ways in which two European cities – Coventry in the UK and the German city of Dresden – that were the targets of aerial bombing raids during the Second World War have sought to memorialise that experience.

Fig 2.6 Coventry City of Peace and Reconciliation sign.
© Andrew Rigby

The Coventry experience

Coventry, a medium-sized city in the middle of England, presents itself as a 'city of peace and reconciliation'. The origins of this identity can be traced to the city's experience during the Second World War and the way in which local opinion-leaders used that experience for constructive purposes (Figure 2.6).

Coventry was a major centre of the British armaments industry during the Second World War and therefore a prime target for the German airforce. The bombing campaigns began in June 1940 and increased in intensity throughout the year. On the night of 14 November 1940 the city suffered its most intense assault. For 11 hours the bombs fell, damaging or destroying nearly 60,000 buildings. Over half of the city's 75,000 homes had been hit.

Local armament factories were struck, yet all were able to resume production within five days. But the attack killed 554 people and left over 1,000 people injured. This scale of death and destruction might seem modest by comparison with what befell Dresden some years later in 1945, but at the time it represented the most concerted aerial assault on a city centre. The greatest civic loss was the medieval cathedral of St Michael.

Both the Nazis and the British government used the raid for propaganda purposes. The German regime used it as a warning of what could befall other cities. The British government said that the bombing demonstrated the utter barbarism of the enemy. The provost of Coventry's cathedral, Richard Howard, however, from the outset pursued a different theme.

Howard was determined that a story about peace and reconciliation, and not about war and hatred, should emerge from the destruction. He proclaimed the need for forgiveness and eventual reconciliation with those

Fig 2.7 Coventry Cathedral – the old and the new.
© Andrew Rigby

responsible for the destruction, and he and his successors actively pursued reconciliation with Germany in the years following the end of the war.

In 1962 a new cathedral, constructed alongside the ruins of the old, was dedicated to the theme of reconciliation. In this manner the faith leaders of Coventry played their part in creating a particular memory of the past, with the ruins of the old and the wonder of the new cathedral acting as powerful symbols not just of the destruction of war but of the possibility of overcoming hatred and division (Figure 2.7).

The city's secular political leaders also played a significant role in nurturing the peace and reconciliation mission of Coventry. Driven by a number of local socialists who believed in international solidarity and friendship, the municipal council pursued an active town-twinning policy, and established relationships with other 'martyred cities' in Europe. It was as if there were two distinct movements emanating from Coventry. From the cathedral Provost Howard and his successors spoke about forgiveness and promoted Anglo-German

reconciliation, while the city leaders spoke about international understanding in the context of the Cold War, and promoted the town twinning movement. In 1947, for example, a Coventry-based delegation of church and civic leaders travelled to Kiel, in the German Federal Republic (West Germany), to mark the first official municipal twinning. In the same year Coventry was represented at the laying of the foundation stone of the new village of Lidice, then in Czechoslovakia (now the Czech Republic), next to the former village where the civilian population had been slaughtered by the Nazi occupiers in June 1942. Further twinning links were established with towns and cities that had also suffered from the ravages of war, including in 1956 Dresden, in what was then the German Democratic Republic (East Germany), and in 1957 Belgrade and Sarajevo (then both in Yugoslavia).

Local peace activists

The third agency responsible for promoting the city as a place dedicated to peace and reconciliation has been local citizens' groups and peace activists. Among them were people who, in the middle of the war, had been making efforts to learn German in order to communicate more easily with the 'enemy'. In 1946 a Coventry German Circle was formed, and in 1962 the Coventry Committee for International Understanding (CCIU) was established as a means of involving local people in the city's twinning movement. The idea was that by befriending people from other countries through exchange visits and suchlike, citizens could make an impact, however small, on international relations. As peacemakers of the Cold War, they would contribute to international understanding at the interpersonal level and thereby reduce international tensions. In its early years, the CCIU enjoyed strong community support and many of Coventry's peace activists and local groups networked together in national and international movements pursuing peace and social justice.

In recent years these three agencies – the cathedral, the municipality and local civil society activists – have come together to organise an annual Coventry Peace Month – four weeks of community activities broadly centred around the peace and reconciliation theme.

It is almost 70 years since the bombing in 1940, and through each of these local opinion-leaders reinforcing each other's message it has now become institutionalised in Coventry's self-depiction as a city of peace and reconciliation. Throughout this period the dominant version of the city's story has never been seriously challenged by significant opinion-leaders, either locally or nationally. It is this narrative and this identity that activists within the city can appeal to and appropriate in order to further their initiatives in such fields as peace education, inter-faith dialogue and community cohesion as they face the challenge of developing and giving substance to the 'peace and reconciliation message' appropriate for the second decade of the 21st century.

The Dresden experience

On the nights of 13 and 14 February 1945 the German city of Dresden was subjected to successive waves of bombing attacks by American and British planes that left 12 sq km of the city centre devastated. The most recent estimate for the numbers killed in the attacks on the city concluded 18,000–25,000 people died in the air raids. (Connolly 2008) Whereas Coventry has memorialised its wartime suffering with remarkable consistency, there have been at least three different phases to the Dresden 'story'.

The Nazi narrative – the destruction of an innocent city

When news of the catastrophe reached Berlin, Josef Goebbels launched a propaganda campaign that exaggerated the number of dead; figures of 100,000–200,000 began to appear in the press. The propaganda also emphasised the bombing raids' criminal targeting of civilians. The barbaric nature of these raids on an 'innocent city', the 'Florence of the Elbe', exposed the Allies as guilty perpetrators of war-crimes, said the Nazis, despite Allied claims to the moral high ground in the struggle against the Nazis. In this context, the story of Dresden as a symbol of the horror inflicted on civilian populations in the midst of war emerged.

The narrative of the German Democratic Republic: an Anglo-American war-crime

Less than three months after the city of Dresden was bombed it was occupied by Soviet troops. On 8 May 1945 the inhabitants fell under the rule of another totalitarian regime which, within a few years, began to exploit the tragedy for its own propaganda purposes.

Initially the official line was that the Third Reich – the Nazi government – was to blame for everything terrible that had happened to Germany. However, by 1949 and the division of Europe between the Cold War blocs of East and West, the political elite within the new entity of the German Democratic Republic (GDR) gave the Nazis' narrative its own twist. The destruction of the city, they said, demonstrated the barbarism of the Western imperialistic war-mongers, and this was the theme that informed the public commemoration services that took place each year on 13 February. The death-toll was quoted as 'hundreds of thousands'. According to official East German sources the raids had taken place without the knowledge or consent of the Soviet Union, as part of a campaign to destroy the areas of Germany that had recently been designated to become part of the Soviet Zone.

Throughout the years of the Cold War public commemoration of 13 February was orchestrated according to the prescriptions of the regime. Personal remembrance and mourning took place privately and in the relatively autonomous spaces of the churches and the arts. One of the most important sites of memory and one of the most evocative physical symbols of the bombing was the ruins of the Lutheran Cathedral, the Church of our Lady, known as the Frauenkirche. Here Dresdeners would gather on the night of 13 February to remember the tragedy that had befallen their city and its people in 1945.

Fig 2.8 Dresden Frauenkirche. © (2005) (wikipedia commons-http://commons. wikimedia.org/wiki/Image: FRAUENKIRCHE_UF.jpg)

The church also became important during the late 1980s as the opposition and human rights movements within East Germany grew. Amid the ruins of the Church of Our Lady protesters gathered to bear witness to their opposition to the state.

Dresden – Germany's holocaust or a symbol for peace in the world?

The political transformation and eventual unification of Germany in 1990 brought many changes. Historical archives were opened up. New research into the bombing raids became possible. There was now greater scope for people to commemorate the bombing and the loss of life in their own way. But with the changes there also came intensified political conflict, and the memorialisation of the bombing once more became a subject for political manipulation.

Along with many other cities of what had once been the GDR, Dresden suffered economically in the years immediately following reunification. Unemployment rates rose, prompting a certain resentment among Dresdeners towards their fellow citizens from the West, who were perceived as displaying a superior attitude to their poor 'cousins' in the east. It was in this climate that the appeal of the right-wing National Democratic Party of Germany (NPD) began to grow, especially among unemployed youth.

By 2004 the NPD was sufficiently powerful to win 9.2 per cent of the total vote in the state elections in Saxony, resulting in them taking up 12 seats in the state legislature. On 13 February of that year, while a memorial rally took place at which speakers tried set the story of Dresden within a context of commitment to international peace, hundreds of ultra-rightists were parading on the streets, commemorating what they portrayed as Germany's 'holocaust'. As Mattheas Neutzner recalled:

While a night of silence was celebrated in the Frauenkirche, (*see* Figure 2.8) while services were held in churches and while moving stage productions provided opportunities for contemplation and reflection, the atmosphere in the streets of the city centre was dominated by the noisy cat-and-mouse tussle between demonstrators and police. Those Dresdeners who felt personal grief and sought to express their mourning were coldly exploited by the marching right-wing factions, and at the same time denied their right to mourn by anti-right-wing activists. (Kunzel 2004, 51)

Each side, leftist and rightist, was presenting a particular interpretation of the bombing. For the leftist anti-fascists the bombing was just retribution on a people and a regime that had unleashed the horror of war on the world. For the rightists the bombing was a war crime involving the unjustified slaughter of innocent civilians. Seeing the demonstrations and counter-demonstrations one year later, in February 2005, one was left with the overwhelming impression of political groupings exploiting historical memory for their own particular purposes. And one consequence of this that made a huge impact on the author was that the autonomous space available for the citizens of Dresden to mourn the loss of family members and neighbours killed in the raids was being once again circumscribed and politicised.

One reason for the erosion of the autonomous space for personal and collective mourning has been that both the rightists' and the leftists' versions of the bombing are coherent enough to resonate with different constituencies among the Dresden citizenry and beyond. Dresden, in 1945 a city of almost 750,000 people, was not innocent, in the sense of having nothing to do with the Nazi regime's practice of 'total war'. The city accommodated approximately 20,000 military personnel, it was an important military transport hub, and more than 100 Dresden companies were involved in the production and supply of military equipment, weapons or munitions. A significant part of the workforce in such factories was forced labour, most of them from eastern Europe, but also including thousands of prisoners of war. The Jewish population of Dresden had virtually disappeared by the time of the bombings, their systematic transportation and murder having begun in January 1942. As Taylor concludes in his authoritative study of the bombing:

Dresden was not an "open city", but a functioning enemy administrative, industrial, and communications centre that by February 1945 lay close to the front line. RAF Bomber Command struck at Dresden in the way it had been attacking German cities for years, which sometimes caused great destruction and sometimes did not. In the case of Dresden – because of unseasonably good weather exactly over the city, an unexpected absence of opposition, a lack of the usual "cock-ups", the inexperience of the city's people, and the local Nazi leadership's appalling neglect of air raid protection – it wrought something terrible and apocalyptic (Taylor 2004, 475–6).

But the bombing of Dresden was also a 'terror' raid inasmuch as the city was burned and destroyed with the deliberate aim of undermining civilian morale.

It was concern about the manner in which the commemoration of 13 February was being expropriated by political extremists that led a group of concerned citizens to establish an organisation, '13 February 1945' with the aim, as articulated by one of its founder members, Matthias Neutzner, 'to address all aspects of the history of our city and its inhabitants in the context of the events of 13 February, and to discuss fundamental questions of peace, humanity and our own responsibilities. We want to explore modern forms of remembrance.' (Kunzel 2004, 53; Neutzner et al 2006).

One of the group's first initiatives was to publish a statement, *Dresden, 13th February – A framework for remembrance*. The aim was to establish the 'space' for a wide variety of remembrance activities, at the same time making clear what should not be tolerated. What was paramount in the document was the recognition that while Dresdeners had the right to express their mourning in their own forms of remembrance, they also had the responsibility – because of their suffering and because of their past complicity with the National Socialist regime – to ensure that such horrors should never happen again. To quote from the declaration:

We are remembering because the events of history constitute a duty and obligation to stand up for peace, against violence and war. We are remembering because the confrontation with our history from the periods of National Socialism and war makes clear our responsibility for the development of a humane, democratic and peaceful society.

It concluded,

We want the date 13 February to be the starting point for an ongoing process of learning and commitment for peace and humanity. We want to develop the decades-long traditions of remembrance both critically and self-critically. We want to maintain peaceful cooperation with the peoples of our former wartime enemies and to promote even closer partnerships. (Kunzel 2004, 55–57)

So the struggle continues, to maintain in creative tension respect for the dead and those who lost loved ones while at the same time presenting this history in such a manner as to strengthen forces for peace and tolerance in the world.

Coventry's suffering from the bombing raids of November 1940 does not compare with that of Dresden in 1945 in terms of the number of people killed and the scale of material destruction wrought upon the city. But at the time it was traumatic enough, and both the British and the German political elites sought to manipulate the experience for their own ends. The British used it to illustrate the barbarism of the enemy, the Germans used it as an illustration of their overwhelming power and capacity to inflict violence on those that dared to oppose them. But through the moral courage of people like Provost Howard of Coventry Cathedral, the commitment to international fellowship shared by many of the local political leaders within the city, and the idealism of local civil society activists, the wartime experience of Coventry was presented to the world as a message of hope for the future through working for reconciliation between former enemies at the international, the national and the local levels. And this narrative has remained consistent and unchallenged for almost 70 years.

By contrast, different groupings and political agencies have sought to use the story of Dresden for their own particular ends. Its significance has been and remains contested into the present day.

List of references

Barsalou, J and Baxter, J 2007 *The urge to remember: The role of memorialization in social reconstruction and transitional justice*, Washington, DC: United States Institute of Peace

Connolly, K 2008 'Panel rethinks death toll from Dresden raids', *The Guardian*, 3 October 2008

Edkins, J 2003 *Trauma and the memory of politics*, Cambridge: Cambridge University Press

Hirsch, H 1999 *Genocide and the politics of memory: Studying death to preserve life*, Chapel Hill, NC: University of North Carolina Press

Jacobitti, E 2000 *Composing useful pasts: History as contemporary politics*. Albany, NY: SUNY Press

Kunzel, G (ed) 2004 *13 February, Dresden 1945,* Dresden: City of Dresden

Neutzner, M, Herman, J, Zwicker, A 2006 *Scars of War: Memorial Depots in Dresden (Kunstplan)*. Dresden: Verlag-DZA

Taylor, F 2004 *Dresden: Tuesday 13 February 1945,* London: Bloomsbury

Winter, J 1998 *Sites of Memory, Sites of Mourning: The Great War in European Cultural History*, Cambridge: Canto

Wood, N 1999 *Vectors of Memory: Legacies of trauma in post-war Europe*, Oxford: Berg

2. Defining values and significance: memory, commemoration and contested landscapes

The enigma of place: reading the values of Bletchley Park

JEREMY LAKE AND FLEUR HUTCHINGS

In 1948 several teacher training colleges were opened as a result of the Emergency Training Scheme, set up after free education was offered in Britain for the first time to all pupils up to the age of 15. One of these was Bletchley Park in Buckinghamshire, where a group of nondescript wartime buildings, huddled around a late Victorian mansion, were painted white and bedecked with flowers and murals (Forsaith 2004). In 1975 the remarkable history of this site – by then a training centre for telecommunications engineers – burst into the public imagination, with the publication of Fred Winterbotham's book, *The Ultra Secret* (Winterbotham 1975).

The core of the Bletchley Park estate, which had split up in 1937, had just before the Second World War been purchased by the British Government as a new and safe location – away from the risk of bombing in central London – for the Foreign Office's Code and Cipher School (which then became known as GCCS) and Secret Intelligence Service (SIS, later MI6). The GCCS had been set up in 1919 from a small core of staff recruited from the crypto-analytical sections of the Admiralty (Room 40) and the War Office, which had been set up during the First World War. Its function was to break the intercepted coded messages of foreign powers and then assess their intentions and actions, to study their methods of cipher communication and to advise on the security of British codes and ciphers.

Ultra was the word given to the top-secret decryption of foreign codes, including those encrypted by the famous – and supposedly unbreakable – German Enigma and Lorenz machines. Bletchley Park has since become the growing focus of literature, film and legend, some of which is factually incorrect but nevertheless testament to the site's global renown. Its codebreakers worked on an international level – co-operation with Polish codebreakers had for example led in 1940 to the breaking of the Enigma code – and made a valuable contribution towards the forging of the post-war Anglo-American special relationship. They were at the forefront of the development of a whole range of subjects from mathematics to linguistics, and most famously the development of high-speed digital processing machines, including the Colossus computer. The site was also a global information hub, developing from a small community of cryptographers into a large complex organised along industrial lines for the efficient processing and analysis of encrypted codes, the housing of computing machines, and for communicating the evaluated decrypts to ministries and military commands and units. It is this that makes it so uniquely important, its contribution to the 'information age' making it arguably the equivalent of England's Ironbridge Gorge for the industrial age, and Portugal's Sagres for the age of exploration.

Future in the balance

The future of the site, however, has often hung in the balance, and there have been well-publicised disagreements about the extent to which the site and its buildings illustrate its national and global significance. By 2003, it was also realised by all those with a stake in the future of this site that a masterplan – to be adopted as planning guidance by Milton Keynes Borough Council – and a management plan for the conservation and careful development of the site was needed. It was agreed that these would be based upon a clear understanding, communicated to and then agreed upon by its key stakeholders, of the historical significance of the site. This significance was communicated by English Heritage as a series of key values to all those with expertise and an interest in Bletchley Park and its place in the local community, as well as relevant themes in 20th-century history. The resulting 'values paper' (Lake 2004) was divided into two parts: an assessment of the values attributed to the site – such as its contribution to victory in the Second World War, the development of signals intelligence, the information age and international relations – and an assessment of how the landscape and the architectural detail of the buildings has been preserved and reflects these values. The paper initially drew on a thesis by Fleur Hutchings and on a chronology for the buildings based on records in the National Archives which was funded by English Heritage and the Bletchley Park Trust (Hutchings 2003, Evans 2003). It was used as a framework for public consultation and – after workshops and correspondence – revised and integrated into the masterplan and conservation management plan which had been commissioned by English Partnerships, the government regeneration agency who were driving forward investment in the site and its integration into the surrounding community. This process also benefited from the results of a thorough survey of the site by English Heritage's research and survey team from late 2003 to 2004 (Monckton et al 2004; Monckton 2006; Lake, Monckton and Morrison 2006).

Assessing the values of Bletchley Park

Signals intelligence

The establishment, development and continuity of intelligence production on the same site during the Second World War is *the* major factor that contributed to the success of GCCS. The working practices developed at Bletchley Park played a fundamental role in the structuring of intelligence-gathering – signals intelligence as it became known – by Britain and its allies for the remainder of the Second World War, the Cold War and beyond (Andrew 2001, 433).

Efficient management of the increasing amount and complexity of intelligence data that passed through Bletchley Park – as the theatre of war expanded – was fundamental to the success of GCCS. It was some of the pre-war latest recruits to Bletchley Park – most notably the Cambridge mathematician, Gordon Welchman – who were to play a critical role in this. Welchman realised that, because the base settings (the rotor starting positions and wheel orders) on the Enigma machines were changed only once a day – every night at midnight – every message intercepted over the ensuing 24 hours could be decrypted, if the base settings could be broken on any single message within that 24-hour period. He commented, just before his death, that this insight was his greatest contribution to the war effort (Welchman 1982,198). The strategy was simple and involved a division of the most important tasks into two pairs of huts, which were sited close to the mansion and stables where all the codebreakers had been formerly based. One pair of huts focused on naval Enigma, and the other on army/air force Enigma and other codes. Each pair of detached huts then separated the tasks of decryption from the analysis, archiving and assessment of the intelligence material, before it was communicated to ministries, military commanders and the battlefield. The huts remained critical to GCCS's operations throughout the war, and the system of paired working and close inter-service liaison was retained in organisational form within the large new blocks which were built between 1942 and 1945. This bringing together of all processes onto one site, and their development into the basis of modern-day signals intelligence, marks Bletchley Park out from the codebreaking efforts of its opponents and its American allies.

A global information hub

By the eve of the Second World War Bletchley Park was already standing at the hub of the world's largest communications system, including the Y signal stations built from the First World War to intercept radio messages (see GCHQ [2003] for a global list of sites) and the 19th-century cable network maintained by Cable & Wireless which had been developed to serve the British Empire (Morrow 1939): Bletchley Park developed a close working relationship with the company and its headquarters in London (GCHQ 2003, 19, 29).

GCCS was able to capitalise on this global network, as well as its leadership of signals intelligence and computing technology, and thus make an invaluable contribution to the US/UK special relationship. The Holden and Brusa agreements in 1942 and 1943 between GCCS and the United States' Sigint authorities, marked the first time in history that intelligence expertise and technology was exchanged formally between foreign powers. By mid-1943 the most stubborn and difficult Enigma decryption problems – particularly of the *Shark* naval enigma codes which had exposed the Atlantic convoys to greater risk of attack from undetected U-boat packs – were being routinely sent to Washington DC. Here, the most powerful bombes (*see below*) were applied to these problems and the solutions relayed back to Bletchley Park within the same 24-hour period (Erskine 2001, 194–6; Budiansky 2001, 359–62).

Information technology

The codebreakers of GCCS had to meet the challenge posed by developments in encoding machinery and high-speed teleprinter transmissions before the Second World War. The German Enigma encryption machine, capable of around 200 million million million combinations (Welchman 1982, 51–2), was joined from late 1941 by the Lorenz teleprinter code which was developed for the German High Command. Together these stimulated Bletchley Park's pioneering use of not only a remarkable range of deductive techniques aimed at finding the daily settings of enemy encryption machines, which were on the cutting edge of developments in algorithmic mathematics, but also the development of rapid analytical machines (RAMs) whose task was to speed up the decryption. The first of these, the so-called bombes, were developed by Gordon Welchman and Alan Turing. Turing was one of a remarkable range of personalities who worked at Bletchley Park, many of whom went on to glittering careers in public life, science, academia and industry. He played a vital role in the decryption of naval Enigma, but is now also best known as a pioneer thinker on artificial intelligence (his paper on 'Universal Computing' was published in 1936) and for his profound impact on computing developments after the war (*see* Table 1).

The RAMs all represent key stages in the development of the modern computer, and its practical application for business, intelligence and defence purposes. The continuing debate about the place of these machines – and especially the celebrated Colossus computer – within the lineage of the modern computer (see for example Budiansky 2001, 315; Copeland 2001, 366–9) simply underlines the need for more research in this field (Simon Lavington and Tony Sale, pers comm, 2004–5).

The debate about Ultra

Several historians have similarly attempted to measure the exact contribution of Ultra intelligence on the battlefield (for example Calvocoressi 2001, 103–111; Budiansky 2001, 332–337). F H Hinsley, one of the key figures of Hut 4 (which decrypted naval codes) and the editor of the standard work on wartime British Intelligence (1979–1990), has cited Ultra's decisive contribution towards the Allies' North African, Mediterranean and Atlantic campaigns, and the fact that it delivered to military commanders the virtually complete German order of battle in Normandy before the Allies' invasion of France in June 1944, in support of his claim that Bletchley Park's work shortened the war by around two years (Hinsley 1994,12–13). Other historians, most recently John Keegan, have stressed that intelligence cannot be evaluated on its own – its use must be linked to the delivery of effective force (Keegan 2003, 383 and 398).

Hinsley has indeed conceded that the influence of intelligence on the decisions of battlefield commanders declined after the 1944 battle for Normandy, arguably with near-catastrophic results later that year for the Allies at Arnhem and in the Battle of the Bulge. He acknowledges that Ultra's major contribution in the European theatre was identifying the secret work on the V-rockets at Peenemünde, Germany and forewarning of the Germans' V-weapon attacks and other developments in weapons technology (Hinsley 1994, 11–12). More significant and relevant, however, are the conclusions of cryptologists and historians (eg Budiansky 2001) that Ultra intelligence – and in particular the continuity of production on one site – was most useful as a constant, cumulative source, continually guiding decisions rather than starring in one-off situations: 'by talking about these particulars, one may get a false picture of the source as a whole. The main value was building up a picture from which conclusions could be drawn' (Kahn 1983, 93). This approach influenced the structuring of Cold War signals intelligence, most notably in the key role that GCCS's successor GCHQ (General Communications Headquarters, based since 1953 at

Cheltenham in Gloucestershire) and the American National Security Agency played in NATO's [North Atlantic Treaty Organisation] Cold War mission.

Assessment of the Site

It follows that Bletchley Park must be understood and assessed as a whole, and in relationship to its landscape setting, rather than simply for its mansion or famous huts. Indeed, and despite some demolition (most notably Block F which housed the earliest Colossus computer and sections that worked on breaking Japanese codes), the archaeology of the site – which can be appreciated through the scale, siting and sometimes the surviving wartime layouts of the huts and blocks – reflects the distinct management processes that developed at Bletchley Park, and its development from a small specialist community into a 'university of signals intelligence' (Millward 2001, 37). This whole complex pioneered the application of process-flow and production-line methods, and close inter-service liaison, to the key stages of receiving, decrypting, evaluating, processing and disseminating data to appropriate ministries and commands. All the key stages in the development of cryptographic, computing and intelligence processes are visible in the surviving fabric, showing how the enterprise grew as its operations increased in scale and complexity. First there is the former mansion, stable yard and parkland, then the timber huts and the later brick, steel and concrete structures that were gradually erected by GCCS.

The archaeology of signals intelligence

Indeed, no other countries' codebreaking operations featured the continuity of production on the same site: Bletchley Park's principal rival, Germany's B-Dienst, being dispersed and poorly coordinated. This is what makes Bletchley Park and Ultra unique. The other Allied codebreaking organisations – the US Army's Signals Intelligence Service and the US Navy's OP-20-G, based in Washington DC – developed on separate sites and in a state of rivalry. The

United States' buildings that contained these operations have been demolished.

The existing Victorian stable yard and mansion were the original heart of GCCS's cryptographic research from September 1939. The huts, which were envisaged as a set of discrete but interlinked working compartments controlled by senior staff working from offices in the mansion, survive close by. Huts 3 and 6 were built for the decryption and evaluation of Enigma army and air force traffic, and Huts 4 and 8 for the decryption and evaluation of Enigma naval traffic. In their scale and internal planning these huts show us how GCCS's success was underpinned by strict rules covering security, the division of its workers into secure compartments, space for key groups to assess and disseminate information and a great deal of routine work in indexing and archiving – as well as operating the rapid analytical machines in other structures (see Table 1).

The planning of the much larger blocks – initiated in July 1941 – responded to a massive increase in the volume and complexity of the traffic, the widening of the theatre of war and the need to better integrate the roles of cryptoanalysis, intelligence and traffic analysis, and develop liaison between the services and the US Sigint authorities. This is particularly evident in Block D, which was planned with Huts 3, 6 and 8 arranged along a central spine and still retains some of its wartime layout.

The archaeology of the information age

Bletchley Park has also retained a unique assemblage of buildings whose planning and gradual growth directly reflects GCCS's development of technology that was then at the international cutting edge. It is the only site in the world that has such a range of structures connected to the birth and formative years of what we might call 'the information age'. Table 1 sets out international developments for each major stage of development in computing technology, followed by a summary of its use at Bletchley Park (under functional development) and the surviving fabric.

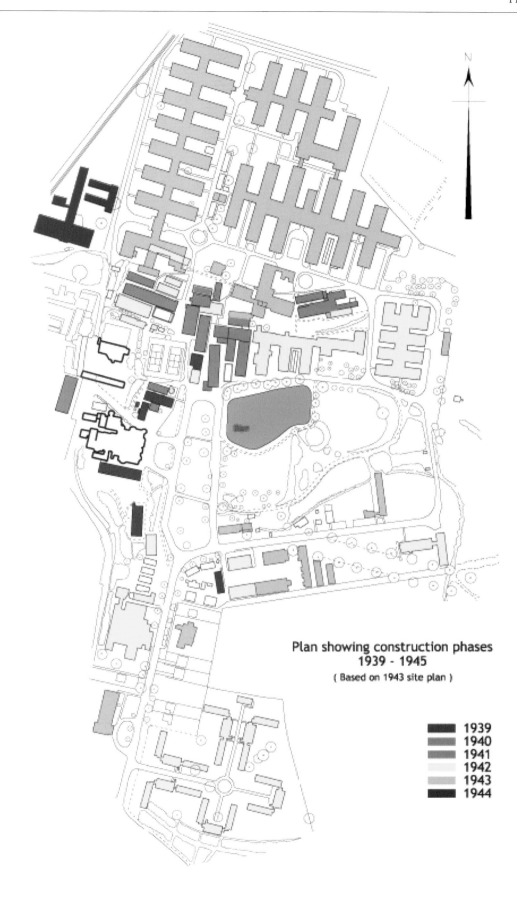

N

Fig 2.9 Plan showing how
the site was gradually
extended from the core of
the mansion and
outbuildings, with at first
the huts of 1939–40, the
brick-built huts for the
bombes of 1941 and the
blocks culminating in H
Block of 1944 which was
built to house the Colossus
Computer.
© English Heritage

Plan showing construction phases
1939 - 1945
(Based on 1943 site plan)

1939
1940
1941
1942
1943
1944

*Fig 2.10 Blocks G and D in
the foreground, with the
pond – a survival from the
18th century formal garden
– and the mansion and
nearby huts in the
background.
© English Heritage*

Table 1: The relationship of rapid analytical machines to fabric
International development: in the 19th century development of manually operated machines using punched cards, culminating, from the 1880s, in machines invented by Herman Hollerith to analyse masses of data (such as the 1890 census of the United States).

Functional development	Fabric
The Bletchley Hollerith section secretly adapted and experimented upon IBM machines manufactured under licence in the UK by the British Tabulating Machine Company. IBM had already supplied machines to the US intelligence services and to the German government, which were then used for the tracing and deportation of Jews (Austrian 1982; Black 2001). Developments at Bletchley were studied by the Americans and used as the model for the establishment of similar but larger plant developed for their intelligence services in Washington DC.	The massive scale and bespoke planning of C Block (which in October 1942 succeeded to the demolished Hut 7 as the Hollerith machine building) was required in order to house what was one of the largest assemblages of these machines ever grouped together. The continual and secret adaptation of these machines is a little appreciated aspect of Bletchley Park's contribution to the development of the modern computer.

International development: *electro-mechanical machines* that used 'small, electrically-driven switches called relays' – by 1940 'a standard component in telephone equipment' (Copeland 2001, 350–1).

From late 1939 Alan Turing and Gordon Welchman (and the engineering team headed by Harold (Doc) Keen) led work to develop a highly sophisticated electro-mechanical device named the bombe, designed to speed up logical deductions made off-line about the daily settings on the Enigma machine (Sebag-Montefiore 2000, 62–6). Orders placed late in 1940 for the mass production of bombes resulted from early 1941 in the construction of larger buildings at Bletchley Park and the establishment of five additional stations for housing them. Later in the war more powerful models were developed in close partnership with the Americans, and there were visits to the United States by Alan Turing and others (Erskine 2001, 191).	The first bombes were housed in the small Hut 1. The brick-built Huts 11 and 11a are built to a larger scale, because they housed bombes that were now being mass-produced and required temperature-controlled environments for reliable functioning. None of the bombe buildings at the five outstations linked to Bletchley Park have survived.

International developments: *electronic machines* that used faster and more powerful thermionic tubes (called valves, the precursors of the transistors and chips used from the mid 1950s);
   sequence or programme-controlled machines, which relied on a programme of instructions fed into the machine on punched cards or paper tape.

From 1942 the development of a series of machines culminated in January 1944 (in June 1944 for the more powerful Mark II) in the Colossus machine, developed in collaboration with Tommy Flowers and other Post Office engineers. It had no need for an internal memory, but it is widely recognised as the world's first electronic digital computer. Like the more powerful ENIAC, developed by the US Ordnance Department in 1946, it was developed as a high-performance electronic digital processor.	F Block, which housed the earliest Colossus computers and related machines, was demolished in 1988. H Block, opened in June 1944, was built to house these machines and related operations. It now survives as the world's first purpose-built computer room.

Post-1945 key developments: *stored programme machines,* whose outputs depended on a series of coded instructions stored in the computer's internal memory and thus dispensed with operator intervention, and the need to reconfigure by hand the cables, plugs and switches that wired machines together.

The contribution of Bletchley Park staff towards post-war developments
Max Newman and Alan Turing contributed to the development of the world's first stored-program computer (Manchester's SSEM) and inspired Donald Michie's (another worker at Bletchley Park) work on artificial intelligence (Copeland 2001; Lavington 1998; Simon Lavington pers comm 2005; Brian Oakley pers comm 2004).
The contribution of Colossus to post-war decryption is less well-known, and is only now being revealed through research. Contrary to popular myth Colossus and other RAM machines were not broken up. They were transferred to GCHQ in Cheltenham and recombined as the powerful Oedipus machine – fully operational by May 1954 and the first GCHQ machine to exploit the potential of high-speed digital storage (Simon Lavington pers comm 2005).

In contrast to the university-based research that sustained many developments in Britain, Germany and the US, the machines developed at Bletchley Park were production, not research models, applied instantly (and subsequently adapted) to the purpose for which they were intended. The archaeology of radio communications is only just beginning to be explored (*see* Martin 2002), and a study of the Y-station network is long overdue: future studies of the computer industry, as a recent entertaining study of the sites and communities of Silicon Valley in California has indicated (Finn 2001), show great potential to draw perceptual and material evidence together.

The inherited landscape

The survival of wartime fabric intermixed with elements of the 18th- and 19th-century park is typical of what befell countless country houses and their estates in the Second World War (Robinson 1989). Cycle racks, a bus depot and a large canteen and recreational centre speak of the varied needs of a workforce that according to records in the National Archives expanded from 2317 in August 1942 to 8941 in January 1945 (John Gallehawk pers comm. 2004). Most of the Bletchley Park personnel – 70 per cent – were WRENS (female naval staff) who carried out administration and worked the on-site rapid analytical machines: many more worked the bombe machines that were housed in several outstations established on newly-acquired sites (called outstations) in the region. Almost everyone was housed away from the site itself, in private homes, hotels, camps and hostels in Bletchley and much further afield. This is in striking contrast to the impact of GCHQ at Cheltenham, where in the 1950s there emerged a socially-ranked gradation of new domestic architecture (Freeman 2002, 22–24 and 30–33).

The late Victorian mansion was in every respect the iconic structure of the site; it was the headquarters building for senior staff, for meetings with American and other partners and the restaurant for all its staff until 1943. As an interesting example of the power or spirit of place at work, one of the former codebreakers recalled that the 'country house atmosphere ... (was) ... essential to the Bletchley ethos which was not institutional, barracky nor even collegiate; the services might have gone round saluting each other but for the code breakers there was a lack of hierarchical administration.' (Mavis Batey, pers comm 2004). Hierarchies of course existed, as did the daily grind of administration and operating the site's analytical machines, but the correspondence of senior officers displays a concern to retain sufficient space to play and relax (Evans 2003). Today the park in front of the mansion conveys the strongest sense of Bletchley Park's wartime use and atmosphere, including the tennis courts, grassed area and lake (a former medieval fish pond), all of which feature in memoirs as an important recreational and contemplative setting for the staff (*Life in the Park* 1999).

The work on Bletchley Park built upon lessons learned from extensive research into military sites by English Heritage. This had already highlighted the fundamental importance of documentary records as a baseline for evaluation and survey (Dobinson, Lake and Schofield 1997), for example of sites associated with explosives manufacture and the Cold War (Cocroft 2000, 2001; Cocroft and Thomas 2003). Another key issue was that of national and international context, for example the links forged between military and civil engineers in the royal naval dockyards (Douet and Lake 1997; Evans 2003) and British and German explosives experts in the late 19th century (Cocroft 2000, 77–83, 146–7).

The methods we have adopted at Bletchley Park have also involved early contact and consultation with key stakeholders as well as rapid documentary analysis. This has made it possible to set out a framework for understanding the site as a whole in its historical context, and to later refine this framework through detailed research and public consultation. This reflected both a growing realisation that complex and extensive sites needed to be assessed and managed as a whole – for example in the approach taken towards airfields (English Heritage 2003; Atkins 2004) – and that site owners and the broader public needed to contribute to open debate about the heritage value of these sites, as well as their value to local communities, the economy and other factors (English Heritage 2008). All this has shown us that the process of research and establishing an initial framework to inform key partners and early consideration of development options do not have to be mutually exclusive, with the latter only following on after the research is complete. It is a process of enquiry that must be seen as constantly evolving. Considerable investment has now been made in the infrastructure at Bletchley Park, led by English Partnerships. The prospects for the site are now improving, and in November 2008 English Heritage announced a £330,000 grant for reroofing the mansion. English Heritage is also now in discussions with the Bletchley Park Trust and Milton Keynes City Council on a conservation area partnership scheme to secure through grant aid the restoration of the historic wartime huts over three years from April 2009.

Acknowledgements

The authors were introduced to Bletchley Park by Graham Steaggles of English Heritage, and are indebted to him and other colleagues (particularly Wayne Cocroft, John Schofield, Andrew Williams, Linda Monckton and Kathryn Morrison) for their support during the development of this project. The authors are also indebted to all those who contributed to the values paper and the associated debate in 2004–5, and in particular staff at GCHQ, Tony Sale, John Gallehawk, Simon Lavington and Brian Oakley.

Note

To see the draft master plan for Bletchley Park, go to http://www.mkweb.co.uk/urban-design/documents/Final%5Fdraft%5F24%2D12%2D04%5FInternet%5Fversion%2Epdf There is a vast and growing literature on Bletchley Park and the development of intelligence. If you want to know more, look at work by Budiansky, Hinsley, Hinsley and Stripp, Keegan, Sebag Montefiore, Smith, and Smith and Erskine. The bibliographies in Lavington, and the Annals of the History of Computing, provide introductions to the history of computing.

Bibliography

Andrew, C 2001 'Bletchley Park in post-war perspective', in Smith, M and Erskine R (eds) Action this Day, London: Bantam Press 431–440

Atkins, WS 2004 'RAF Scampton. Historic Characterisation'. Unpublished report for English Heritage

Austrian, G 1982 Herman Hollerith, Forgotten Giant of Information Processing, New York: Columbia University Press

Black, E 2001 IBM and the Holocaust, London: Little, Brown and Company

Budiansky, S 2001 Battle of Wits, London: Penguin Books

Calvocoressi, P 2001 Top Secret Ultra. Cleobury Mortimer: M & M Baldwin

Cocroft, W D 2000 Dangerous energy: the archaeology of gunpowder and military explosives manufacture. London: English Heritage

Cocroft, W D 2001 Cold War monuments: an assessment by the Monuments Protection Programme. London: English Heritage (typescript report)

Cocroft, W D and Thomas, R J C 2003 Cold War: building for nuclear confrontation, 1946–89. Swindon: English Heritage

Copeland, B J 2001 'Colossus and the dawning of the computer age', in Smith, M and Erskine R (eds) Action this Day, London: Bantam Press 342–69

Dobinson, C, Lake, J, Schofield, J 1997 'Monuments of war: defining England's twentieth-century defence heritage', Antiquity 71, 288–99

Douet, J and Lake, J 1997 Thematic Study of the Royal Naval Dockyards. Unpublished report for English Heritage

English Heritage 2003a Twentieth-century military sites: current approaches to their recording and conservation. London: English Heritage

English Heritage 2003b Historic Military Aviation Sites: conservation management guidance. London: English Heritage

English Heritage 2008 Conservation Principles. London: English Heritage

Erskine, R 2001 'Breaking German Naval Enigma on both sides of the Atlantic' in Smith, M and Erskine R (eds) Action this Day, London: Bantam Press 174–196

Evans, D 2003 BP: The development and historical function of the fabric. Unpublished report for English Heritage and Bletchley Park Trust

Evans, D 2004 Building the Steam Navy. The Royal Dockyards and the Victorian Battle Fleet. London: Conway Maritime Press

Finn, C 2001 Artifacts: An Archaeologists's Year in Silicon Valley. Michigan: MIT Press

Foot, W 2006 Beaches, Fields, Streets and Hills. The Anti-Invasion Defences of England. York: Council for British Archaeology

Forsaith, P 2004 Dora Cohen and the Bletchley Park Training College. Oxford: Oxford Brookes University

Freeman, P 2002 How GCHQ Came to Cheltenham, Cheltenham: GCHQ

GCHQ 2003 Locations and Organisations Associated with BP, 1939–45. Cheltenham: GCHQ

Hawkins, B, Lechner, G, Smith, P (eds) 2005 Historic Airports. Proceedings of the International 'L'Europe de l'Air' Conferences on Aviation Architecture. Swindon: English Heritage

Hinsley, F H (ed) 1979–1990 British Intelligence in the Second World War, 5 vols London: HMSO

Hinsley, F H 1994 'The influence of Ultra in the Second World War' in Hinsley, F H and Stripp, A (eds) Codebreakers: the Inside Story of Bletchley Park, Oxford: Oxford University Press, 1–14

Hinsley, F H and Stripp, A (eds) 1994 Codebreakers: the Inside Story of Bletchley Park, Oxford: Oxford University Press

Hutchings, F 2003 'The cultural significance of Bletchley Park'. Unpublished MA Thesis, Brandenburg Technical University, Cottbus, Germany

Kahn, D 1983 Kahn on Codes – Secrets of the new Cryptology, New York: Macmillan Publishing

Keegan, J 2003 Intelligence in War. London: Pimlico

Lake, J 2004 The National and International Values of Bletchley Park. A Discussion Paper. www.english-heritage.org.uk/characterisation (accessed on 2/02/2009)

Lake, J, Dobinson, C, Francis, P 2005 'The evaluation of military aviation sites and structures in England', in Hawkins, B, Lechner, G, Smith, P (eds) Historic Airports. Proceedings of the International 'L'Europe de l'Air' Conferences on Aviation Architecture. Swindon: English Heritage, 23–34

Lake, J, Monckton, L, Morrison, K 2006 'Interpreting
    Bletchley Park' in Schofield, J, Klausmeier, A and
    Purbrick, L (eds), *Re-mapping the Field: New
    Approaches in Conflict Archaeology*. Berlin:
    Westkreuz Verlag

Lavington, S 1980 *A History of British Computers*.
    Manchester: Manchester University Press

Lavington, S 1998 *A History of Manchester Computers*.
    Swindon: British Computer Society

Life in the Park. 1999 Bletchley Park Archive, 13
    November 1999

Martin, R 2002 'King's Standing Radio Transmitter
    Station, Crowborough'. *Industrial Archaeology
    Review*, **24**, 91–102

Millward, W 1994 'Life in and out of Hut 3', in Hinsley, F
    H and Stripp, A (eds) 1994 *Codebreakers: the Inside
    Story of Bletchley Park*, Oxford: Oxford University
    Press, 17–29

Monckton, L, Morrison, K, Grundon, I, Williams, A 2004
    'Bletchley Park', *Architectural Investigation Reports
    and Papers B/010/2004*, 4 vols, English Heritage

Monckton, L 2006 'Bletchley Park, Buckinghamshire: the
    architecture of the Government Code and Cipher
    School', *Medieval Archaeology*, **40**, 2, 291–300

Morrow, G L 1939 'Wireless and Imperial Defence.
    Maintaining Communication in Time of War', *The
    Wireless World*, 10 August 1939, 119–20

Robinson, M R 1989 *The Country House at War*, London:
    Bodley Head

Sebag-Montefiore, H 2000 *Enigma. The Battle for the
    Code*. London: Phoenix

Smith, M 2001 *Station X – the Codebreakers of Bletchley
    Park,* London: Channel 4 Books

Smith, M and Erskine, R (eds) 2001 *Action this Day*,
    London: Bantam Press

Welchman, G (1982) *The Hut Six Story*, Kidderminster:
    M&M Baldwin

Winterbotham, F 1975 *The Ultra Secret*, London:
    Weidenfeld & Nicolson

3. Public archaeology, public history: case studies in conservation and management

Interpretation as a means of preservation policy or: whose heritage is the Berlin Wall?

AXEL KLAUSMEIER

From 1989–2004

This paper has two aims: first, to explain briefly how the remains of the Berlin Wall have been treated since its fall in November of 1989 and to point out its significance as a monument. Secondly, the strategy of commemoration that the Berlin Senate has agreed upon will be presented which sets some ambitious goals with funding of €46.4 million for implementation by 2011 (*Berliner Zeitung* 2007, 19).

The concept involves very different commemoration projects and concepts that will be implemented at several different sites. It is easy for anyone to realise that commemorating the history of the Berlin Wall and the victims is complex and difficult because many interest groups, each with their own very different concepts of commemoration, all claim that their own concerns are especially significant.

A look back

After the fall of the wall in 1989, there was a consensus in support of clearing away as thoroughly and quickly as possible what was probably the most famous structure of the 1960s – the hated border installations surrounding West Berlin. The structure, euphemistically called merely 'the wall', actually consisted of a wide space with a staggered system of successive barriers.

The wall was loathed because of its immediate function, which was on one hand to divide Berlin and thus by extension Germany, Europe and the world, and on the other, to lock up the population of the German Democratic Republic (GDR) [former East Germany] and to keep countless families and friends apart. Another reason for hating it was because of its position in global politics; it was where the political and economic blocs of the capitalist West and communist East clashed as nowhere else. The end of this confrontation and of the Cold War are closely related to the events of the autumn of 1989 and consequently to the fall of the wall, brought about by the people of the GDR. As a result of these events the structural elements of the former border installations were largely removed, beginning in June 1990 (Gaddis 2007, 9, 295).

Despite the rush to dismantle the fabric of the wall, as early as 1990 the Berlin State Office for the Preservation of Historical Monuments made great efforts to preserve parts of it, against considerable public resistance (Deutsches Nationalkomitee 1997, 93–100; Dolff-Bonekämper 1999, 317–325; Feversham and Schmidt 1999). The Office first carried out exploratory walks along the former border and later put preservation orders on individual sections. During the years 1990 to 1992, a total of seven former sections of the wall and other border installations, initially still under the direction of the East Berlin Institute for Preservation of Historic Monuments, received preservation orders.

These preservation orders met with sometimes severe resistance from inhabitants and state politicians, who in their euphoria about the opening of the border, wanted to see all traces of the installations disappear as quickly as possible. Thus, there was not simply a lack of political will to preserve remnants and traces of the wall as historical testimony; rather there was an expressly articulated will to do the opposite. People saw the structural elements of the border installations as both alien and as a continuing injury to the urban space, and they were deemed no longer acceptable.

Consequently, with proverbial German thoroughness, demolition was carried out on a grand scale. All that remained of 155km of border installations around West Berlin – often through involuntary and random actions – were those that had been categorised as insignificant, such as the patrol road in the centre of the death strip (a strip of cleared land running parallel with the wall itself, which was booby-trapped, mined and offered a clear field of fire for the East German border guards), which was easily transformed into a pedestrian walk, and some pieces in museums, such as the Deutsches Historisches Museum and The Allied Museum in Berlin.

For the public, politicians and urban planners the former border soon dropped out of sight and out of mind. Up till 2004 the structure that had once significantly shaped everyday life in Berlin was commemorated on only two days a year: 13 August, the anniversary of the erection of the wall in 1961, and 9 November, the anniversary of its entirely unexpected fall in 1989.

Reviving interest in the wall

In 1999, Polly Feversham and Leo Schmidt investigated what had happened to the border installations following the collapse of the GDR and identified it in cultural-historical terms (Feversham and Schmidt, 1999). Since around that time, there has been a more favourable attitude in Berlin to documenting the remaining elements of the Berlin Wall and to protecting them against further destruction. The Berlin Senate, commissioned the Conservation department of Brandenburg Technical University (BTU) Cottbus to document, from 2001 to 2003, all surviving elements of the inner-city border. Published in 2004, this report lists and records in detailed maps about 800 remnants and traces, focusing solely on the depth of the wall strip and its eastern hinterland (Klausmeier and Schmidt 2004).

The report revealed that the wall had not vanished. Briefly, the roughly 42km of what had once been the inner city border and the 155km of the former border around Berlin form a quite unique historic, if not cultural landscape

– a landscape full of memory and memorials. Apart from the central area surrounding the Brandenburg Gate, the Reichstag and Potsdamer Platz, a grass-covered area – mostly covered by unplanned vegetation – extends through the city from north to south, providing an idea of the width of the area once covered by staggered barriers.

Identifying the wall remnants

The only place where one can experience the sequence of the former barriers as a total entity – albeit framed by an artistic-architectural staging – is at the official Berlin Wall documentation centre at Bernauer Strasse, although sharp-eyed observers and those who know the city's history can spot significant elements of the border installations along the entire length of its former course. Nevertheless, the existing remnants and traces reflect a fundamentally different image of the border from the one collectively remembered, in particular by people from the former West. They are nothing like the typical features that nearly everyone feels that they know, such as the watchtowers, the arc lights or the patrol road. What is left evokes the complexity of the border, its staggered fixtures and expansions as well as the attitude of its builders.

The surviving physical remnants are primarily elements that were encountered east of the barriers and could never really be seen from the western side and – because of their particular position within the border area – were out of sight for most citizens in the former East. The familiar images of the border installations have all but vanished; very few of these fragmented preserved remnants of the border installations can be decoded by the untrained eye. It is as if one needs optical aids – an adequate mediation strategy, so to speak.

The former edifice was of historic and worldwide significance and may still be so today. But what remains of it could hardly be more banal. The mostly fragmented structural remnants consist of cut-off double iron girders, hideous metal gates covered by graffiti, dented metal fences, severed cables and wires, and derelict switch boxes that once provided electricity to the border, left in place to this day. There are also almost imperceptible concrete seams along the walls of houses or in the ground and neglected square concrete boxes, knee or waist-high – so-called flower-box barriers (see Figures 3.1 and 3.2).

Fig 3.1 (above) Hinterland
wall of the former border
checkpoint at Bornholmer
Bridge, Berlin.
© Axel Klausmeier

Fig 3.2 (left)Reused
hinterland fence in
Potsdam-Griebnitzsee.
© Axel Klausmeier

Fig 3.3 Surviving remnant of border fence, the most Western blocking element, near Potsdam, Gross-Glienicke.
© Axel Klausmeier

Fig 3.4 Hinterland fence in Potsdam-Griebnitzsee, next to the villa in which Stalin lived during the Potsdam Conference in 1945.
© Axel Klausmeier

Nothing in these objects instils fear today or conveys their once overshadowing character. Their current significance lies specifically in their fragmentary nature; it is this characteristic that tells us something about the population of the GDR and how the wall was conquered peacefully. Did the numerous 'wall-peckers' – people who laboriously hacked out pieces of the smooth concrete wall – view the fragments of what they labelled 'Border Wall 75' (1975 being the year in which one major phase of alteration/enhancement in the wall's construction was finished) as anything other than souvenirs? These preserved remnants, by the way, are all the more valuable now even if, because of their fragility, they generally represent a problem to the people in preservation of historical monuments who are struggling to preserve them.

Why the fragments are significant

The material nature of the object on one hand and its cultural and historic significance on the other are on quite different levels. Remembrance, nevertheless, requires sites and images of places in order to establish the links that make history and the nature of history come alive. The significance of material testimony of remnants and traces lies in the message they convey. In 1849 in his book *Seven Lamps of Architecture*, the Victorian art critic John Ruskin wrote that without architecture human beings would be unable to remember (Ruskin 1989, 176). For that reason, it is very important to protect and preserve the fragmented remnants of the wall, following an assessment and selection process.

Although the individual construction pieces and the void created by the clearing of the border installations represent alien elements in Berlin's densely built-up urban space, both kinds – the remnants and the void – help us visualise the former course of the border as a kind of negative. The void, with its random vegetation amidst a pulsating urban space is culturally quite significant in the sense of the first article, second paragraph of the Burra Charter (an international charter for the conservation and management of places of cultural significance): 'Cultural significance means aesthetic, historic, scientific or social value for past, present or future generations', because it reminds us of the former location and course of the border installations. Indeed, it is the sometimes irritating urban void that speaks so clearly and unabashedly about what it meant to have a barrier in the centre of a city of approximately 3.5 million inhabitants: a fissure through the city's living organism.

Paradoxically, even nowadays, it is the void that conveys best what the border looked like because a void is defined by its delineations, for instance, by the growth along its edges, the adjacent buildings or the firewall along its seams. In this case, a particular challenge in terms of preservation is that fundamental issues concerning such monuments are tied to objects that neither can be registered in catalogues and lists nor protected by exclusive definitions. Rather, their protection must be essentially built up by a mediating and interpretative preservation (Breuer 1997, 20).

In other words this rich landscape of memory has been treated and perceived as a traditional cultural landscape. Our research methods, too, are rather traditional – in contrast to its subject. We take the material resource seriously, departing from it to engage in a kind of landscape inventory, in which we also refer to historical information of all kinds for explanation, identification and definition of the structural elements that have been found.

Debates about adequate commemoration

The need for structural preservation of individual fragments of the former border fortification, which often require extensive explanations because of their derelict condition, is as urgent as the need to convey their significance as a monument. Without interpretation, the 'historic monument – the Berlin Wall', preservation will have little meaning for coming generations.

As David Lowenthal warned us, 'the past is a foreign country' (Lowenthal 1985). A glimpse at German classrooms seems to confirm his statement because German students' knowledge about the division of Germany is rather sketchy (*Der Tagesspiegel* 2007, 2004). To quote what history teacher Regina Wessendorf told the Berlin newspaper, 'for most pupils the wall is distant history, and of the former political figures, pupils barely remember Erich Honecker' (*Der Tagesspiegel* 2007).

A shift in perspective

2004 was an important year in the history of the commemoration of the Berlin Wall. In the summer, at the so called Checkpoint Charlie Museum, located at the former crossing point in the wall between East and West, museum director Alexandra Hildebrandt recognised a need to commemorate the victims of the Berlin Wall. She met this need in an extremely simplified way, arguably a banal theme park fashion, by using original 'Border Wall 75' elements and 1065 wooden crosses to symbolise the former situation at the border as well as to commemorate those who had died there. The question of authenticity – of the original course of the wall – did not matter to her. Nevertheless, this new magnet for tourists raised many questions of context concerning the original location, documentation, information and commemoration. The new installation was both highly questionable and fervently debated.

Hildebrandt's initiative made the issue of how to commemorate the wall much more immediate and topical. Its impact pressured the Berlin Senate to draw up a precise and subtle commemoration concept for the history of the wall and its victims in the autumn of 2004.

The resulting debate was very complex and there is no space for a full discussion of it here. However, Hildebrandt's action had triggered a media buzz – perhaps the most positive thing that can be said for it. Indeed, the attention was suddenly focused on the topic of the Berlin Wall, throughout Germany, not simply by the controversial installation but also by the first public debate on how the wall should be treated and its victims commemorated. The increase in public interest stimulated other memorial sites and historical institutions in Berlin, in particular, the Berlin Wall Documentation Centre at Bernauer Strasse to reflect critically on their work, and think about how to convey and coordinate their offerings, and become more visitor-friendly. This flurry of discussion and action was much greater even than that of the previous year, when Leo Schmidt's provocative suggestion to nominate the historical landscape of the Berlin Wall for inclusion on the World Heritage List was met by a broad lack of understanding.

Soon a commission of experts was specifically established for the purpose was making preparations for a unified commemoration concept by the Berlin Senate. Now the goal was to develop a concept to commemorate the way the city had been divided up, the Berlin Wall itself and its victims. The commission of experts that presented its work in April 2005 consisted of various local government representatives and representatives of institutions such as memorial sites and academia, political parties, preservation of historic monuments, the Senate Administration for Urban Development, the Senate Chancellery, the tourist board, the central district of Berlin as well as commissioners for culture and media of the Senate Administration for Science, Research and Culture.

Bernauer Strasse exemplifies the fractured city

The concept through which central locations along the course of the wall was to return them to 'a recognisable state and where visitors could experience the former border' (Klaus Wowereit, Mayor of Berlin: www.berlin.de/sen/kultur/kulturpolitik/mauer/m1.html). The concept was not to commemorate the wall solely in one place, but to make an expanded memorial site at Bernauer Strasse the centre, because the history of that street is an excellent example of how the wall affected the city. At this street Berlin's urban space was brutally split in 1961. Families and lives were separated here. People dug tunnels under the street in order to escape, and the GDR regime ordered soldiers to fire at escapees at Bernauer Strasse. In addition to the existing documentation centre (where the number of visitors has doubled to 300,000 a year in recent years and which will expand and eventually feature a permanent exhibition), the memorial, and the Chapel of Reconciliation, there will be an information pavilion nearby, a clear delineation of the still existing traces such as the border, tunnels, crosses for the dead, and relics of watchtowers, as well as documentation in the form of films and markers with personal testimonies. The intention is expressly not a 'Berlin Wall miniature park' but rather a complement to existing relics in the form of 'objective' documentation.

There will be additional important sites for commemoration, including the former border crossing at Checkpoint Charlie, the so-called East Side Gallery (a 1.3km-long strip of former hinterland wall near Ostbahnhof), the Brandenburg Gate and about ten more locations along the former wall. There will be a public competition to design the individual locations. In various places there will be photo and video installations, some of which may be displayed temporarily only, for instance, at the 'nationally symbolic' Brandenburg Gate. In commemoration of the confrontation of the super powers during the Cold War era, a permanent exhibition is planned at the former Allied border crossing Checkpoint Charlie. This exhibit is intended to complement the existing museum at Checkpoint Charlie, which embodies the horror of the wall, its builders and victims in 'show' fashion. Until this public-private partnership at Checkpoint Charlie is up and running, a large temporary display will inform visitors about the history of the border crossing, successful and failed escapes as well as the confrontation of Soviet and American tanks and the period following the fall of the wall. There will also be directions to other relevant sites of commemoration and a website about all of it.

The commemoration plan also encompasses seven locations at various points along the former wall, each with different perspectives. Wherever there are prominent remnants of the wall or for example watchtowers, the commemoration will focus on the particular structures or fragments and on the historical layers of the former border demarcations and the changes they underwent.

The interpretation concept will be rounded out to include the topography of the wall and will deal with its role in dividing east from west, as well as with later perceptions of the wall. Among the locations will be the so-called 'Palace of Tears', once an integral part of the former rail-crossing point at Friedrichstrasse in the very heart of East Berlin, and Checkpoint Bravo at the former border crossing Drewitz between West Berlin and the former East German district of Potsdam. 'Division and connection' is the last theme within the concept. It refers to marking and documenting paths of the former wall. Finally, the intention is to secure and complete the 'historic mile', a double row of cobblestones, with information panels.

The development of the concept for the Berlin Senate was the first important impetus in Berlin towards creating a comprehensive vision for commemorating the wall, the division of the city and the wall's victims. It is clear that the plan will have to be amended as it proceeds. It also has to face the fact that the State of Berlin owns very few of the necessary plots of land and that numerous people who will be affected by implementation of the concept will have to be consulted. Then there is the issue of financing in times of very tight budgets. Nevertheless, at the core of the debates will be the mediation of the significance of the Berlin Wall as a monument because widespread public awareness of a structure's significance is like oxygen (Rhys Jones 2003, 9) in the struggle for its preservation. In the final section some aspects of mediation and interpretation will be addressed, which apply to the preservation of any monument.

Strategies of interpretation and mediation

According to Jan and Aleida Assmann (Assmann J 1992; Assmann A 2003), built structures are a means of communication because they constitute our material storage of memory and knowledge about developments in cultural and art history; thus they are of utmost interest to cultural studies. They inform us through their substance about the circumstances of their origin and the people who made and changed them. They tell us about those people's lives, values, goals, dreams and limitations. This is true for the original builders as well as for later generations, who lived with the objects and, changed them, changed how they used them or chose to neglect them. Indifference and neglect, in this case, are telling phenomena, both of which must be taken seriously. By the same token, the way we treat built structures or buildings will inform later generations about our present methods and attitudes.

There is another dimension to the way in which a built structure is an object of communication. Different institutions and interest groups connect their different goals and interests with the object in question. When assessing whether to preserve a building, the goal is to work out its significance to gain a common understanding about its particular character. It is particularly difficult to get people to understand the significance of 'uncomfortable monuments' (Huse 1997). Thus, when we speak up now, many years after the fall of the former border fortification, wanting to preserve its many remnants and traces, we have to take account of all aspects of people's past experience of it and their attitudes towards it. This means encompassing past and present East-West relationships, national and international aspects, division and suppression (as well as overcoming both of these), and commemoration of the victims. This often 'uncomfortable heritage' of the GDR period is a physical reminder of a country that has long disappeared – to a generation that is still trying to come to terms with its more recent past (*Frankfurter Allgemeine Sonntagszeitung* 2007).

Different strategies of interpretation have already been developed such as anchoring the topic in school curricula and institutions of continuing education. This happened rather quickly as part of the wider reviewing of the history of a dictatorship. The next goal will be to secure the financial framework for a long-term implementation of the concept. The wall will become even more popular in 2009 because Germany will be celebrating two significant anniversaries, preparations for which are already underway, coded as '60/20'. There will have been 60 years of the Federal Republic of Germany and 20 years of a unified Germany, after the fall of the wall.

Goals of investigation

Our Department of Conservation at BTU Cottbus will continue to build on its work on the history and cultural significance of the Berlin Wall. In spring 2007, we received funding from the German Research Association (Deutsche Forschungsgemeinschaft) in order to investigate the wall in a larger context. Together with several partner institutions, especially with historians, we will shed new light on various aspects of the wall. We want to connect the built structure to the political decisions that led to its construction. We will also examine the structural alterations to the wall and analyse in particular the existing remnants and traces of the approximately 155km of border installations around the former West Berlin.

The purpose of this work is to set out the cultural and political significance and meaning of the Berlin Wall, which changed not only between 1961 and 1989, but also from 1989 to the present day. Using the files of the border guards, which have been kept intact and complete, we want to retrace the structural development of the border installations and see how the wall was perceived in the contemporary media of East and West. This will help us form a precise and nuanced impression of its complex historical significance.

We will establish a database for the remnants of the wall as well as the infrastructure that was necessary to make the structure function as intended (such as barracks and military training areas – to name only two items). This will make it possible to make a fresh assessment of the economic aspects of the border regime and to understand in an entirely new way the border troops and their two main tasks: namely, defence of the state border and preparedness to attack West Berlin and the former Federal Republic of Germany.

Thus we hope to draw more attention to the entire system of the Berlin Wall – to a system of political influence in all major spheres of everyday life and to one of oppression of individual liberties. Our mapping of this landscape of memory will facilitate preservation and enable future generations to continue the process of interpretation.

Zusammenfassung

Die Reste der Berliner Mauer: Eine streitbare Denkmallandschaft

Die Berliner Mauer ist bis heute das weltweit bekannteste Bauwerk der DDR geblieben. An den Berliner Sperranlagen prallten einst die politischen und wirtschaftlichen Blöcke des kapitalistischen Westens und des kommunistischen Ostens wie nirgendwo anders aufeinander. Doch nach dem Ende des Kalten Krieges und der weitestgehenden Abräumung der baulichen Elemente der einstigen Grenzanlagen geriet der ehemalige Grenzstreifen zusehends aus dem Blickfeld der breiten Öffentlichkeit, der Politiker und der Stadtplaner.

Lange Zeit galt die Mauer als fast vollständig verschwunden, doch kann sie sich seit etwa 2004 wieder eines größeren öffentlichen Interesses erfreuen. Dazu trug im Besonderen die im Spätherbst 2004 als Kunstaktion deklarierte, jedoch die einstige Grenzwirklichkeit verfälschende und banalisierende Installation der Grenze am Checkpoint Charlie bei. Doch seitdem ist viel geschehen: Der Senat von Berlin hat ein Gedenkkonzept für diese einzigartige Denkmallandschaft entwickelt, bei dem den erhalten gebliebenen baulichen Zeugnissen eine wesentliche Rolle zukommt.

Seit 1999 beschäftigt sich der Lehrstuhl Denkmalpflege der Brandenburgischen Technischen Universität Cottbus mit diesem unbequemen Erbe und bemüht sich inmitten von zumeist emotional geführten Debatten um die penible Dokumentation der baulichen Reste und Spuren, deren denkmalpflegerische Kontextualisierung sowie um die Vermittlung des außerordentlichen kulturellen Wertes dieser häufig unscheinbaren Objekte. Es geht um die wissenschaftliche Erfassung dieser einzigartigen Denkmallandschaft, die nicht nur aus den Resten und Spuren der einstigen Grenzanlagen selbst besteht, sondern für deren Betrieb eine ausgeprägte Infrastruktur im Hinterland nötig war, die nicht zuletzt aus Kasernen und Truppenübungsplätzen, Wohnsiedlungen für Offiziersfamilien und zahlreichen Infrastrukturgebäuden bestand.

Bibliography

Assman, J 1992 *Das kulturelle Gedächtnis. Schrift, Erinnerung und politische Identität in frühen Hochkulturen*. Munich

Assmann, A 2003 *Erinnerungsräume. Formen und Wandlungen des kulturellen Gedächtnisses.* Munich

Berliner Zeitung, 2007 9 November 2007, p 19

Breuer, T 1997 'Landschaft, Kulturlandschaft, Denkmallandschaft als Gegenstände der Denkmalkunde'. In: *Die Denkmalpflege*, 55/1, Pp5–23. Munich/Berlin: Deutschen Kunstverlag

Dolff-Bonekämper, G 1999 'Denkmalschutz für die Berliner Mauer' in Schneider B and Jochum R (ed) *Erinnerungen an das Töten: Genozid reflexiv*, pp317–25. Wien: Böhlau Verlag

Feversham, P and Schmidt, L 1999 *Die Berliner Mauer heute. /The Berlin Wall Today*. Berlin: Verlag Bausesen

Frankfurter Allgemeine Sonntagszeitung 2007 'Wo die DDR vergraben liegt. Die Atombunker der DDR sind jetzt Baudenkmäler und Ausflugsziele – ein Besuch unter der Erde' 28 October 2007

Gaddis, J L 2007 *Der Kalte Krieg*. Eine neue Geschichte. Munich: Pantheon

Huse, N 1997 *Unbequeme Baudenkmale. Entsorgen? Schützen? Pflegen?* Munich: ZAK

Klausmeier, A and Schmidt, L 2004 *Wall Remnants – Wall Traces. The Comprehensive Guide to the Remnants and Traces of the Berlin Wall*. Berlin: Westkreuz Verlag

Lowenthal, D 1985 *The Past is a Foreign Country*. Cambridge: Cambridge University Press

Ruskin, J 1989 *The seven lamps of architecture*. (reprint of 1880 edn). New York: Dover Publications Inc

Rhys Jones, G 2003 'Foreword' *in* Wilkinson P (ed) Restoration. *Discovering Britain's Hidden Architectural Treasures*. London: Headline Book Publishing

Schneider, R 1997 'Grenzanlage Bernauer Strasse – Friedhof, Museum, Denkmal'. in Deutschen Nationalkomitee für Denkmalschutz (eds): *Verfallen und vergessen oder aufgehoben und geschützt? Architektur und Städtebau der DDR – Geschichte, Bedeutung, Umgang*, Erhaltung. Bonn

Der Tagesspiegel 2004 'Für den Jahrgang 89 ist der Mauerfall nur ferne Geshichte', 9 November 2004

Der Tagesspiegel 2007 'Wer war Honecker?', 9 November 2007

3.Public archaeology, public history: case studies in conservation and management

The memorial landscape at Peenemünde

CHRISTIAN MÜHLDORFER-VOGT

History of Peenemünde and its public interpretation

What does the first large military research centre in the world, founded at Peenemünde, Germany, have to do with 20th century 'landscapes of war'? After all, there were no direct battles, as there were on the battlefields of Verdun or Ypres.

The more we consider this question, the more convinced we are that this 25km² area of remote countryside on the northern part of the island of Usedom, at the edge of the Baltic Sea, represents an ideal-typical landscape of war. The growing economic, scientific and logistical structures of the 20th century, often known as the military-industrial complex, made the waging of modern warfare possible.

The research centre founded in Peenemünde in 1936 was the first large military research centre in the world. Today its technical, military and logistical traces characterise the local landscape.

First we will give some background to Peenemünde's history and will explain the purpose of the Historical Technological Information Centre (hereafter HTI). Then we will show how the *Denkmallandschaft* (landscape of monuments) at Peenemünde typifies the complex military sites of the 20th century. Finally we want to discuss the potential and the problems of this project.

The origins of the rocket

In an international context Peenemünde might be the most notable place in the federal state of Mecklenburg-Vorpommern, because on 3 October 1942 the rocket Aggregate 4 (better known as the V2) was launched here and reached space for the first time in history. Its historical origins can be traced to the Treaty of Versailles of 1919 that followed the defeat of Germany in the First World War.

The Versailles Treaty prohibited Germany from developing or possessing long-range artillery. Nobody could imagine in 1919 that a rocket would ever be an effective weapon, but the result of the ban was indeed that Germany went on to develop a completely new weapon, the rocket. Another German military invention, the V1 – the forerunner of a cruise missile –was tested in Peenemünde too.

In the early 1930s, shortly before Hitler came to power, a secret military training area near Berlin was founded for tests and development. But soon it was too small and could hardly be kept secret. So the National Socialist regime started searching for a new site. Ideally, they wanted to find a length of straight coastline, to allow the complete visual observation from the new research centre of the intended 300km flights. The scientists and engineers were to construct a new rocket, propelled by liquid fuel and capable of carrying a warhead weighing one tonne.

Finally they found an area close to the small fishing village of Peenemünde, at the northern end of the island of Usedom, with just 400 inhabitants. Today this island in the Baltic Sea lies directly on the Polish border.

What happened at Peenemünde

A power station was built at the site between 1939 and 1942, capable of producing 30 megawatts (Figure 3.5). Most of the energy it generated was consumed by the process of liquefaction of oxygen, which was used as rocket fuel and was produced in a building erected at the same time. Today the old power station is the biggest industrial monument of the federal state of Mecklenburg-Vorpommern and our

museum is housed in it. The museum's outer area of 120,000m² contains 90 per cent of the former fishing village, which was destroyed during the construction work for the power plant.

The HTI (Historical Technological Information Centre) Museum at Peenemünde is primarily concerned with a historical critique of the Nazi regime; the technology displayed here, such as the V1 and V2, are the pegs on which we hang our explanations of the social history.

The Nazis saw the V1 and V2 rockets as 'wonder weapons'. Although it was clear at the latest by 1943 that the war was lost for Germany, the leaders believed that these weapons would turn the tide in their favour. Thousands of rockets were fired at towns such as London, Antwerp and Liege, killing around 10,000 people.

The first great air raid by the British Royal Air Force on the research centre took place on the night from 17 August to 18 August 1943. Approximately 700 people were killed. Just a few months later, the mass production of V1

and V2 rockets was shifted to the underground concentration camp Mittelbau-Dora in central Germany. Testing and basic research continued at Peenemünde until the end of the war.

An estimated 20,000 prisoners died in the human tragedy that was the Mittelbau-Dora underground concentration camp, because of the inhuman working and living conditions. The V1 and V2 are probably the only weapons that caused more loss of life in their production than in their offensive use (Erichsen and Hoppe 2004, 231).

The museum

The HTI at Peenemünde focuses on the social history that informed the rocket research. The museum was opened on 8 May, 1991. It is the second largest museum of the federal state of Mecklenburg-Vorpommern, attracting around 240,000 visitors every year. At the time of writing the body responsible for the museum is the

Fig 3.5 The Peenemünde crane track in foreground and power station in background.
© Historisch Technisches Informationszentrum Peenemünde

town of Peenemünde, with a population of 300. A curious consequence of this is the fact that the museum's budget is over 10 times more than that of the body that is responsible for running it. Soon the regional government will take over responsibility for the museum.

The museum contains a section on the theme 'rocket heirs', explaining the importance of the technical know-how developed at Peenemünde to the USSR, the USA, Great Britain and France during the Cold War.

As the complex history of Peenemünde might be hard to understand if it focused solely on the scientific themes, other kinds of art and culture play important roles in the interpretation programme. Every summer, for example, plays by Bertolt Brecht and George Tabori are performed at the power station, and there are music performances by jazz or rock musicians. In the autumn there are classical music concerts.

The path through the landscape

The idea of explaining the extensive infrastructure of the research centre by means of a historical path for visitors was first discussed in the 1990s, but nothing came of it, due to a factor connected with the post-war history of Peenemünde. After 1945, the Red Army and then the army of the German Democratic Republic used the 24km² around the north part of the island and it was therefore out of bounds to civilians. Although, with the reunification of Germany in 1989/90 part of this area became accessible again, around 70 per cent still cannot be entered because of the danger of unexploded bombs, shells, and so on, left by the armed forces. This means that many historical sites that should have been networked to each other by the proposed teaching path cannot be accessed.

In summer 2006, historians from the HTI museum identified the historical sites that were accessible, initially picking out 22 features, which were then reduced to 13 for the 22km historical path and the *Denkmallandschaft* (memorial landscape) was opened in May 2007. Each historical site shows two signs: a larger sign with explanations and historical photographs or documents, and a smaller one with a map telling visitors their whereabouts on the route.

The aims and criteria of the memorial landscape determined the choice of the historical sites. First, we aimed to attract more tourists, the most important target group for the HTI.

The memorial landscape should increase the attractiveness of the north of Usedom island to tourists. The tourist marketing concept 'Usedom 2015' stresses that HTI is the only cultural institution of the island with an international 'unique selling point'.

Secondly, as with the HTI itself, the memorial landscape should inform visitors about the Nazi regime in a historically critical way. The historical sites should give information about the complex system of the research centre (Erichsen and Hoppe 2004); the goal-directed coordination and organisation of the individual work steps could only succeed by using modern methods of project management. Although no conflict took place as part of Peenemünde's operations (apart from the air raid), its infrastructure – recognised today as as a military industrial complex – was however, an indispensable element of the waging of modern warfare.

The memorial landscape should achieve the following:

- represent the complexity of the military, industrial and scientific complex
- represent the development (in this respect the reception history – analysis of how the site has been perceived over time by different groups – of Peenemünde also plays a role) and point out the historical context (Mühldorfer-Vogt 2007)
- individualise the historical protagonists as real people
- the interpreted landscape should also reflect what it means to be an inhabitant of Peenemünde and how the site has contributed to their identity.

Some key features of the memorial landscape

Before building of the research centre could start a large part of the north of the island had to be raised 1.5m higher with sand from the Baltic Sea to create a firm base for construction on what had been very marshy ground. As the north of the island was frequently flooded, this measure also served as a protection against high tides. A 12km-long dam was built in 1939 along the course of the River Peene. On the right in Figure 3.6 you see what is now known as Lake Kämmerer, originally a branch of the river. With the building of the dam it was separated from the river, creating a lake. The construction of

Fig 3.6 The dam, built to protect the centre against high tides, created a lake. © Historisch-Technisches Informationszentrum Peenemünde

the research centre completely changed the topography of the north part of the island.

South of the research centre are the so-called Peenebunkers, shelters near the river, reminiscent of Roman buildings (Figure 3.7). Rockets were supposed to have been stored here, but measurements prove that this was not technically possible. With the help of our database, set up in 2006, we will no doubt find further historical sources to shed light on this. It will not be difficult to alter the signs at the site, if we find new information because the panels are printed foils, applied to metal signs, which can be quickly replaced.

Fig 3.7 The Peenebunkers, whose purpose has yet to be established. © Historisch-Technisches Informationszentrum Peenemünde

Fig 3.8 The derelict oxygen plant, which produced the liquid oxygen that fuelled the rockets.
© *Historisch-Technisches Informationszentrum Peenemünde*

The fuel for the aggregate 4 rocket (V2) was liquid oxygen (plus alcohol). For the liquefaction of oxygen the oxygen plant, built next to the power station between 1939 and 1942 needed 25 megawatts. Nowadays the massive derelict plant dominates the Peenemünde site (Figure 3.8).

Another important feature in the memorial landscape is the platform for the suburban fast train. This was roughly 200m from the eastern plant (Werk Ost), the heart of the research centre. All important research took place in the eastern plant and the world's first supersonic wind tunnel was used here. The rail line was integrated into the 107km system of the suburban fast train.

Most of the 15,000 workers (scientists, engineers but also concentration camp prisoners) used the train, which was therefore extremely important for the functioning of the research centre. The electricity for the trains was generated by the coal-fired power station. The district heating system – more than 7km of

pipes – was also operated by the power station.

Running the research centre necessitated the use of thousands of slave labourers. Because of the lack of records we do not know how many slave labourers died while working at Peenemünde. They were housed in two camps in the north of Usedom that were part of the Sachsenhausen concentration camp; one was known as Karlshagen I camp. Figure 3.9 shows what is left of the camp's watchtower. Conservation of this historical site was carried out in 2006 by teenagers as part of an international project. Such projects play an important role in our educational work.

Around 1,200 male prisoners from different nations lived in Karlshagen I camp, among them a Soviet, Michael Dewjatajew. The story of concentration camp prisoner Michael Dewjatajew is an outstanding opportunity for us to present historical characters as real individuals – an important factor when teenagers are a principal target group for the museum's outreach work.

Dewjatajew was a Red Army pilot, but the Germans did not know this. Had they done so he would not have been sent to do forced labour at Peenemünde's airfield, along with nine other prisoners. In February 1945 the nine men succeeded in overwhelming their German guard and took off in a plane. Although they were pursued by two German fighter planes, they managed to reach the Russian lines in the east. Because, however, of Stalin's doctrine that forbade Russian soldiers from falling into German captivity, they were condemned to spend the next 10 years in the Gulag, accused of being collaborators. This story makes the airfield of Peenemünde another important feature in the historical path.

Besides giving us the story of Michael Dewjatajew, the airfield provides a link to and background for the next stage of Peenemünde's history, the Cold War. During the 1950s the Red Army and then the 9th fighter squadron of the National Volks Armee (the armed forces of the German Democratic Republic) used the airfield and the former research centre buildings. The strategy of the Warsaw Pact assigned great importance to the 9th fighter squadron and because of this the HTI will create make a major permanent exhibition about this theme in the next five years.

The chapel was built in 1872 and is one of just four buildings that are still preserved from Peenemünde as it was before 1936 when construction of the research centre started (Figure 3.10). The chapel has therefore become a focus of local identity for Peenemünde's 300 inhabitants. In the late 1960s, however, 52 bodies were found in a mass grave in the cemetery beside the chapel: most of them had bullet

Fig 3.9 Peenemünde's slave labourers lived in nearby Karlshagen I Concentration Camp: the remains of a camp watchtower.
© Historisch-Technisches Informationszentrum Peenemünde

Fig 3.10 The chapel, a building dating from before the building of the research centre.
© Historisch-Technisches Informationszentrum Peenemünde

holes in the back of the head. Probably these bodies were concentration camp prisoners. The chapel site therefore gives us a link to the next historical site, the memorial in Karlshagen, 7km from Peenemünde.

After exhumation the 52 bodies were solemnly reburied at Karlshagen, and that area was designed as a memorial, according to the then-prevailing Soviet-dominated aesthetic known as 'socialist realism'. From the late 1960s till the 1980s innumerable ceremonies took place here with the GDR's National Volksarmee. Here, for example, soldiers had to swear an oath to the state version of anti-fascism. The Cold War theme is thus a further connection to the potential future perspectives of our project.

In its 725-year history the little place of Peenemünde has had a surprising place on the political world stage and in its wars. In 1630, during the Thirty Years War, the Swedish king, Gustavus Adolphus, landed here with his troops: this landing place will be the next site in the planned expansion of the historical path.

Problems and perspectives

In the next few years the 190m crane runway has to be restructured as an important landmark of the memorial complex (*see* Figure 3.5). As with other huge objects in the HTI, such as the suburban fast train or the so-called Walter-Schleuder (the catapult of a V1), we only want to preserve and not 'restore' this object: the visitor should be able to recognise how more than 8m tonnes of coal were transported in the crane runway's 50-year working life.

An important influence on the museum's plans is the fact that every year more than 30,000 children and students take part in activities such as workshops and guided tours. They form a very important target group of the HTI. If reconstructions and restorations became too much like a theme park, the museum could lose its credibility as an authentic educational site. Nevertheless we know that preservation has a public role and the activity of preservation is an attraction in itself. All the preservation works are carried out publicly so visitors can communicate with the restorers.

One reason for increasing the number of exhibits in the museum is biological: as time passes, the death of most eyewitnesses of the research centre, during the Second World War and the Cold War, increases the significance of the exhibits. The HTI is very proud to possess more than 140 hours of video clips with eyewitnesses' testimonies of the research centre and these become more precious with the passage of time.

For more than 60 years no civilian could reach the north part of the island, this part of Usedom today represents an extremely important ecosystem and contains, among other things, a large population of eagles. Another form of expansion for HTI could be to integrate the ecological dimensions of the site.

But the limitations of this project should not be underestimated. It was hardly the original aim of this museum – or any museum for that matter – to act as the main engine for promoting commercial tourism on behalf of an entire district. We often find, however, that tourism is influencing our discussions and we debate the part it should play. Although the tourist economy frequently finances some measures, tourists tend to expect rather more of a V2 theme park, something that is not compatible with a serious museum.

Another debating point is what an appropriate marketing strategy for the museum should be. While cultural tourists form an important target group for the HTI, this group is not perceived as playing an important role for the wider tourist economy. As a result the museum receives no support with marketing this aspect of its work.

Zusammenfassung

Diverse Ruinen, denen zwischen 1936 und 1945 als Funktionsgebäude ursprünglich ein wichtiger Stellenwert in der Heeresversuchsanstalt in Peenemünde zukam, werden seit Mai 2007 im Rahmen der „Denkmallandschaft" ausgewiesen. Dieser mehr als 20 km lange historische Rundweg umfasst 13 historische Stätten wie z.B. den Bahnsteig der historischen S-Bahn, die Sauerstofffabrik, aber auch das KZ-Arbeitslager Karlshagen I. Gemein ist diesen vollkommen unterschiedlichen Stätten, dass sie für das Funktionieren des Militärisch-Industriellen Komplex des totalitären NS-Regimes jeweils ein wichtiges Mosaiksteinchen bildeten. Zugleich sind heutzutage einige dieser Stätten ohne weitere Hinweise für die zahlreichen Besucher kaum noch zu erkennen, da sich inzwischen die Natur Teile dieses ehemals größten Forschungszentrums wieder einverleibt hat.

Charakteristisch für die Heeresversuchsanstalt ist die Tatsache, dass die gesamte Topographie des Nordteils Usedoms durch dieses Großforschungszentrum nachhaltig verändert wurde. So wurden weite Teile der 24 km_ umfassenden Gesamtfläche mit Hilfe von Ostseesand aufgeschwemmt, eine Ausbuchtung des Peenestroms durch einen Deich von diesen abgetrennt, das Ergebnis hiervon bildet heute der Kämmerer See.

Am Beispiel des früheren KZ-Häftlings Michail Dewjatajew sollen in diesem Kontext weitere Vermittlungsebenen der Denkmallandschaft dargestellt werden. Das Schicksal dieses ehemaligen Rotarmisten wird einerseits bereits in der Dauerausstellung des Museums thematisiert, es wird aber auch an verschiedenen Stationen unseres Rundweges abgehandelt, so z.B. am Flugplatz. Von hier aus gelang es Dewjatajew mit neun weiteren Häftlingen, einen deutschen Wachsoldaten zu überwältigen und sich dann mit einem deutschen Jagdflugzeug hinter die Ostfront abzusetzen. Ziel dieser Individualisierung ist es, den zumeist anonymen Opfern „ein Gesicht zu geben". Dieses Angebot an zusätzlichen Identifikationsmöglichkeiten ist deshalb so wichtig, bilden doch Kinder und Jugendliche eine wichtige Zielgruppe unseres Museums.

Das Schicksal Dewjatajews steht auch stellvertretend für den Anspruch, historische Entwicklungslinien und Brüche auszuweisen. Konkret von der sogenannten Stalin-Doktrin betroffen, die den Rotarmisten verboten hatte, in deutsche Kriegsgefangenschaft zu gehen, wurde Dewjatajew nach seiner erfolgreichen Flucht bis Mitte der 50er Jahre ins Gulag verschickt. Die Stationen Peenemünder Kapelle sowie Karlshagener Ehrenmal stehen ebenfalls für diesen epochenübergreifenden Zugang.

Jede Station besteht aus einem doppelten Metallschild: Auf der linken Seite erhält der Betrachter die jeweiligen historischen Informationen. Falls verfügbar werden hier auch historische Fotos abgebildet. Das rechte kleinere Schild weist in Form einer Landkarte den Lehrpfad sowie den Standort des Betrachters aus. Diese Karte ist mit einer Spezialfolie auf dem Metall angebracht. Dies ermöglicht unkompliziert die Erweiterung der Denkmallandschaft, indem lediglich die Folie ausgetauscht werden muss.

Ein direktes Ergebnis der deutschen Nachkriegsgeschichte ist die Tatsache, dass aufgrund des Wirkens zuerst der Roten Armee und dann der NVA nach 1945 Teile des Usedomer Nordens noch immer munitionsverseucht sind. Daher sind highlights wie z.B. der Prüfstand VII, die Stätte, von der am 3. Oktober 1942 das erste Aggregat 4 (V 2) gestartet wurde, derzeit nicht zu begehen. In der mittelfristigen Planung hingegen ist es geradezu zwingend, diese Stätten den Besuchern zugänglich zu machen.

List of references

Erichsen J and Hoppe B (eds) 2004, *Peenemünde – Mythos und Geschichte der Rakete 1923 – 1989*, Berlin: Nicolaische Verlagsbuchhandlung GmbH

Mühldorfer-Vogt C 2007 '15 Jahre HTI – ein Museum im Spiegel seiner Zeit' *in* Albrecht, M (ed) *Technikgeschichte kontrovers: Zur Geschichte des Fliegens und des Flugzeugbaus in Mecklenburg-Vorpommern*, Schwerin: Friedrich-Ebert-Stiftung, Landesburo Mecklenburg Vorpommern

3. Public archaeology, public history: case studies in conservation and management

The making, breaking and rebuilding of 20th century Coventry

CHRIS PATRICK

Coventry today is the product of the dramatic changes that occurred during the 20th century. This paper will explain how Coventry transformed itself into a centre for engineering, and how the production of armaments led to it being targeted by Nazi Germany during the Second World War. The impact of war production and of the air raids of 1940–41 on the fabric of the city will be examined, looking at what was lost, what was gained, what evidence remains and how the bombing acted as a catalyst for a further transformation in the post-war period.

The making

Coventry was one of the major cities of later-medieval England. By the mid-19th century it had become something of a picturesque backwater, captured in romantic drawings of decay and used by the Victorian writer, George Eliot as the model for *Middlemarch*, her novel of provincial town life. Although the city was no longer the economic powerhouse of the Midlands, much of its medieval fabric survived. The famous novelist Henry James, who visited the city in the 1870s, celebrated its preservation and ranked Coventry alongside Shrewsbury, York and Chester (James 1905, 35).

The industrial revolution was a latecomer to Coventry. The great civic building projects of the Victorian period, that transformed neighbouring cities such as Birmingham, had passed Coventry by. This contributed to the preservation of the city's medieval fabric, captured in watercolour paintings (Figure 3.11).The city, however, was on the cusp of major economic and social upheavals.

The weaving of silk ribbons and watch manufacture had dominated Coventry's 19th century economy. By the 1870s both were in decline and the search had begun for new sources of wealth and employment. The cycling boom of the 1880s revived the economy of the city. The engineering skills of the local workforce soon made Coventry the principal centre for bicycle innovation and manufacture in Britain.

The Daimler Motor Company was established in a disused cotton mill in Foleshill in 1896, an event that is generally considered to represent the birth of the British motor industry. Once again, the transferable skills of the workforce, the available workshop space and the growing machine-tool and component industry, meant that Coventry was the ideal location for the venture.

Gradually, through the 1890s and 1900s, Coventry attracted more and more entrepreneurs starting various types of engineering companies. The restructuring of the city's economy acquired its own momentum from the links across different parts of the engineering sector. These links offered important opportunities for diversification into new markets.

In 1905 Coventry's trade directories listed 29 motor manufacturers. By the First World War, Coventry manufacturers such as Humber, Hillman, Rover, Singer, Standard, Siddeley-Deasy and Daimler accounted for 14 per cent of the UK's vehicle production workforce (Thoms and Donnelly 1986, 13).

Arms manufacture arrives in Coventry

In 1905 the presence of appropriately skilled workers engaged in the production of machine-tools and other precision engineering industries led to the establishment of the

Fig 3.11 Butcher Row, Coventry around 1900. © Coventry City Council

Fig 3.12 The naval gun shop at Coventry Ordnance works, 1917.
© Coventry City Council

Coventry Ordnance Works on a greenfield site at Red Lane. The company was set up by a consortium of British shipbuilding firms – John Brown, Cammell Laird and Fairfield – aiming to challenge the duopoly of Vickers and Armstrong-Whitworth.

At first the works struggled to gain government contracts until a massive expansion in the demand for naval and land armaments in 1914 (Figure 3.12). The Ordnance Works was greatly expanded during the First World War, with the addition of workshops to the eastern part of the site. By November 1918, its products included naval guns, aeroplanes, tanks, anti-aircraft guns, 400,000 cartridge cases and millions of fuses and detonators (Thoms and Donnelly 1986, 22). In 1938 the works were taken over by the Royal Navy and the complex became a maintenance and storage depot until it finally closed in the 1970s (McGrory 2003, 133).

Large parts of the works survive today, intermingled with streets of terraced housing built for the workforce. The most striking structure is the 1915 naval gun shop, a vast shed, 300m long, for the production of gun barrels for warships (*see* Figure 3.12). The barrels would have been tested onsite at an adjoining underground range and then loaded onto wagons and delivered by rail.

The production of naval guns so far from the sea demonstrates how specialist engineering work often went where the skills and know-how already existed. Today the gun shed and the other surviving buildings of the Ordnance Works complex are part of an industrial estate and are in need of further study. The buildings currently have no statutory protection and their long-term future is far from secure.

The First World War saw the construction of other purpose-built munitions factories on farmland sites in Coventry's suburbs. One such factory partially survives at Swallow Road in the Holbrooks area of the city. The buildings have been heavily altered but it is still possible to make out the narrow, north-lit wooden-roofed buildings laid out in a grid arrangement. Another survivor is the 1916 Hotchkiss et Cie machine-gun factory in Gosford Street in the city centre. This much altered factory is now Coventry University's William Morris Building.

Firms such as the Coventry Ordnance Works were obvious candidates to benefit from the demands created by war, but almost all of Coventry's engineering firms were heavily involved in the war effort. The factories of motor firms such as Daimler at Radford, Standard at Canley and Siddeley-Deasy at Parkside were massively expanded to produce thousands of shells in addition to lorries, ambulances and tanks.

Of greater long-term significance for the city was that Daimler, along with Standard and Siddeley-Deasy, had been heavily involved with aircraft production. This established the city as a centre for aero-engineering. While most motor manufacturers reverted to making vehicles after the war, Siddeley-Deasy saw the future opportunities of the infant aircraft industry and continued with aircraft production. In 1919 it entered into partnership with the Tyneside armaments firm Armstrong-Whitworth to form Armstrong-Siddeley, concentrating aircraft production in Coventry at a former RAF airfield in Whitley and at Parkside (Thoms and Donnelly 1986, 33).

Coventry bucks the trend

While many of Britain's industries slumped after the First Word War, Coventry's industrial sectors – motor vehicles, aircraft, electronics, synthetic textiles and machine tools – contin-

ued to expand. The machine-tool industry in particular bucked the depression trend, as manufacturers wanted improved machinery to cut their production costs. Changes in the motor industry saw the growing market becoming increasingly dominated by a few large firms, particularly those, such as Standard and Daimler, which had inherited factories that had been expanded for war production.

The growth in the city's economy resulted in a massive growth in population. The demand for skilled labour, coupled with the comparatively high wages, had attracted immigrants before the First World War. The extra momentum provided by war production saw the trend continue into the 1920s and 1930s, attracting workers from depression-hit areas such as south Wales and north-east England. The population had risen from 46,000 in 1881, to 106,000 in 1911. In the inter-war period Coventry became the fastest growing British city, with the population rising from 167,000 in 1931 to 224,000 by 1939 (Figure 3.13; Lancaster nd, 67).

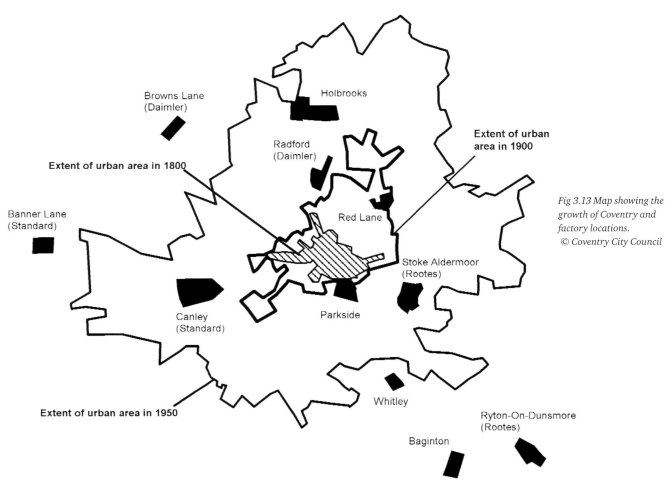

Fig 3.13 Map showing the growth of Coventry and factory locations.
© Coventry City Council

This population growth placed massive pressure on housing, with builders struggling to keep up with demand. The expansion of factories during the First World War had seen new facilities established on farmland outside the city centre, along with vast estates of semi-detached housing for the workforce. This pattern continued in the inter-war period until the supply of housing finally ran out in 1940 because of the bombing, resulting in the establishment of the National Service Hostels in May 1941. Fifteen hostels were eventually built in Coventry, providing accommodation for thousands of war workers.

Preparing for war

By the mid-1930s it was obvious that Coventry's engineering industries would have a crucial role to play if Britain was to achieve air parity with Nazi Germany. The government decided that the RAF needed 8,000 new planes, but to achieve this, new sources of production were needed. Representatives of the Midlands motor manufacturers were invited to a meeting at the Air Ministry in May 1936, where they were encouraged to enter the aero-engine business (Richardson 1972, 65).

This was to be the start of what was known as the shadow factory scheme, in which the government paid for the construction and fitting out of brand-new factories to build aircraft engines and then paid the motor manufacturers to manage production. The factories were to produce components for Mercury and Pegasus engines to go into the newly designed Blenheim bombers. The engines would then be assembled at Austin, at Longbridge, Birmingham or by the Bristol Company at Filton.

Four factories were built in Coventry: two for Standard in Canley; one for Daimler in Radford; and one for the Rootes Group at Stoke Aldermoor (*see* Figure 3.13). Production began in 1938 but it soon became apparent that this would not be enough and that larger engines, and more of them, would be needed to power the new Lancaster and Stirling bombers.

Rather than disrupt the existing factories, the decision was taken to build four more factories, three of them in Coventry: one at Ryton-on-Dunsmore for Rootes; one in Browns Lane, Allesley, for Daimler; and one in Banner Lane, Tile Hill for Standard. Along with the Rover factory at Solihull, they were to build 800 Bristol Hercules engines per month with the factories working in pairs, each making half of the engine, as a measure to spread the risk of losing production to bombing (Richardson 1972, 68).

Standard Aero Engines No 2 Factory, Banner Lane, was the largest of the shadow factories and was highly controversial, even in 1939, as it was a major incursion into the newly-established 'green belt' and was initially resisted by the city council. The factory was in production from July 1940 and comprised four large workshops with office accommodation at the front, and 22 engine test houses to the rear.

By August 1943, Banner Lane employed more than 6,000 workers. By the summer of 1945 it had produced, along with its sister factory at Canley, some 20,000 Hercules engines (Hulka and Lowe 2004, 16). After the war the factory was acquired by Standard, and later become the home of Massey Ferguson Tractors from 1946 until its closure in 2003.

Finding the traces

Before the building at Banner Lane was knocked down in 2004, a programme of building recording was undertaken as part of the planning permission for the site (Hulka and Lowe 2004). The factory had retained many of the features stemming from its wartime use. The exterior of the machine shops and assembly shops still showed traces of their wartime camouflage paint, and the air-raid shelters for the workforce were still underneath these structures.

Each shop had 12 shelters. There were four single shelters, each accommodating 73 employees and eight double shelters each accommodating 146 employees. To reach the shelters from the machine shops there was a concrete staircase protected by a steel door, designed to withstand a blast. This led to a corridor with escape hatches above and chemical toilets at either end. The shelters took the form of U-shaped loops leading off the corridor with benches running along the side of each wall.

To the rear of the machine shops were the engine test houses. There had originally been 22 houses, arranged in pairs to form 11 blocks. There were two types; 12 H test houses and 10 M test houses. It is not clear whether they were for testing two types of engine (perhaps H for Hercules and M for Mercury) or whether they were for two different types of testing (Figure 3.14).

Since Banner Lane closed in 2003, both the Rootes No 2 factory at Ryton-on-Dunsmore (latterly Peugeot) and Daimler No 2 at Browns Lane (latterly Jaguar) have also closed and both these factories were demolished in 2008.

In addition to the shadow factories, Coventry's established aircraft manufacturers were also turning out complete planes. Armstrong-Siddeley had merged in 1935 to form Hawker-Siddeley and produced over 1800 Whitley bombers at their factories at Parkside, Whitley and Baginton, before being diverted in 1944 to make Lancaster and Stirling bombers (550 and 106 of these respectively) (Richardson 1972, 69).

The breaking

The concentration of war production in Coventry meant that by 1940 it was only a matter of time before the city became a target for air raids. The city was on the receiving end of 40 air raids between June 1940 and June 1941. It was, however, the raid on the night of the 14 November 1940 that would famously change the appearance of the city forever (Figure 3.15). On that night the city was attacked by 400 enemy aircraft that dropped 500 tons of high explosive and 30,000 incendiaries. Around 75 percent of the city's factories, and over 40,000 homes, were damaged or destroyed. The final death toll was 554 (Richardson 1972, 84).

The city centre was particularly badly hit. The historic streets of Broadgate, Smithford Street and West Orchard were devastated. Most notoriously, the Cathedral of St Michael burnt to the ground because fire crews could not reach the incendiary bombs that had fallen and been trapped between the buildings inner and outer roof space. The army was called in to carry out emergency demolitions of dangerous structures, and even the demolition of St Michael's tower and spire was considered.

The bombing of the city centre appears to have had little impact on the city's buried medieval archaeology and archaeological evidence for the bombing itself is not as commonly encountered as one might perhaps expect. When Second World War archaeology is encountered it is more by accident than design and usually during the excavation of earlier sites.

A recent excavation of a medieval undercroft in Bayley Lane (Figure 3.15) revealed that the

medieval structure had been reused as the cellar of some 19th-century court type housing that had been destroyed in November 1940. As the building burnt, it collapsed into the cellar, along with the possessions of the tenants, creating a time-capsule that included someone's savings – found in a corroded cash-box beneath an equally corroded bedstead. Watches, furniture from a child's dolls house and bottles of OK sauce were also found.

Research showed the house to have been the home of Albert and Elsie Radford. After this news featured in the local press relatives came forward with their memories of pre-war life in Bayley Lane. It demonstrated the fact that what was lost in November 1940, along with the buildings and the people, was the death of a way of life in the city centre where extended families lived in close-knit communities.

The massive scale of the bombing meant that thousands of tons of rubble and objects

Fig 3.14 Engine test house at the former Standard Aero Engines No 2 Factory, Banner Lane.
© CgMs Consulting

Fig 3.15 Bayley Lane 1940.
© Coventry City Council

were removed from the devastated city centre and dumped elsewhere. A report in the *Boston Sunday Globe* wrote of Coventry: 'there are probably more second-hand bricks here today than anywhere else in the world, you can drive out of Coventry in any direction and on the outskirts of the town you will see vast fields solidly covered with dumped truckloads of brickbats and rubble' (cited in McGrory 1997, 119). RAF aerial photos of 1946 clearly show rubble dumped on Stoke Heath and other open spaces on the city outskirts. Archaeological excavations carried out at such places today frequently find melted bottles and sandstone from the city centre redeposited in medieval moats and hollow-ways (old sunken roads).

That the bombing of 1940 caused massive damage to the city is not disputed; the blame for the destruction of medieval Coventry, however, cannot be completely attributed to Nazi Germany. The radical replanning of the city centre had been under discussion since the 1920s. Car ownership in Coventry was twice the national average, and the traffic was putting the historic road system of the central area under immense strain. In 1931 the city council created the new Corporation Street by demolishing a huge swathe of the city, with scenes that foreshadowed the wartime destruction. Next to go was the Butcher Row area (*see* Figure 3.11), razed to make way for the new Trinity Street. Butcher Row and the streets around it represented Coventry at its most picturesque, with rows of tightly packed, jettied, timber-framed buildings. Even at the time, its demolition was viewed as an appalling act of municipal vandalism but accepted in the name of progress.

Further progress of this sort was to come in 1938, when Donald Gibson was appointed Coventry's first city architect. Gibson took a blank canvas approach to planning and soon produced plans for a new modern Coventry in which little more than the Cathedral of St Michael and Holy Trinity Church would be spared. The opportunity for a blank canvas came sooner than expected on 14 November 1940. Gibson later recalled watching the fires to see which areas of the city were burning and then examining his plans to see which parts of them it would now be easier to implement (Gill 2004, 62).

The rebuilding of the city

By 1941 plans were being drawn up for the rebuilding of Coventry. The newly formed department of architects, led by Donald Gibson, and the established engineers department, led by Ernest Ford, both had town planning responsibilities and they drew up two competing plans.

Gibson's plan was the more radical and involved sweeping away most of the existing buildings and establishing a new road layout separating the car and the pedestrian with two-tier shopping areas. He wanted the city to be strictly zoned with civic and commercial zones, with housing and industry banished to the suburbs (Figure 3.16). Ford's plan was less radical but this was probably motivated more by pragmatism about the cost than any interest in conservation, Ford having been the vandal of Butcher Row. Ford wanted to keep the historic street plan but to widen the streets to accommodate the extra traffic. Some of the historic buildings would also be retained.

Eventually the city council approved the Gibson plan. Rebuilding could not start, however, until July 1947, when the government declared 274 acres (111 ha) of the city an area of extensive war damage. Previously there had been no legal framework for a local authority to purchase land and dictate its use.

The levelling stone for the new city was laid on 8 June 1946 and Princess Elizabeth opened the new Broadgate area in 1948. The first building to be built was Broadgate House. Progress was slow as the project suffered from lack of materials and manpower; it was not until 1953, 13 years after the destruction of 1940, that the building was finally opened.

Showpiece developments were low on the council's list of priorities compared with industry, housing and education. In order to get Coventry's shopping centre up and running again, rows of temporary prefabricated shops were erected to prevent shoppers being attracted to less damaged towns and losing the habit of shopping in the city. Some of these sturdy 'temporary' shops survived into the 1990s. Some slightly later ones from the 1950s are still standing today at the junction of Well Street and Bishop Street.

Around Coventry you can still spot wartime damage, with the telltale signs of buildings that have lost their upper storeys and gaps in rows of terraced houses. On a row of 16th-century tim-

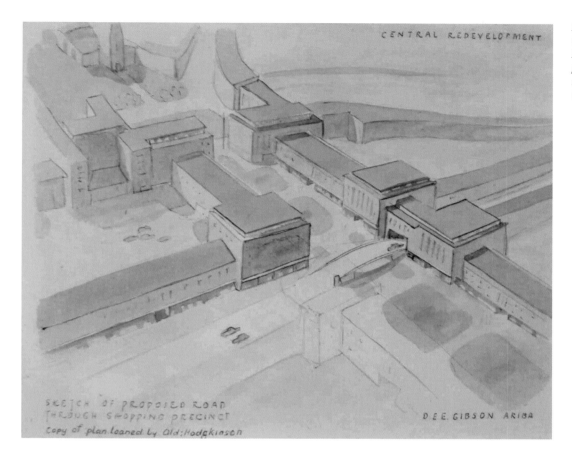

CENTRAL REDEVELOPMENT

SKETCH OF PROPOSED ROAD
THROUGH SHOPPING PRECINCT
Copy of plan loaned by Ald: Hodgkinson

D.E.E. GIBSON ARIBA

Fig 3.16 Watercolour by Coventry's city architect, Donald Gibson, showing proposed city redevelopment.
© Coventry City Council

ber-framed houses in Far Gosford Street, temporary asbestos sheet roofing is visible, perhaps the result of an unresolved compensation claim for war damage.

Conserving what is left

Conservation was even lower on the list of council priorities. The bombing had left many islands of historic structures around the city centre, and this isolation made them vulnerable to 'progress'. A survey undertaken by the National Buildings Record in 1958 found 100 timber-framed buildings remaining. The post-war austerity measures that had aided their preservation, however, were over. As a result, there was a dramatic increase in the pace of development and by 1966 there were only 34 such buildings left (Gill 2004, 68).

Eventually, the wilful destruction of the city's heritage began to stir public opinion. It led to the revival of an idea originally floated by Donald Gibson 20 years earlier, whereby timber framed buildings would be moved to be alongside 'their own kind'. Gibson had envisaged a 'garden of rest' for the city's historic buildings, centred around

Bonds Hospital on Hill Street. It evolved into the Spon Street Townscape Scheme where many buildings, cleared from areas such as Much Park Street were dismantled, restored and re-erected on Spon Street. It was a controversial plan at the time and would not be regarded as good practice today, but it undoubtedly saved many buildings that would otherwise have been destroyed.

From boom to slump

Coventry's boomtown growth continued into the post-war period with production capacity boosted by the newly-vacated shadow factories and all seemed to be business as usual. By the later 1950s, however, it was becoming apparent that the city's economic base was shrinking and becoming increasingly over-dependent on the motor and aircraft industries.

Coventry lacked the industrial diversity of neighbouring Birmingham and if the bottom was to drop out of either or both of these industries, then the city could find itself in trouble. This is basically what then happened in the 1970s when Coventry's manufacturers failed to diversify into new markets and became less competitive, leading to financial losses and eventually factory closures. By the 1980s the city had returned full circle to the slump of 100 years earlier.

One only has to examine aerial photographs of Coventry taken in the 1970s to see how the landscape of the city has changed in the last 30 years. The fate of the former Armstrong-Siddeley factory at Parkside is typical of any number of industrial sites in the city. The factory closed in 1994 and the whole complex was demolished, except for the former Swift Cycles office block, which was saved after a struggle and successfully converted to form part of a hotel.

This is a familiar pattern for Coventry: if the will is there the office elements of former industrial complexes can sometimes be saved, but the actual manufacturing space is almost always lost. Usually the best we at the city council's archaeology office can achieve is a thorough photographic record of a complex, but this will often only happen if the site is the subject of a planning application. Sadly, many sites are lost without record as no permission is needed to demolish a factory. Landowners are sometimes unwilling to grant access for building recording, fearing that any discoveries may hinder their future plans.

The Daimler No 2 Factory at Browns Lane was demolished in 2008 so that the owners can avoid having to pay tax on the vacant factory. They are quite within their rights to do so, as no permission is required to demolish it and no planning application is pending. Fortunately, they were willing to grant access for building recording and this historic complex will not be lost without a record having been made of it.

The economic reality is that the demolition of factories to create business and technology parks is merely the city once again restructuring its economy and is part of an ongoing process that many of the city's Victorian entrepreneurs would doubtlessly recognise and approve of.

The Coventry city centre was changed forever by the air raids of 1940-41. Many of the great medieval buildings such as St Mary's Guildhall survive today, but the historic streetscapes of more humble timber-framed buildings have vanished. The grand plans for the city's rebuilding fell victim to the economic realities of the post-war period and Gibson's plan remains only partly executed, leaving Coventry with a strangely disjointed city centre where historic buildings are left stranded amongst car parks and roundabouts or facing the backs of faceless 1960s office blocks.

In conclusion, the bombing of 1940 remains the defining event of Coventry's experience of the 20th century. Reminders of the events are never far away and remain a source of tremendous local interest and pride. Wartime archaeological remains and monuments, which were once treated as something to be removed to 'get to the good stuff' (usually the medieval deposits), are now rightly regarded as an opportunity to learn more about ordinary people living in extraordinary times.

List of references

Gill, R 2004 'From the Black Prince to the Silver Prince: Relocating Mediaeval Coventry' in Harwood, E and Powers, A (eds) The Heroic Period of Conservation. Twentieth Century Architecture 7, London: The Twentieth Century Society

Hulka, K, and Lowe, J 2004 Description and Analysis, Former Massey Ferguson Factory, Banner Lane, Coventry. CgMs Consulting Report Ref 4807

James, H 1905 English Hours. Oxford

Lancaster, B nd 'Who's a Real Coventry kid? Migration into Twentieth Century Coventry' in Lancaster, B and Mason, T (eds) Life and Labour in a 20th Century City. Warwick: 57–78

McGrory, D 1997 Coventry at War. Stroud: Sutton Publishing

McGrory, D 2003 The Illustrated History of Coventry's Suburbs. Derby: Breedon Books Publishing Co Ltd

Richardson, K, 1972 Twentieth-Century Coventry. London: Macmillan

Thoms, D W and Donnelly, T 1986 'Coventry's Industrial Economy 1880–1980' in Lancaster, B and Mason, T (eds) Life and Labour in a 20th Century City. Warwick: Cryfield Press, 11–56

3. Public archaeology, public history: case studies in conservation and management

Public access to Second World War British heritage in Malta

JOSEPH MAGRO CONTI

This paper briefly addresses some issues in the conservation and presentation of the recent heritage of war in Malta, the way this heritage is made accessible to the public, and the social and economic effects of the way it is managed.

Not many academics have attempted to explore what the remains of Malta's Second World War defences mean to people in Malta today and little has been done to investigate and analyse the values, issues and conflicts arising from attempts to conserve Second World War defences (Magro Conti 2002). Second World War defences in Malta have been used as educational aids, and have made a contribution to the islands' tourism. But they have also played a special part in contributing towards the reconciliation of national identity with the British past.

So far there has been no coherent management policy established for making informed decisions about the fate of these sites. Their future is threatened by increased development pressure, competing for the land, which is necessarily limited. When claims are put forward for the conservation of Malta's Second World War defences, a range of interest groups in the islands often react with prejudice and hostility because of political, aesthetic and economic reasons and priorities.

Some argue against the conservation, saying that items from such a recent past are not heritage, and people are especially hostile to preserving objects that relate to aspects of painful pasts, particularly those within living memory; these, they say, should not be promoted for educational and leisure purposes (Borg 1996; Grima 1996). In the last 20 years, however, the Maltese public has shown increased interest in heritage in all its diversity mainly owing to the influence of the media and increased opportunities for widening intellectual and cultural capital, for example through better education and museums. Awareness about Second World War fortifications in Malta has only developed during the past decades owing to the lobbying of a local non-governmental organisation, the Maltese Heritage Trust, *Fondazzjoni Wirt Artna* (FWA) and the action taken by the Malta Environment and Planning Authority (MEPA) to statutorily protect samples of this recent heritage before it is too late to save them.

The islands of Malta and their fortifications

Geography gave the Maltese archipelago a strategic location at the crossroads of the Mediterranean, with favourable sea currents and the fine harbours. These factors contributed to the archipelago's rich archaeological and historical heritage. Since antiquity a series of foreign powers have used the islands as their base for commerce and military purposes.

In 1964 Malta obtained independence from the United Kingdom and is now a republic run by a parliamentary democracy. Malta has many cultural heritage items (including a concentration of World Heritage Sites), and an overwhelming presence of fortifications, ranging from prehistory to the Cold War.

The strategic military importance of Malta to the British during the Second World War was summed up by a letter from King George VI to the people of Malta – written on 15 April 1942 – awarding the whole community the highest possible civilian award for bravery, the George Cross. The King referred to Malta as an 'island fortress'.

The fortress nature of Malta stems from three factors: nature, the man-made fortifications, and the determination of its people to overcome adversity. High natural cliffs on Malta's south-west coast give it some natural defences against incursions by sea. More accessible low-lying areas of coast have been protected by fortifications since the Bronze Age, including Roman, Arab, and medieval additions. There was a notable period of building (1530–1798) under the Knights of the Order of St John. At the start of the 19th century the British intervened in the struggle between the Maltese and Napoleon, resulting in a long period of British rule (1800–1964) and further military building. In the 19th century the British constructed new mechanised forts, coastal batteries and fortified lines, as well as upgrading earlier defences to accommodate the latest artillery.

During the Second World War the British further constructed about 400 pillboxes from which to defend the island, heavy and light anti-aircraft batteries and a large number of smaller defences, amenities, airfields and naval facilities. Civil defence was a significant feature of the islands' defence strategy and many air-raid shelters were cut in the rock, which became emblematic of local resistance to the Germans. British heritage of the Second World War is also manifested in Malta by underwater ship and aircraft wrecks, military cemeteries, and vast public and private collections of military objects.

Between 1955 and 1964, during the Cold War era, the British and NATO forces provided new types of defences in the Maltese Islands with at least 20 secret underground installations, mainly consisting of emergency flour silos and mechanised mills, stores, command centres and a forward scatter station (a type of radar installation) (RCHME 1997 3a).

Public involvement in management and access to heritage

Tilden (1977) was one of the first to argue that providing better public access, explanation and presentation, is a way towards improving conservation: with the following model:

- through understanding – awareness
- through awareness – appreciation
- through appreciation – conservation.

The growing theoretical concern about involving the public in heritage led to the development of 'community archaeology' through which control of heritage sites is partially handed over to the local community (Marshall 2002, 211; Moser et al 2002, 220). This approach has become a cornerstone of modern heritage management.

In addition to Tilden's maxim, Start calls for public 'participation' as the active way beyond passive awareness and defines it as the 'enjoyment and understanding of archaeology and local history, consequently leading to the acceptance of one's own heritage, acquiring a sense of ownership and lending oneself to be *committed towards involvement* [emphasis added] in heritage management' (Start 1999, 49). It is expected that by facilitating better access to heritage one encourages further public participation and involvement, thus truly handing over part of the management.

There are great challenges in developing access policies and strategies that address and satisfy the diverse groups of people who may have very different interests from those of historians and heritage managers. It is likely to be necessary to identify a range of interest groups or what commercial marketing people call the 'audiences' who make up what is known as the marketing mix. These groups range from archaeologists to tourists, and include sponsors, politicians, people living near the heritage sites, and even those opposed to ongoing projects. Thus, heritage managers must be aware of the 'marketing mix' of the heritage they manage, as what may be applicable for one group is not necessarily valid for the others.

In Malta tourists are often the largest audience that come in contact with heritage sites and with the communities near these locations and it is therefore tourists who are often the catalysts who provide opportunities for the local communities and for themselves to experience and appreciate both the tangible and intangible heritage of the Second World War.

One of the principles of the International Council on Monuments and Sites (ICOMOS) is that 'tourism and conservation activities should benefit the host community'. In practical terms this means ensuring that attracting tourists by conserving sites and making them more accessible contributes socio-economic benefits to the host community (ICOMOS 1999: Principle 5), especially employment and empowerment of locals in site management. In this context, accessibility means both physical access to a site and intellectual access in terms of making the meanings of sites and collections more readily comprehensible to visitors. Some achievements have been made in Malta by non-governmental organisations and the local councils who are attracting visitors to air-raid shelters. Although they have done little more than involve volunteers who provide services out of pride and altruism rather than for personal financial gain, nevertheless attracting visitors has had positive economic multiplier effects on local business.

However, in the opinion of the author, the backbone of community involvement and public access to heritage should be the provision of a proper volunteer programme (Magro Conti 2007). Rahtz (1999: 12–13) defines the fulfilment of volunteering as 'learning by doing . . . [by which] immediately one was introduced to a wide field of other disciplines'. The positive contribution of volunteer participation can be seen in the Defence of Britain project, intended to encourage public participation, where from 1995 to 2002 600 volunteers participated in what Morris (2001) described as a 'mass observation of history', in documenting anti-invasion sites of the Second World War.

Having been a volunteer of FWA in projects involving Second World War sites and other heritage sites, the author can testify that active involvement through volunteering brings about a higher level of commitment than just passively participating as a visitor. FWA volunteers have helped in site maintenance, surveys, research, re-enactments, as well as guiding and facilitating visitors in hands/minds-on displays. The presence of committed local volunteers alongside paid staff may be the key factor in making the management of a site sustainable and it is therefore not a topic that should be brushed over in any management/business plan of a heritage site.

Development of public access and participation

Malta has hundreds of Second World War defences but very few are managed and open to the public. Up to the mid-1990s the National War Museum represented Malta's history during the Second World War. The lavishly illustrated publications by Quentin Hughes (1969; 1993) and Stephen Spiteri (1990) on the subject of Malta's fortifications, including those of the Second World War, further popularised the subject and helped many Maltese and others understand and appreciate these structures.

In 1995 a private company opened the war rooms that had served as the British High Command centre during the Second World War, but recently this museum closed down (Pace 1995). Also in 1995 a volunteer non-governmental organisation opened the Aviation Museum at Ta' Qali, an ex-RAF airfield and this is still going. In 1996 FWA restored and opened the first of the defences – the R15 pillbox (Farrugia 1996; 2000) (Figure 3.17). Some people criticised this initiative, saying that the 'pillbox' was ugly, brought back memories of war and that it symbolised British colonialism (Borg 1996; Grima 1996). However, the project was pursued and in 2001 FWA opened a public air-raid shelter at Vittoriosa, calling it the Malta at War – Home Front Museum (Farrugia 2001) (Figures 3.18. 3.19 and 3.20).

Fig 3.17 Re-enactors at the R-15 pillbox.
© Fondazzjoni Wirt Artna

Fig 3.18 Vittoriosa Shelter welcome sign.
© Fondazzjoni Wirt Artna

125

Fig 3.19 Vittoriosa Shelter logo.
© *Fondazzjoni Wirt Artna*

Fig 3.20 Vittoriosa Shelter, gas door interpretation.
© *Fondazzjoni Wirt Artna*

Public interest grows as access increases

Public reaction to the opening of the shelter was highly positive because shelters symbolised local endurance at a time of adversity. The Malta at War Home Front Museum is one of the most visited sites in the islands by tourists and locals – including school groups. Soon after FWA opened the shelter and museum at Vittoriosa, some local councils also opened air-raid shelters and these sites became suddenly seen as significant and as a symbol of the locality's pride, demonstrating the sacrifice, hope and attainment of victory through local resistance. This new perception contrasts to the attitude shown by some towards the British 'foreign' machines of war, with which they do not feel any connection; the shelters represented the Maltese people rather than the foreign servicemen (Zerafa 1995).

The Vittoriosa shelter, in common with the other sites managed by FWA, is used for educational activities in support of Malta's national curriculum. Students visit during school terms and participate in summer school activities. Occasionally FWA arranges special awareness-raising events for all, offering guided tours, re-enactments, hands-on facilities and specialised lectures. These have been highly successful owing to the opportunities offered to the public to interact with the guides, the re-enactors and the hands-on facilities similar to the model recommended by McDavid (2002, 307).

Many of the visitors have formed their view of Malta's wartime through hearing firsthand personal accounts from their parents or grandparents who experienced the Second World War and life in the shelters, or in the British Services. FWA is attempting to record some of these personal experiences of Second World War survivors, both civil and military, as well as collecting paraphernalia such as photos and other mementos as part of an ongoing initiative to record the intangible aspects of Second World War heritage.

Fieldwork and academic research has also lately begun to record the tangible heritage and socio-economic aspects of Strait Street in Valletta (Schofield and Morrissey 2007), which was a leisure hub for many British servicemen. Before the war the street had mainly consisted of bars, brothels, lodgings and music halls. By the early 1970s, owing to the departure of the British military services from Malta, Strait Street had a sudden decline.

The authorities had tolerated the activities in Strait Street seeing them as a morale booster to the troops. This aspect of the British military presence has been shrouded in taboo by locals for decades and therefore attracted little attention for study. However, Schofield's researches met with enthusiastic help from several locals who offered information and access to places that had been closed for decades. The Malta Maritime Museum acquired an authentic wooden shopfront of one of the bars as part of its interpretation of daily life of British servicemen (Figure 3.21).

The sites discussed above and their opening to the public or to researchers, were evidence of increased interest, locally and beyond, in Malta's role during the war. Public access to them provided added revenue for the tourist industry.

Public access to Malta's Second World War sites

During the past few years both non-governmental organisations and state-run museums have begun to reach audiences who find it difficult or impossible to visit the sites. Efforts have focused on people who have mobility problems because of disability or age. So far little has been done to tackle access barriers for people with other types of disabilities such as visual impairment, though a seminar in 2004, organised by Heritage Malta (the national agency responsible for state museums), did discuss the challenges (*see below*).

There are difficulties in providing physical access facilities for people with mobility problems at historic monuments and museums because the buildings were not intended as visitor attractions or to cater for disabled people. Door widths and changes in levels are major problem areas and physical changes to the historic fabric may require alterations that are often not compatible with conserving the historic monument.

Apart from physical access, we need to work towards 'intellectual' inclusion of the public in general. Inclusion entails inter-activity; where one makes an effort to enable the public to understand and participate in learning about sites and collections. More often, given that we are living in a consumerist society where even heritage has become a commercial commodity, marketing to attract 'customers' to museums has also to include strategies to encourage intellectual stimulus.

In Britain, for instance, heritage sites have a duty to provide adequate access to disabled people and there have been significant advances in the provision of physical access at museums and historic buildings. In 1999 English Heritage (England's statutory heritage protection body) issued a policy document on *Easy Access to Historic Properties* (English Heritage 1999). Some museums, such as Tate Modern, London, have even their own information booklet for disabled visitors (Tate Modern 2002). Leading by example English Heritage

Fig 3.21 Malta Maritime Museum, wartime bar exhibit
© Heritage Malta

127

has also launched archaeological fieldwork training for people with disabilities (English Heritage 2007, 30).

New access provisions come into effect

In Malta the *Equal Opportunities (Persons with Disability)* Act, 2000 was the first law to require reasonable provision of physical access in public buildings for disabled people. In 2001, to meet its obligation under this new legislation, Malta's National Commission for Persons with Disability published *Access for all – design guidelines* (KNPD/MEPA 2001). The guidelines were approved by MEPA (Malta Environment and Planning Authority) as a planning consideration and as a standard for the provision of reasonable physical access to disabled people and for compulsory adoption in all new public buildings.

The guidelines cover items such as ramps, rails, lifts, door openings, non-slip surfaces, toilets, signage, lighting and escape routes. Planning applications for refurbishment or for new museums must be audited for their accessibility. At this stage, stakeholders, such as the museum curator, the architect, planners, conservator and the disability amenity group, come together to work out solutions that provide the best physical and intellectual access without compromising the conservation standards of the historic building. Care is taken in the case of historic buildings where proposed alterations are required to provide access to disabled people that they do not compromise the architectural integrity.

In 2004 Heritage Malta, the national agency responsible for state museums, including the Malta Maritime and National War museums, organised a seminar *Access to Culture for Persons with Disability*, for heritage and museum professionals. The aim of the seminar was for people to think about enhancing the visitors' experience through improved accessibility and interpretation at state museums.

Heritage Malta is also training staff to help disabled visitors better, consulting with organisations that work with disabled people. It will provide information technology to widen access to the heritage. Speaking at the seminar, Joseph Camilleri, president of the National Council for Disabled Persons (KNPD, Malta), quoted a study that states that about 10 per cent of Europe's population are disabled in some way or another (Randall 2003). He also listed some of the reasons why cultural venues have not thought about making themselves accessible to disabled people because of prejudiced ideas about disabled people having low expectations, and the costs of making sites accessible.

All museums in Malta urgently need to produce basic printed material for disabled visitors, audio information for visually impaired people and to train museum staff to adequately welcome disabled people. There is also a need to increase the numbers of disabled people employed within museums.

At the National War Museum the exhibits are all at ground floor level and are fully accessible to disabled people, though the space around exhibits is very crowded (Figure 3.23). The museum is being refurbished and toilets have been provided for the disabled. At the Malta Maritime Museum the exhibits are displayed on five levels and a lift for the disabled and toilets were recently installed. The Aviation Museum is housed within an ex-RAF hanger and all exhibits, archive and workshops are at ground level.

The air-raid shelters are difficult to make accessible as they are underground and reached by means of narrow flights of steps and have very tight spaces. They are unsuitable for people with mobility problems and are claustrophobic. They also lack disabled toilets. However, the Vittoriosa shelters have a small exhibition space at ground floor and are accessible to the disabled. The pillboxes are also difficult to access as the only means is through a small hatch.

Fig 3.22 Malta Maritime Museum, model ships kept in a reserve open store, where they can be viewed on request.
© Heritage Malta

Other heritage venues, such as Malta Experience and the Malta George Cross multimedia shows provide good physical access and disabled toilets. However, none of these museums offer facilities for the partially sighted or blind, except where such people are allowed to touch artefacts and are offered personal guiding (Figure 3.24).

Intellectual access to Second World War heritage in Malta is also subject to this review. An eye-opening quote for the author is one by Parker Pearson (1993: 225) who insists on the need for a change in perception in museums where 'instead of welcoming "visitors", we should be encouraging "participants" (Pearson 1993, 225). The variety of interpretation and presentation services currently in use in Malta's museums and sites dealing with the subject under review consist of a number of basic traditional methods as well as others where more effort has been invested to offer greater stimulus to visitors.

Fig 3.23 Exhibits such as this Italian E-boat (centre) used in the failed attack against the Malta's Grand Harbour, are crowded into the Malta National War Museum.
© Heritage Malta

Fig 3.24 Malta Maritime Museum: Exhibits such as ships' maintenance tools, used as tactile aids for people with visual impairment.
© Heritage Malta

Visitors may roam the sites and museums without a guide, especially they are short of time, taking in information from exhibits and interpretation panels whose content and quality vary. Sometimes they are minimalistic, sometimes too detailed. Most of the sites now have a welcoming panel and some provide an illustrated leaflet with a plan of the site or museum with numbered cross-references to small numbered signs on walls indicating the original use or theme of the rooms, spaces and equipment.

All sites have a permanent exhibition addressing historical, military, technological, and socio-economic aspects of the period, containing the traditional glass cases exhibiting original artefacts with labels and models as well as large illustrated panels describing equipment or activities within particular areas. Often, these are hard to read or the information is too technical. However, there is still a need for the curator and the graphic artist to get feedback from visitors about their interpretation panels for potential improvement.

The Vittoriosa shelters, for instance, also have some of the subterranean rock-cut chambers fully kitted out, complete with authentic and replica artefacts of the period, usually based on evidence from contemporary photos and accounts by survivors. Although some people (Shanks and Tilley 1987; 1992) consider that these tableaux present a falsified idea of the past, they nevertheless offer a valid visual aid and a stimulus of debate to visitors. They are easier to understand than an explanation in words or text. Using these tableaux as a reference, the guides tell visitors about the daily life of soldiers and civilians.

In some of the state museums audio guides are being introduced for self-guided visits and such a facility will be available soon at the National War Museum. Audio guides have already been provided at the Palace Armoury Museums also managed by Heritage Malta. Many visitors find that a more rewarding explanation is given by joining in a tour delivered by the museum's own guide, someone who is specialised in the subject and who is already familiar with questions that visitors may have. This is standard in FWA sites, such as the shelters at Vittoriosa, where guided tours are provided at set time intervals so that visitors may plan their visit better.

A more ambitious level of provision for visitors is live interpretation and re-enactments by staff and volunteers in period uniforms (parts are original and some are faithful replicas in design and materials). This has become a hallmark of sites run by FWA, which offers such events on special occasions, though at Fort Rinella and the Saluting Battery (both Victorian period) they take place daily. At the state museums re-enactors are invited to participate at special events.

Themed open days at these sites have also become popular, especially with locals, because they offer a variety of activities and experiences for all the family or groups. On such themed days all kind of presentations are offered, including special treats such as the showing some rare period documentary or propaganda film footage, temporary themed exhibitions and lectures, or a gun drill using a Bofors anti-aircraft complete with the shrill sound of an authentic wartime air-raid siren. Many may enjoy these presentations as if they were at the theatre. However, the guided tours and discussions that follow help many to recognise the price our forefathers had to pay so that we enjoy the peace of the present, at least in Europe.

Another standard service at FWA sites, including the shelters, is the educational activities, tied in to Malta's national educational curriculum. During the past 20 years the national educational curriculum has increased its coverage of Malta's role in the Second World War. Museums have thus also increased the facilities and activities they offer for schoolchildren. The Aviation Museum, run by staff and volunteers, facilitates school groups, allows visitors to view ongoing conservation at their workshops and also allows visitors to climb in a cockpit of one of their aircraft, surely a big stimulus for some, especially the youngsters. At the Malta Maritime Museum visitors are allowed to touch some of the exhibits. The museum also has a friends' association that helps in raising funds and awareness.

All museums now have bookstands, which apart from generating revenue, help to raise more understanding, awareness and appreciation of the subject. Publications about Malta's experience during the Second World War have increased during the past two decades, especially ones containing personal experiences. An important inclusion in the history of the Second World War in Malta is the events that led to several prominent Maltese citizens being deported to British camps in Uganda for being staunch supporters of the *redenzione* – integration with Italy and for being sympathisers of Mussolini's fascism (Borg 1991; Frendo 1991; Mizzi 1983, 1996a, 1996b; Soler 1986).

The Malta Experience and the Malta George Cross at Valletta are basically commercial establishments that offer good quality multimedia shows about the history of Malta, including the Second World War and are a very good introduction to tourists.

The Malta Maritime Museum and the National War Museum offer access to information through their archives and open storage and this will shortly be available at the Aviation Museum and at FWA sites. Access to online data is much needed and may be shortly available for the National War Museum collections. As for the built defences, the MEPA is carrying out an overhaul of its digital inventory of immovable property, including the heritage from the Second World War, which will also be made available online.

This paper briefly discussed how Malta's Second World War heritage has become increasingly significant among the Maltese. This is a big shift compared to 20 years ago, when the same heritage tended to be dismissed as relics of colonialism and the symbols of war. Heritage managers can now build on the emerging interest in Second World War heritage in Malta by recognising that they can make better use of what has been done so far. Heritage managers need to see that the care of these sites should no longer be left exclusively to state agencies, but must involve some responsibility for their preservation from the general public.

The increasing initiatives taken by the various agencies in Malta managing heritage of the Second World War are contributing to the preservation of public history and making it accessible to local and visiting audiences. Efforts in making this tangible and intangible heritage more physically and intellectually accessible include a variety of forms ranging from traditional permanent museum exhibitions, to interactive experiences, re-enactments and specialised guided tours, as well as improved physical access to all, including people with mobility problems, promotion on the internet, increased tourism marketing, facilitating school groups and research in archives. Through these strategies wider audiences and niche tourist markets are being attracted.

Some issues of the Second World War, however, remain sore points for interpretation and are often avoided or glossed over or overshadowed by the interpretation of marvels of technology, heroism and victory. Notwithstanding this, the interpretation, presentation and accessibility of Second World War heritage in Malta has stimulated debate about who 'owns' the past, and whether the present generations need to conserve this dissonant heritage, and whether or how to make moral judgements on the heritage of recent conflicts.

Public involvement in heritage management is about making the past relevant to society by understanding the needs and expectations of the public in all its diversity, but especially that of the locals, thus making the site more relevant to the public by communicating its significance. Understanding interest groups is essential to develop a good relationship and provide better service at the site.

Developing opportunities for the public's physical and intellectual access to heritage has become an essential component of heritage management, and a public participation programme should facilitate management objectives and convey the museum curators' message – that they want the public to participate and 'own' the museum in order to achieve sustainable museum management and to ensure permanence. Therefore, providing physical and intellectual access to heritage should be a creative process that continues to develop, and be open to as many audiences as possible. There is still a pressing need for heritage managers and curators to engage directly with the public, especially in generating awareness at grassroots level and in securing the long-term commitment of volunteers.

ESTRATT

Il-wirt tal-fortifikazzjonijiet f'Malta hu kkunsidrat bħala fost l-aħjar eżempji ta' patrimonju militari fid-dinja. Matul l-aħħar għaxar snin kien hemm żieda ta' nteress fil- preservazzjoni, konservazzjoni u riabilitazzjoni ta' difiżi tat-Tieni Gwerra Dinjija mibnijja mill-Ingliżi f'Malta. Uħud mill-pubbliku għadhom m' aċċettawx il-konservazzjoni ta' dan il-wirt pjuttost riċenti, waqt li oħrajn iqisu d-difiżi Ingliżi tat-Tieni Gwerra Dinjija bħala parti integrali mill-wirt nazzjonali Malti u għaldaqstant iffaċilitaw aċċess lill-pubbliku għal ċerti siti u mużewijiet. Dan il-kuntrast joffri sfidi għallamministraturi ta' dawn il-monumenti storiċi, minħabba li huma kkunsidrati riċenti, li jirrappreżentaw vjolenza u li jitqiesu minn xi wħud bħala simbolu ta' kolonjaliżmu. Dan il-kapitlu jagħti rendikont qasir fuq id-dibattitu dwar il-wirt tal-gwerra u l-wirt riċenti, u jispjega r-rwol tal-wirt ta' gwerra riċenti fi żvilupp lokali u reġ jonali, iħeġġeġ it-tkattir ta' l-għarfien dwar is-suġġett permezz ta' parteċipazzjoni u inizjattivi fil-komunitajiet fl-immaniġġar tal-patrimonju tat-Tieni Gwerra Dinjija, u jagħti rendikont ġenerali ta' kif xi siti qed ikunu aċċessibbli għal pubbliku ġenerali fl-aspetti amministrattivi, preżentazzjoni, aċċess fiżiku u ntelletwali.

List of references

Borg, J 1996 'Monuments to shame', *The Malta Independent on Sunday*, 31 March 1996, p 31

Borg, R 1991 *Malta u l-Faxxizmu. rajja tas-Snin Tletin* Malta: Sensiela Kotba So`jalisti.

Development Planning Act, 1992, revised 1997. Malta

English Heritage, 1999. *Easy Access to Historic Properties.* Swindon: English Heritage

English Heritage, 2007 'Inclusive, Accessible, Archaeology.' *Conservation Bulletin*, Issue 55, 30

Equal Opportunities (Persons with Disability) Act, 2000. Malta

Farrugia, M 1996 'The last of impressive fortifications', *The Malta Independent on Sunday*, 25 February 1996, p 20

Farrugia, M 2000 *The R15 Reserve Post at San Pawl Tat-Targa l/o Naxxar*. A Brief History. Malta: Fondazzjoni Wirt Artna

Farrugia, M 2001 *Couvre' Potre Air Raid Shelter. A Brief History and Description*. Malta: Fondazzjoni Wirt Artna

Frendo, H 1991 'Plurality and polarity: Early Italian Fascism in Maltese colonial politics', *in* Fiorini, S and Mallia-Milanes, V (eds) *Malta. A Case Study in International Cross-Currents*, Malta: University of Malta, 227–240

Grima, J A 1996 'But no pillboxes! Musings on the latest craze. . .'. *The Malta Independent on Sunday*, 7 January 1996, p 30

Hughes, Q 1969 *Fortress. Architecture and Military History in Malta*, London: Lund Humphries

Hughes, Q 1993 *Malta: A Guide to the Fortifications*. Malta: Said International

ICOMOS [International Council on Monuments and Sites] 1999 *International Cultural Tourism Charter: Managing tourism at places of heritage significance*. Adopted by ICOMOS at the 12th general assembly in Mexico, October 1999 http://www.international.icomos.org/charters/tourisme.htm accessed 16 December 2008

KNPD/MEPA 2001 *Access for all – design guidelines*. Malta: Kunsill Nazzjonali Persuni b'Di abilita'

Magro Conti, J 2002 'Values, issues and conflicts in the conservation of Second World War defences *in* Malta'. Unpublished Master's dissertation, University of York

Magro Conti, J 2007 'Community involvement in the management of prehistoric sites' *in* Hodder, I and Doughty, L (eds) *Mediterranean Prehistoric Heritage. Training, Education and Management.* McDonald Institute Monographs, University of Cambridge, 57–68

Marshall, Y 2002 'What is community archaeology?' *World Archaeology – Community Archaeology*, **34**, 2, 211–219

McDavid, C 2002 'Archaeologies that hurt; descendants that matter: a pragmatic approach to collaboration in the public interpretation of African-American archaeology' *World Archaeology – Community Archaeology*, **34**, 2, 303–314

Mizzi, L 1983 *Ghal-Holma ta' Hajtu*. Malta: Pubblikazzjoni Bugelli

Mizzi, L 1996a 'The conspiracy trials', *Sunday Times of Malta*, 22 December, 1996, 68–69

Mizzi, L 1996b *Mixlija B'Kongura u Tradiment*, Malta: PEG Ltd

Morris, R 2001 'The Defence of Britain Project', notes taken during the Defence of Britain Conference, Council of British Archaeology, Imperial War Museum, London, 24 November 2001

Moser, S, Glazier, J, Phillips, J E, Nassr el Nemr, L, Saleh Mousa, M, Nasr Aiesh, R, Richardson, S, Conner, A, Seymour, M 2002 'Transforming archaeology through practice: strategies for collaborative archaeology and the Community Archaeology Project at Quseir, Egypt'. *World Archaeology – Community Archaeology* **34**, 2, 220–248

Pace, S 1995 'Lascaris War Rooms refurbished', *Sunday Times of Malta*, 26 February 1995, p 61

Parker Pearson, M 1993, 'Visitors Welcome' *in* Hunter, J and Ralston, I (eds) *Archaeological resource management in the UK: An introduction*. Stroud: Alan Sutton/Institute of Field Archaeologists, 225–231

Rahtz, P 1999, 'Learning by doing', in Beavis, J and Hunt, A (eds) *Communicating Archaeology*. Bournemouth University School of Conservation Sciences, Occasional Paper 4, Oxford: Oxbow Books, 11–20

Randall, B 2003 'Integrated Solutions', *Inside Housing*, 14 November 2003

RCHME 1997 *NATO Forward Scatter Station Stenigot – Historic Building Report* Swindon: RCHME

Schofield, J and Morrissey, E 2007 'Titbits Revisited: Towards a Respectable Archaeology of Strait Street, Valletta (Malta)' in McAtackney, L, Palus M Piccini, A (eds) *Contemporary and Historical Archaeology in Theory*. Papers from the 2003 and 2004 CHAT Conferences, BAR International Series 1677, 89–99

Shanks, M and Tilley, C 1987 *Social Theory and Archaeology*. Cambridge: Polity Press

Shanks, M and Tilley, C 1992 *Re-constructing Archaeology: Theory and Practice*, 2nd edn. London: Routledge

Soler, E 1986 *The King's Guests in Uganda: From Internment to Independence* 1939–1964, Malta: Lux Press

Spiteri, S 1990 *British Military Architecture in Malta*. Malta: Heritage Interpretation Services

Start, D 1999 'Community Archaeology: Bringing it back to local communities', in Chitty, G and Baker, D (eds) *Managing Historic Sites and Buildings*. London: Routledge/English Heritage, 49–59

Tate Modern 2002 *Access*. London: Tate Gallery.

Tilden, F 1977 *Interpreting Our Heritage*, 3rd edn. Chapel Hill: University of North Carolina Press

Zerafa, I 1995 Spirit of enterprise at Mosta: Wartime horrors soon to be re-lived in shelters being opened for viewing, *Times of Malta*, 19 June 1995, 28–9

3. Public archaeology, public history: case studies in conservation and management

Orford Ness – A landscape in conflict?

ANGUS WAINWRIGHT

A case for preservation?

Orford Ness – a former secret weapons testing ground on England's east coast – highlights the issues involved in understanding the history and aesthetics of a place, developing a management philosophy and how this affects practical decisions.

The National Trust is Europe's largest conservation organisation, with 3.5 million members and 250,000 hectares of land. Set up over 100 years ago, it has acquired, for the benefit of the nation, many places of historic interest and natural beauty and has built up considerable expertise in the understanding and management of these ornamental landscapes.

Management plans are the basis of the responsible management of Trust properties. These plans draw together the results of specialist surveys, describe the aims of management and explain how the property is to be managed within the constraints of finance and specialist interests. The defining and describing of the aesthetic qualities of properties, however, has not been developed to the same extent as the surveys of other aspects. In most cases this deficiency has not harmed the aesthetic qualities of Trust properties, as the preserving of important historical or biological elements and processes has coincidentally preserved aesthetic attractions. But the fact remains that the sum of the objects described in these surveys do not adequately capture the essence of a landscape.

This problem is well illustrated at Orford Ness, Suffolk. Here the landscape has a disturbing effect on the viewer, partly due to the violent contrast of its man-made and natural elements and partly due to its exposed and somehow hostile nature. Some of the features that go to make up this unique landscape

have historical or biological importance but others do not.

Those interested in the preservation of these features have been faced with a number of difficulties. It is easy to argue for the preservation of attractive features, even though historically they may be unremarkable. It is more difficult to make a case for the preservation of what many would consider ugly features even when they are rare, and nigh on impossible when these ugly features are also commonplace. Unfortunately it is just such ugly and seemingly commonplace features that are an essential part of what makes Orford Ness unique.

More than a rare habitat

Orford Ness lies more or less on the eastern extremity of England's east coast. The shingle spit that makes up most of the property belonging to the National Trust stretches for about 16km. The shingle spit protects from the sea a thin strip of grazing marsh and mudflat; dividing the spit from the mainland is the River Ore. To most locals Orford Ness is known as 'the island' because of its isolation and apparent separation from the mainland.

In geological terms this landscape is a great rarity, being one of the three major shingle formations in the British Isles. It is the only one which consists of both a shingle spit and a triangular area of sand and gravel pointing out to sea, properly known as a cuspate foreland. The shingle surface preserves a complex pattern of ridges deposited over many centuries that record the stages in the formation of the land form. Orford Ness is the largest vegetated shingle spit in Europe, as well as being the second largest but best preserved area of vegetated shingle in Britain. This shingle structure is very dynamic, building up in

some areas and eroding in others and the beach can change shape overnight.

Orford Ness also has an internationally rare and highly specialised flora. This botanical interest is enhanced by the variety of habitats it contains. These include mudflats, salt marsh, reed beds, brackish lagoons, shingle beach and neutral grassland. The property is also notable for its bird life, being an important over-wintering and breeding ground for sea birds, waders and wildfowl. The national and international importance of the geology and biology of the property is reflected in its

designation not only as a national nature reserve, and as a Ramsar site (one protected under the Ramsar convention on wetlands, named after Ramsar in Iran, where it was signed in 1971) but also as a special protected area.

Despite its international importance for nature conservation, however, it is its long history of military experimentation which has most impact on the visitor. The landscape is dominated by the structures and detritus of 70 years of intense scientific activity (*see* Figures 3.25 and 3.26).

3.25 Former atomic weapons test laboratories at Orford Ness: among the almost featureless shingle, the visitor experiences a disturbing compression of perspective.
© Joe Cornish/National Trust

3.26 A former atomic weapons test laboratory at Orford Ness becomes habitat.
© *Joe Cornish/National Trust*

Many who visit Orford Ness dislike it at first, as did many decision-makers within the National Trust. Roughly when the Trust acquired the land in 1993 a school of thought developed that advocated 'tidying up' and allowing the place to be converted back to a 'wilderness'. This was a shocked reaction of those used to judging the rural charms of bucolic lowland farms, wild upland moors or elegantly landscaped parks. As the new curators, our job was to step beyond such gut reactions and endeavour to understand Orford Ness on its own terms, to appreciate the order in disorder and the beauty in ugliness. We had to listen to its stories, learn to savour its attractions and finally persuade others to fall in love with it. The following paragraphs summarise how we went about developing our case.

The history of weapons research

The history of Orford Ness begins with the reclamation of the salt marshes during the Middle Ages. The town of Orford was an important port protected by the impressive 12th-century keep of Orford Castle. The military connection began in 1915 when the Royal Flying Corps adopted it as a research station. Research work was divided into three subject areas: machine guns and gun sights, testing of bombs and bomb sights, and navigation and aerial photography. By 1918 the staff had expanded to 600.

After the First World War activities at the station were reduced drastically. However an important episode in 1935–6 was the brief residence of Robert Watson-Watt and his team working on the development of radar. It was at Orford Ness that the possibilities of radar as a practical air defence system were first demonstrated before the team moved to a larger site. Given the pivotal role of radar in the defence of the British Isles during the Second World War, it is chastening to think that the history of the world might have been quite different had it not been for the faltering efforts of a few young men using outdated equipment in three dilapidated wooden huts at Orford Ness.

During the Second World War the pace of work increased. Experimental work concentrated on bomb ballistics and firing trials. Bomb ballistics experiments increased in sophistication as the speed and height of aircraft increased. Bombs grew larger too, culminating in the 22,000lb earthquake bomb. Firing trials were aimed at improving the lethality of allied ammunition and improving the protection of allied aircraft against German ammunition.

The site was handed over to the Atomic Weapons Research Establishment (AWRE) in 1959. Initial work on the atomic bomb concentrated on the ballistics of the weapon and telemetry (remote reporting of information). Later, enormous concrete test cells were built on the shingle beach to carry out environmental tests on the weapon. These tests were designed to mimic the rigours which a weapon might suffer before detonation. They included vibration, extremes of temperature, shocks, 'G' forces, and so on. Although we are told the weapons did not include any fissile material, the high-explosive initiator was present. A test failure would have resulted in a catastrophic explosion. For this reason the tests were controlled and recorded remotely and the cells were designed to absorb and dissipate an explosion without affecting the other facilities or the nearby village of Orford.

From 1971 and 1973 Orford Ness briefly became RAF Orford Ness with the construction of an immense Anglo-American 'over-the-horizon' radar installation known as Cobra Mist. Such technologies have an advantage over conventional radar in that its beams can 'look around corners' (the curve of the earth in this case) and are not forced to travel in straight lines, making them ideal as an early warning system that can detect low-altitude objects at long distance. The site was finally abandoned by the military in 1986. The buildings are now used to transmit BBC broadcasts.

Between 1986 and the acquisition of the property in 1993 by the National Trust, the site was exposed to the devastating effects of the triple forces of easterly gales, scrap-metal merchants and vandals.

The Cold War remembered

The first half of the 20th century was dominated by wars of a previously unimaginable scale. The second half has been dominated by the Cold War, carrying with it the threat of a 'hot war' on such a scale that whole nations could be destroyed. Staggering advances in science have produced weapons that have rendered the conventional view of the battlefield redundant, threatened civilian populations with death on an unprecedented scale and the natural environment.

What will be the memorials to the turbulent decades of the later 20th century? In earlier periods, when the nation's wealth was spent to fight off real or imagined threats, buildings were used both strategically and as a means of displaying power. Orford Castle itself is a classic example; it was built to the latest design by King Henry II to counterbalance the power of the barons in the region. By the end of the Second World War such fortifications had been rendered redundant by the increased range, accuracy and destructive power of contemporary weapons (the result of scientific work carried out at places such as Orford Ness). It was now by parading this technology that power was displayed.

Today redundant weapons are preserved in various museums but these will never set the imagination going in the way that the great medieval castles do. Much of the appeal of these structures stems from the contrast between the dominating scale of the architecture and the effects of time and nature on their fabric. Some castles are still capable of holding us in awe, especially where their imposing ruined form is set in opposition to the forces of nature, such as at Dunstanburgh on the windswept Northumbrian coast of northern England. The impact of this castle in its landscape is closely comparable with that of the AWRE test cells standing in the shingle wastes at Orford Ness (*see* Figure 3.25).

Like these medieval castles, the buildings at Orford Ness can be looked at in a number of ways: as part of the documentation of past events, as symbolic of deepseated aggressive urges within our culture, or as dramatic forms in the landscape – the contrast between man-made structures and their natural environment can enhance an appreciation of both.

Again like the ruins of medieval castles, these buildings also say a lot about our continuing confrontation with the forces of nature and the ability of these forces to adapt to our structures and, given time, to destroy them. In the harsh environment of Orford Ness the destructive powers of nature are most evident in the form of the massive shingle banks thrown up or scoured away in the course of a stormy day. Since writing the original version of the article three of the Orford Ness buildings have disappeared into the sea and one has collapsed in a storm. The next to go will be that most iconic of coastal buildings – the lighthouse.

First steps in the management plan

Defining and promoting the aesthetic, symbolic and historical importance of the property was the first step in the production of a management plan. The next step was to identify those features that contribute most to these categories. These were summarised along with nature conservation aspects in a statement of significance that attempted briefly to define those key aspects and features of the place that the Trust must preserve.

When describing Orford Ness one is apt to use adjectives such as bleak, mysterious, secret or hostile. Although these words describe the dominating impression of the shingle areas, they do not describe other areas of the property. Just as one might define different habitat areas and develop different management pre-

scriptions for each, it was important to try to define areas with different aesthetic characteristics more precisely.

Three character areas

For aesthetic purposes the Orford Ness property can be divided into character areas, that is to say definable areas with unique aesthetic characteristics. These character areas gain their distinctiveness from their particular geology and past history of management; and for this reason they may well be meaningful in nature conservation and management terms as well. To a large extent they also define areas with distinctive histories. The three main character areas are:

- the old airfield
- grazing marshes (King's Marsh and Lantern Marsh)
- the shingle

Obviously these areas can be further subdivided.

The old airfield

For visitors alighting from the boat that brings them to the site, the old airfield is the first area they see. Anyone primed to expect an exposed windswept site will be surprised, as the initial impression given by this area is of a rather enclosed piece of well settled and unspectacular pasture. This feeling is created by the high river banks that cut off any view of the sea on one side, or the countryside on the other, and by the arrangement of common-place pitched-roof military buildings dotted around the perimeter of the grazed fields. The domestic feel of the main group of buildings has led to it becoming known as 'the street'.

The visitor walks across the old airfield on one of the concrete roads and into the main site, dating mostly from the First and Second World Wars. The dilapidated 'ghost town' atmosphere that characterised this area when the Trust took over has now been altered, as many of the buildings now house the offices and workshops of the site staff. Visitors now see the river wall and the AWRE concrete buildings beyond and will be tempted to investigate these by crossing the bridge to reach the shingle.

Despite the obvious signs of human activity – past and present – in this area, the feeling of mystery and secrecy which with much of Orford Ness is imbued is also evident here. This is due to the silence, broken only by birds' calls and rattling corrugated iron, the dilapidated and overgrown buildings, and the incomprehensibility of the function of many of the structures.

Without an understanding of the history of military buildings and the specific work that took place at Orford Ness it would be easy to dismiss these dilapidated buildings. From the historical and archaeological standpoint various criteria can be used to decide which buildings and structures were most important both here and elsewhere on the property. These are:

Rarity

These criteria would include unusual buildings, such as the model bombing range and older buildings, such as the First World War 80-man barrack hut.

Functional group value

Buildings forming part of a group devoted to a special function and buildings associated with the bombing range fit into the category meeting this criteria.

Aesthetic or symbolic value

One of the criteria – for assessing whether or not to preserve – focuses on buildings with a special aesthetic value either individually or as part of a group. Structures with a symbolic function might include the concrete perimeter fence; this is one of the few signs that the area was once a secret site. The fact that part of this fence has been removed confuses today's visitors as it looks as if there was nothing to stop the least skilled Russian spy from walking onto what we are told was one of the nation's most secret sites.

Buildings with special historical associations

These criteria could encompass buildings in which important technical developments such as the development of early radar occurred or with historical events such as the early atom bomb test.

The buildings in 'the street' seem to us unremarkable. We are familiar with this sort of plain, functional, prefabricated architecture from any number of military sites, industrial estates and farms. It is difficult now to appreciate how revolutionary these structures were when they first appeared and how important the technical advances made in their design and manufacture were to post-war architecture.

Orford Ness is remarkable in preserving a variety of First World War examples of hut types; added to this is a range of similar buildings of all periods, up to the 1950s. Buildings of each period tend to be characteristic of the styles and concerns of their period. It is essential that this rich and varied building stock is preserved.

King's and Lantern Marshes

These two marshes are effectively divided by the Cobra Mist building and the BBC transmitter masts (this area is not owned by the National Trust). Like the airfield these marshes are enclosed areas, but here the atmosphere is lonelier. This is the preserve of waterfowl attracted by the flooded borrow pits (aggregate extraction pits), bomb craters and ditches; the silent barn owl also has its haunt here. Towards the top end of Lantern Marsh, the marsh narrows considerably and, where salt water penetrates the shingle beach, it is colonised by salt marsh plants. The immense bulk of the artificially raised shingle ridge overshadows this stretch. This is one of the few areas where it is obvious to anyone that the sea is eating into the land and driving the beach forward over the marsh. Both marshes are dominated by the monolithic presence of the Cobra Mist building, its featureless grey surface only enlivened by the shadows of passing clouds.

The shingle

Access to this, the most distinctive part of the property, is gained by crossing the tidal stony ditch by bridge. The bridge takes you to a network of concrete roads leading to the AWRE buildings.

The disposition and peculiar shape of the AWRE buildings and the flat, almost featureless, landscape they inhabit, lead to a disturbing compression of perspective and a difficulty in judging distances (*see* Figure 3.25). The scale of the buildings is overbearing, and in this exposed landscape the individual can feel overpowered and reduced in their presence. The visitor is drawn from one building to another and only during the long walks between the buildings is their monumental scale appreciated. As they loom larger and larger, anticipation grows; this slow process is one of the attractions of the place.

Once visitors reach a building the sense of mystery increases rather than diminishes. What are now silent, shadowy, rubble strewn and roofless interiors give little clue to what only a few years ago housed banks of gleaming and humming machinery tended by an army of white-coated technicians. The ruinous condition, scale and inscrutability of the structures conjure up comparisons with the temples and funerary monuments of past civilisations. The obliteration of any evidence of function and the heavy metal grilles through which one looks strongly underline the secrecy of what went on here – visitors can only ponder.

The areas between the buildings are scattered with debris; close inspection reveals that the concrete and iron is disintegrating, lichens have colonised pieces of broken asbestos roofing while horned poppies and other plants are establishing themselves amongst heaps of bricks. This process of colonisation and decay of the man-made by nature is one of the key aesthetic qualities of Orford Ness.

The lighthouse and the sea beyond will probably be the next target for a visitor with any energy left. The lighthouse is an obvious landmark with a well-known and reassuringly benevolent function, a friendly face after the rigours of windswept beach and the vast and incomprehensible AWRE buildings. To the north the beach stretches away for 3km to the dimly visible small town of Aldeburgh.

Aesthetic qualities

To sum up the aesthetic qualities of a place is difficult but some key points can be drawn out.

- the key aesthetic qualities are the sculpture-like impact of the immense buildings in a spacious landscape and the contrast of the man-made with the natural.

- the key symbolic significance of Orford Ness is its ability to symbolise the role of technology in late 20th-century warfare and the awesome destructive forces it unleashed as well as the political, moral and social repercussions.

- the key natural process is the colonisation of and the destruction of man-made artefacts by nature; the dynamism of this process is very evident in the changing beachscape and the obvious decay of modern 'permanent' materials such as reinforced concrete.

Other aesthetic qualities can be summed up by such words as exposed, hostile, disturbing, mysterious, inscrutable, conflicting, bleak, soli-tude, peaceful, stillness. Orford Ness is a paradoxical wilderness, an essentially wild place that is dominated by the works of man.

Management philosophy

Following the analysis of the aesthetic qualities of the property a general philosophy of non-intervention has been adopted. This stems from a need to protect not only the fragile aesthetic qualities described above, but also the features of nature conservation and geomorphological value, such as breeding bird colonies and shingle ridges. The challenge for the National Trust in the management of the property is to both preserve the evidence of the past use of the site and at the same time to allow natural processes to run their course.

The philosophy will be applied with varying degrees, from character area to character area, according to practical constraints and a parallel management aim to enhance the natural history value of the property. This management approach is about to be tested by English Heritage (England's statutory heritage protection body), which is in the process of trialling a proposed new heritage protection system that will see the structures at Orford Ness given some legal protection for the first time. The process will also see the creation of a management agreement between The National Trust, English Heritage and local government. We have yet to see if English Heritage will accept the Trust's management approach.

The philosophy goes into practice

Shingle area

On the shingle the non-intervention philosophy is imposed most rigidly. No form of tidying is done and on most of the buildings no form of conservation takes place.

From an archaeological point of view it has to be admitted that, in allowing the natural decay of these buildings, we are allowing the loss of the structural detail that contributes to their archaeological value. Much of this detail will be preserved, however, in the contemporary architects' plans and documentation and in a newly commissioned specialist survey (Cocroft and Alexander forthcoming). The main structure of the buildings and their impact on the landscape should survive for many years yet, thus the area's symbolic value will be maintained for future generations. The ongoing process of the structures' decay, which in the view of the National Trust is such an important part of the aesthetic interest of Orford Ness, should be allowed to run its course.

An unfortunate side-effect of putting this philosophy into practice is that unattended access is barred to much of the area. This is because health and safety requirements would necessitate the removal of many dangerous ancillary structures and the blocking of all entrances. Such action would greatly harm the architectural and historical value of the buildings.

Marshes

The distinctive aesthetic character of King's and Lantern marshes has been somewhat altered by the Trust with the reintroduction of grazing. This change has only been allowed because it will increase the value of the area to nesting and over-wintering birds. Fences are kept to a minimum to maintain the open aspect of the area. Of course, there is a historical precedent for grazing; some of the marshes were grazed from at least the medieval period up to recent years. In the future it is possible that some areas may be returned to mudflat by the controlled removal of the protective banks. This would add to the aesthetic diversity of the property and provide more valuable wildlife habitat.

Airfield

Intervention and change of character are most evident on the airfield site. This is where Orford Ness's new life as a National Trust property is centred. The smooth running of the estate requires a range of buildings including wardens' accommodation, vehicle stores, volunteer dormitory, education room and interpretation area. Wherever possible these functions have been married up with the most historically important buildings as a practical way of preserving them.

As the airfield and the nearby buildings make up the main public part of the property the requirements of health and safety legislation has meant that some dangerous buildings have been demolished. Where buildings have been removed, wall footings and concrete bases have been left so that the keen expert can still 'read' the site and the buildings have been recorded. Rubble is piled in localised areas so as to avoid covering any significant features. Despite these changes and the inevitable activ-

ity that is centred around the area, something of the dilapidated, ghost town atmosphere has survived. As elsewhere, tidiness is not an end in itself but only a method of ensuring visitor safety and the smooth running of the property.

Access routes

Visitors to the site have to use a small ferry. The short boat ride adds to the excitement and anticipation of the visit. It also restricts the numbers who can visit the site to about 100 per day. Control of visitor numbers is important on a site where the feeling of solitude is so important and where a single moving figure is visible from almost anywhere.

Movement around the site is restricted to a number of original concrete tracks. Visitors are asked not to leave these tracks, both for their own safety due to the presence of unexploded ammunition and weapons and also to avoid damage to fragile habitats. The route has been designed to take the visitor past a number of interesting buildings, two of the taller of which (the marine navigation beacon and the bomb ballistics building) have been restored to provide the housing for interpretation and which offer commanding views into the inaccessible areas.

From these buildings the route takes the visitors towards the concrete test cells. From this viewpoint the buildings are arranged one behind the other in recession giving them scale and drama. It has been pointed out (Davis 2006) that this contrived and controlled routing of visitors through the site has many similarities to the way picturesque landscape parks were arranged. Perhaps we could imagine Orford Ness becoming a landscape park for the 21st century!

Interpretation

The interpretation of Orford Ness poses many challenges. One problem is catering for diametrically opposite views of the historic significance of the place, depending on how one views the Cold War. For some, the place symbolises the West's successful defence of freedom against the communist menace, to others it represents the subversion of a political system and scientific endeavour by unbalanced leaders. The Trust's interpretation endeavours to provide fuel for the debate but not to come down on one side or another.

Orford Ness may arouse an immense range of reactions apart from these political standpoints. Artists react to the aesthetics, ornithologists to the bird life. Those who worked on the site remember the exciting technical work with which they were involved and social life of the 'island', memories that contrast violently with the dereliction and silence of the place today. As a reminder that Orford Ness is about people as well as nature and science these recollections form part of the display.

For those with an interest in the history and natural history of the site, interpretation areas are provided in buildings across the site and through a guidebook that takes the visitor on a number of signed routes. The interpretation attempts to explain the often complex technical work that took place and to explain the significance of often inconsequential looking lumps of concrete.

The powerful but fragile aesthetic of the place must be open to appreciation by the visitor. Signs, interpretation and direction markers need to be carefully designed so as not to erode this quality. Directions are stencilled onto the concrete roads and, where they are necessary, signs use a plain military pattern typeface rather than the National Trust's more friendly typographical style. Interpretation boards are all hidden within buildings so they can be ignored by those who do not want information to impinge on their appreciation. The individual should be allowed to develop their own personal interpretation of the meaning of the place. Indications of Trust ownership should not be overt; the visitor should have the feeling that they are trespassing on a wild and secret site. The Trust is trying the difficult task of giving the visitor a safe visit while trying to preserve the feeling of danger and mystery that pervaded the place when the Trust first took it over.

Historic interest, natural beauty?

People tend to expect a visit to Orford Ness to be much like visiting most other National Trust properties – a safe experience. A visit to this National Trust property can be both physically and emotionally rigorous. Visitors are often surprised to find a derelict industrial complex washed up on a wild seashore, evoking the destructive energy of the atomic bomb. Managing these expectations and preparing the visitor for the place is an important responsibility for the staff.

At the top of The National Trust's letterhead it says the Trust is 'for places of Historic Interest or Natural Beauty'. That Orford Ness is historically interesting cannot be disputed, but is it beautiful? If awe and drama are part of natural beauty and if man-made structures make a contribution, then Orford Ness is beautiful. Not far away in the same county, the National Trust helps preserve a rural landscape immortalised by the popular 19th-century painter, John Constable, a nostalgic landscape of a rural past. At Orford Ness it looks after a landscape of stark contrasts, symbolic of the real and current concerns of our time. Though these landscapes are so different, understanding and managing their aesthetic qualities is equally challenging.

List of references

Cocroft, W and Alexander, M 2009 *Atomic Weapons Research Establishment, Orford Ness, Suffolk Cold War Research and Development Site*. Swindon: English Heritage Research Department Report Series 10/2009

Davis, S 2006 'Military landscapes: Scientific ruins and Cold War monuments at Orford Ness'. Unpublished M.Phil thesis, University of Cambridge

3. Public archaeology, public history: case studies in conservation and management

Conservation of First World War landscapes: A landscape architecture perspective

HARLIND LIBBRECHT, JORIS VERBEKEN, SYLVIE VAN DAMME, GEERT BAERT

The paper discusses research carried out by the Department of Biosciences and Landscape Architecture of the University College of Ghent. The project began with a proposal by the city council of Ypres (Ieper), to analyse 34 castles and manor houses in the region of Ypres, in western Flanders, Belgium.

When studying the region of Ypres and the Ypres Salient, it is inevitable that one will encounter the history of the First World War. The project was enlarged therefore to become a landscape study, including the entire evolution of the landscape in the region. Within that story, the First World War is only one chapter, although a very important one – so important that it transformed the entire landscape. Our research findings will result in proposals for the future landscape of the region of Ypres.

The paper explains the role of the landscape architect in the protection of the First World War landscape on two different levels; that of site planning and that of environmental planning, illustrating the approach with case studies.

Project description

The region of Ypres, better known as the Ypres Salient, remains forever linked to the First World War. This was the battlefield where Allied and German troops fought each other for several years, the trenches and shelters sometimes separated by no more than tens of metres. Hundreds of thousands of soldiers of different nationalities, along with many Flemish civilians, lost their lives in the Ypres Salient.

Much of the 'war landscape' has disappeared: trenches and bomb-craters have been filled, and most of the war fields evened out. Yet indelible memories of the war still mark the landscape. These include the Menin Gate Memorial, numerous war cemeteries from the different nations and Hill 60, near the village of Zillebeke, one of the last relics of the battlefield itself.

An important element from the landscape architectural point of view, are the castles, manor houses and parks that were in the Ypres Salient (*see* Figure 3.27). During the battle, many of these castles were used by the troops as a headquarters, a shelter or a hospital. Some were damaged, others were totally destroyed. A

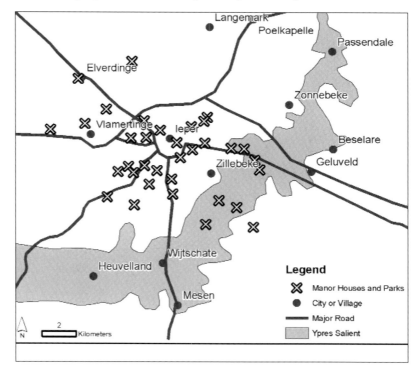

Fig 3.27 The Ypres Salient and the manor house and parks.
After Priem 1998

Legend
- ✖ Manor Houses and Parks
- ● City or Village
- ▬ Major Road
- ▨ Ypres Salient

Fig 3.28 La Hooghe Castle at Zonnebeke.
© *In Flanders Fields Museum, Ypres, Belgium*

typical example is the property of La Hooghe at Zonnebeke, a grand castle, built in the Renaissance style, with Classicist influences. The park round the castle had majestic lawns and a large pond and was well known for its splendour and beauty (Figure 3.28). After the war, only the large pond remained as a testament to the past. The theme park of Bellewaerde currently occupies part of the property. Ironically, few visitors are aware that their children are playing on the spot where so many soldiers died.

The environment of the Ypres Salient and its history of war is likely to receive much attention in the next few years. In 2014 the 100th anniversary of the outbreak of the First World War will be commemorated. There is also the possibility that this First World War battlefield will be recognised as a cultural landscape (UNESCO 2008). War and peace tourism, besides its humanitarian and general political value, is very important for the local economy, with Flanders declaring its ambition to become the top location of war/peace tourism in the period 2014–2018 (Durnez *et al* 2007).

Detailed landscape research of the parks and gardens in the Ypres Salient area could be valuable as part of a multidisciplinary approach to the war territory. The research findings could, for example, provide the basis for a visual reconstruction of the original state of the castle parks and would help with interpretation of the importance of these properties during the war.

Objectives of the project

The first part of the project analyses the evolution of the landscape structure of the wider environment of the Ypres Salient. The second part considers the evolution of castles, manor houses and parks. Both parts inform each other throughout the research.

The project looks at whether castles, parks and manor houses influenced the hedgerow landscape structure of the period before the First World War, and whether the war itself had an impact upon this landscape. It also explores how the landscape architect can contribute to the policy of commemorating the war landscape.

Evolution of the landscape of the Ypres Salient

Any research on the evolution of the landscape structure of the Ypres Salient needs to consider the subject before, during and after the First

World War. We can analyse the landscape structure before the war using historical maps, historical descriptions and photo archives. Extensive research of aerial photographs and British trench maps enable us to track developments during the war; at the documentation centre of *In Flanders Fields Museum* in Ypres there is a well documented archive of aerial photos of the battlefield. With the aid of Birger Stichelbaut's work it is possible to identify the photos by location (Stichelbaut 2006). The geographically referenced photos, together with the British trench maps, enable us to pinpoint exact locations of earlier park structures, trenches and bomb craters, resulting in very well-founded (historical) battlefield research. This research will help identify whether the micro-elevation structure of the First World War can be detected in the recent digital Flemish elevation model (DHM). It will also enable us to work out the evolution of the battlefield (trenches and positions) and the link between the location of the First World War trenches and the current parcelling structure, plant structure (hedgerow structure) and the elevation.

Changes to the landscape after the First World War will be evaluated through a focus on landscape identity. A number of documents and protocols will be used as a framework for identifying and describing landscapes in their current and historical context. These include the European Landscape Convention in 2002, the protection of historical landscape parks as described in the UNESCO World Heritage Convention (UNESCO 2008), and *Using Historic Landscape Characterisation* (Clark *et al* 2002), as coordinated in the English context by English Heritage, England's statutory heritage protection body (Fairclough 2002).

Analysis of the vistas will be through viewshed analysis – a GIS [geographical information system] application that can define visibility from a specific viewpoint or between given points in a terrain. By means of detailed research and fieldwork in cooperation with the Regionaal Landschap West-Vlaamse Heuvels (Cuvelier 2008), we will make an inventory of remaining old landscape elements and vegetation (hedges, trees, pollards etc)

Morphological and functional evolution of the castle parks

The morphological and functional evolution of the castle parks must also be examined within a time frame that is not limited to the dates of the conflict. Distinction should be made between two types of castles: first, there are the old castles (16th and 17th century and older), whose function was defensive, and the need to make them defensible determined the choice of their location. Later on, when such buildings no longer required to be defensive the castles were transformed. The second types of castles (manor houses) were those built in the 19th-century landscape parks, mainly by northern French industrialists, who were attracted to the region of the hills of western Flanders (West-Vlaamse). The project will examine the links between the site characteristics and the structural characteristics of the parks, and the structural and physical characteristics of the landscape. By investigating property structure and land registry, we can find out where grounds or plots were available for the construction of vast castle domains and what may have motivated the choice of site.

During the French Revolution (1789), many church properties were confiscated. Since the formation of the Belgian State in 1830–31, the exploitation law was promulgated, and communities were fined for not living up to this law. We also know from the research that in the 19th century almost all old castle parks were designed in the French style, and later transformed into the English landscape style.

During the First World War the staff officers of the different units occupied the castles which were seen as high-status accommodation. Later on during the war because of their reinforced basement construction some of them became shelters and hospitals. Soldiers who died there were buried in the castle grounds as the existence of small cemeteries in almost all castle parks bears witness. Later on, the large cemeteries were created. These cemeteries appearing as new landscape elements have defined the landscape structure.

The fact that castles were used as camps and shelters turned them into military targets. Some were seriously damaged, and some were completely destroyed. Once again, aerial photographical research and the British trench maps will provide the basis of investigation.

Commemorating First World War landscapes: three case studies

These case-studies will illustrate the role of the landscape architect in commemorating the First World War.

Sites where artefacts can still be seen, or where artefacts are already opened up, are the easiest to understand for the general visitor. In case of the First World War archaeology, there can be reference to the bunkers in the landscape: the visitor can easily imagine the uses of the bunkers and the story is therefore easier to tell.

It is part of a landscape architect's task to help visitors to understand a site. When drawing up a design for a visit to an archaeological site, this can be done in a similar way to the method used more often for natural sites. A 'layer' of various facilities for visitors is sensitively superimposed on the landscape (Figure 3.29). This layer can be made of floating timber walkways and some out-post balconies to get an overview of the site (Figure 3.30).

The layer must be designed with the utmost respect for what is underneath. The construction should be made with a minimal amount of con-tact points to the soil, reducing the impact of the added layer on the site. The site will be protected and the construction can, if necessary, easily be removed. It is, in a way, a sustainable solution. The walkway makes the visit organised and easy for all users, if all points of interest are visited. If people feel that they are missing interesting spots, they can leave the path. It may be possible to connect Hill 60 with the Caterpillar bomb

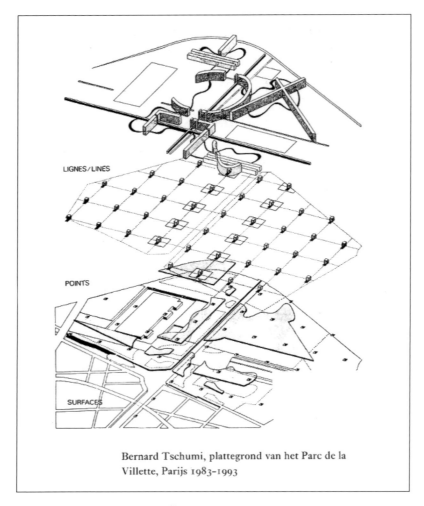

LIGNES / LINES

POINTS

SURFACES

Bernard Tschumi, plattegrond van het Parc de la Villette, Parijs 1983–1993

Fig 3.29 (above) Example of a 'layer' of visitor facilitation.
(After Leupen et al 1995, 63)

Fig 3.30 (right) Floating timber walkway at Playa Barrañán, A Coruña Galicia, Spain.
© Sonia Navas Aranda

Hill 60

Hill 60 is one of the only remaining untouched battlefield sites of the First World War. The name derives from its elevation of 60m above sea level. The site is linked to the former De Vierlingen manor house and park. In the park the bomb crater caused by the depth charge known as 'the caterpillar' still remains.

Design proposal

The first step in making a design is to analyse the site. Site analysis often starts for the land-scape architect with an inventory (LaGro 2001). This inventory assesses what can be detected visually: architecture, vegetation, soil circumstances, elevation, views, and so on. It is often necessary to work on a project with a mul-tidisciplinary team of experts (Lynch 1984). For example, when working on archaeological sites, the landscape architect should get the advice of the archaeologist. In this way the spirit of the place can be captured holistically.

crater at the other side of the historic railway. Sustainable land management could be achieved by using the spot for sheep pasture. Along the path the story of the site is told.

There are different ways of telling the story. Reconstruction is already a tried and tested method in the Ypres Salient district, but the results are not always satisfactory. For example at Bayernwald the trenches were reconstructed. The idea was good, but it is often forgotten that maintaining or restoring trenches was a daily routine for the soldiers living in them. At Bayernwald it can be seen that even in peacetime, after a few years without any maintenance (a process often overlooked in proposals for reconstruction) the sides of the trenches are falling apart. This makes the visit quite impossible, which in turn can result in the closing of the site.

Kemmelberg (Mount Kemmel)

In the region of the West-Flanders hilly landscape, Mount Kemmel's occupation by people goes back to the Iron Age. Important Iron Age structures have been found on the site (Doorselaer *et al* 1987), as well as structures of the First World War. The Belgian paved road that goes over the hill was later mainly maintained for the organisation of cycle races. The cyclists decided that it became too dangerous to cross the hill. It may now be possible to exclude all traffic from this road.

Design proposal

The goal is to build a rack railway to take visitors up the hill. The example of kocjanske jame, Slovenia shows us that this can be done without making too much impact on the forest landscape (Figure 3.31). The rack railway would make it possible for all users to reach the top of the hill, to visit the Belvedere, and enjoy the view. An existing secondary road would enable local traffic to reach the hotel on the side of the hill. Every tourist organisation wants to have its say on the hill, resulting in a mess of confusing signs (Figure 3.32). Coordination is very important. Westtoer (tourism company) tries to organise the coordination for the environment of Ypres.

No-man's-land

The landscape architect can help protect landscapes of war on the larger scale by defining zones where land users are subject to urban development restrictions, curbing the erection

Fig 3.31 A rack railway at kocjanske jame [kocjan Caves], Slovenia makes minimal impact on the landscape.
© *Sonia Navas Aranda*

Fig 3.32 Confusing signs for visitors to de Palingbeek leisure park, Province of West-Flanders.
© *Sonia Navas Aranda*

of new buildings or the use of agricultural processes (for example, muck-spreading – manure treatment of the land). This type of zoning might help preserve the open landscape of the Ypres Salient.

An important challenge to the landscape architect is to convey to visitors that an apparently 'open field' where visible remains are totally absent, nevertheless contains an important hidden history. How can the landscape architect visualise and help others to imagine what is no longer there? One possibility might be to plant hedges on the edge of the plots where the trenches were first dug. The first trenches were protected by the hedges. Starting from there the whole network of trenches was developed. This network can be analysed making use of both aerial photographs and British Imperial War Museum's trench maps.

A grassy border on either side of the hedge would make it easy to maintain the hedge. In this way, the no-man's-land can be visualised by the visitor. To create a project like this, it is important to collaborate with the local farmers, and make them aware of the importance of the possibilities raised. The grassy border can function as a joint use zone for the visitor. Possible ways of visiting the no-man's-land can be organised with a GPS walk using sound and image.

In between the two hedges on both sides of the no-man's-land it would be possible to create cattle pastures, managed by the local farmers, so the scenery of the no-man's-land becomes a long green belt in the landscape: this belt could start in Nieuwpoort (Belgium) and end – conceivably – at the Swiss border.

Between 1915 and 1917, after the second battle of Ypres (22 April to 24 May 1915), the battlefield remained almost unchanged. This might be the most relevant period in which to visualise the no-man's-land in the Ypres Salient. To visualise an evolution in the landscape, both for showing what happened to the manor houses and parks, and what happened on the battlefield, virtual landscape techniques could be extremely useful. Examples are already in use in museums all over the world, a good example being the recently opened Virtual Archaeology Museum (MAV) in Ercolano (Herculaneum) near Naples, Italy (www.museomav.com).

The landscape's managers will need to update the look of the virtual images after about five years, to avoid them looking stale and dated. This is the experience of the Ename Center for Public Archaeology and Heritage Presentation in Oudenaarde, Belgium, where they started in 1996 with the development of the timescope, and have now arrived at the third generation of this timescope.

This paper has presented some fresh ideas to enlarge the collaboration between different disciplines involved in the protection of the First World War landscapes. We hope that this will result in further international research collaboration.

Inleiding/ Samenvatting

Deze paper bespreekt een project van het departement Biowetenschappen en landschapsarchitectuur van de Hogeschool Gent.

Het project startte met een vraag, gesteld door het stadsbestuur van Ieper, om een analyse te maken van de vierendertig Kastelen en Landhuizen in de omgeving van de stad.

Wanneer men de omgeving van Ieper en de Ieperboog bestudeert, is het onvermijdelijk om niet in aanraking te komen met de geschiedenis van Wereldoorlog I.

Daarom werd het project uitgebreid tot een landschapstudie met inbegrip van de evolutie van het landschap in de streek. Binnen dit verhaal omvat Wereldoorlog I slechts één hoofdstuk van de geschiedenis, weliswaar een heel belangrijk hoofdstuk, zo belangrijk zelfs dat het de hele landschappelijke structuur heeft gewijzigd.

Het onderzoek zal leiden tot voorstellen voor het toekomstige landschapsbeeld van de streek rond Ieper.

De paper bespreekt de rol van de landschapsarchitect bij de bescherming van de landschappen van Wereldoorlog I op twee verschillende schaalniveaus.

Het eerste niveau is dat van de site, waar enkele mogelijke oplossingen worden geboden voor een duurzaam bezoek van de sites.

Drie case-studies worden besproken aan het einde van de paper. (Kemmelberg, Hill 60, no-man's-land)

Het tweede schaalniveau situeert zich binnen de ruimtelijke planning: hoe kan de landschapsarchitect bijdragen tot de bescherming van het landschap op grotere schaal.

Eén case-studie illustreert dit aan het einde van de paper.

Bibliography

Aeolus, B 2005 *Stadsrandbos Project Antwerpen*. http://www.milieuraad.be/uploads/1563Rapport Lot_2.pdf accessed December 2008

Clark, J, Darlington, J, Fairclough, G 2002 *Using Historic Landscape Characterisation*. English Heritage and Lancashire County Council. http://www.english-heritage.org.uk/upload/pdf/a4report.pdf accessed December 2008

Cuvelier, D 2008 Regionaal Landschap West-Vlaamse Heuvels from http://www.rlwh.be/ accessed December 2008

De Landtsheer, K 1981 *Bijdrage tot het Archeologisch onderzoek van de gemeente Kalken (Laarne) (O.Vl.), prospectie, analyse, synthese*, Gent:Rijksuniversiteit Gent

Doorselaer, A, Van, R, Putman, K, van der Gucht and Janssens, F 1987 *De Kemmelberg, een Keltische bergvesting : voorstelling van het aarden vaatwerk*. Vereniging voor oudheidkundig bodemonderzoek in West-Vlaanderen

Durnez, J, Van Gheluwe, P *et al* 2007 *Beleidsnota bij de ontwerpbegroting 2007*.

Fairclough, G 2002 *Historic Landscape Characterisation: Template Project Design – for EH-supported county-wide HLC projects*. 1st edn London: English Heritage http://www.english-heritage.org.uk/upload/pdf/hlc_template_project_design.pdf accessed December 2008

Hofkens, E and Roosens, I 2001 *Nieuwe impulsen voor de landschapszorg de landschapsatlas, baken voor een verruimd beleid* in Roosens I (eds), Ministerie van de Vlaamse Gemeenschap. Afdeling Monumenten en Landschappen

LaGro, J A 2001 *Site analysis: linking program and concept in land planning and design* Chichester:Wiley

Leupen, B, Grafe, C , Körnig, N, Lampe, M, de Zeeuw, P 1995 *Ontwerp en analyse*, uitgeverij 010, Rotterdam, 63

Lynch, K 1984 *Site Planning*. Massachusetts: MIT Press

Stichelbaut, B 2006 'The application of First World War aerial photography to archaeology: the Belgian images.' *Antiquity* **80**, 307 161–172

United Nations Educational, Scientific And Cultural Organisation (UNESCO) 2008 *Operational Guidelines for the Implementation of the World Heritage Convention*, WHC. 08/01 January 2008. Paris: UNESCO World Heritage Centre

AFTERWORD

Translation of a speech made at the opening of the Landscapes of War exhibition, Museum of Military History of Valencia, by Santiago Grisolía, President of Consell Valencià de Cultura, Valencia, 6 October 2008.

President of the Valencian Federation of Municipalities and Provinces, Mr Colonel Director of the Museum of Military History of Valencia, ladies and gentlemen:

When I started to think about my words for this presentation, it came to my mind that, with all probability, I would be the only person, among the speakers and the audience, who had ever lived through a war. You know which one I mean. Due to my age, I was never sent to the front-line. Still, in a civil war, the front-line always manages to find you wherever you are. Instead of fighting at the front, I worked as a nurse in a war hospital in Cuenca. You would believe me, even if you had not seen a war hospital, if I said that war hospitals are one of the most hideous faces of history. For example, I had always believed that I had a vocation for medicine until I worked for that hospital, when I lost it.

What all that misery really aroused in me was a profound love for peace. In fact, over the years, I have even taken part in various committees for the promotion of peace in UNESCO as well as other international organisations. Moreover, I was involved in the foundation of the Queen Sofía Centre for the study of violence, which also analyses the biological and psychosocial grounds for the phenomenon of war. What I mean is that I feel a pacifist as any well-meaning person does. However, from an objective point of view, if I was obliged to define myself, I confess that I am merely an 'agnostic pacifist'; I do not believe that we are able to erase war itself unless we are determined to take on the price of ending all liberties worldwide. But many specific wars, different from one another, which break out in real life, are preventable. I avoid citing examples from the past as that would be mere prattle. Kant, 'the optimist', wrote a book on permanent peace; he did not advocate a peace imposed by a sort of 'universal monarchy' either. That peace would clash with liberties. Nonetheless, Kant believed in the gradual creation of spaces of peace, promoted and consolidated by the progress of civilisation and by the gradual rapprochement or gathering of different and free countries around specific humanist principles.

This exhibition showcases, precisely, the collaborative work between several institutions belonging to different European nations that share a high level of civilisation around humanist principles. One of these principles is democracy, of course. Another one is the great value we place on historical experience. Although it may seem that human beings always, 'stumble against the same stone', the stone is not always actually the same one, and the historical accumulation of knowledge is the only thing which, in the end, saves us after the first shock.

One section of this exhibition deals with the material remnants of the past Spanish Civil War, and the other one is about the Second World War. These remnants are both monuments and documents, and neither the monuments nor the documents must be lost or destroyed. The Spanish Civil War was, undoubtedly, a European issue: the prelude to the great European war, which eventually became a world war. The Spanish people have had the pitiful honour of being the pioneers in some distinctive features of war. We invented irregular war in the 19th century; our cities were the first to suffer bombardment in the 20th century, and we subsequently invented air-raid shelters. All these features were later seen in the European war.

The Europeans have always been fighting each other. Nonetheless, a general war between the European nations is very improbable at the moment, unlike in the 1930s. I would be inclined to say that it is even inconceivable. Therefore, the progress of peace is really possible, anywhere and at any time. Because if universal peace is not what we are living at present, at least what we have now is a large space of peace, and long lasting enough to be worth perpetuating.

In conclusion, I believe that the international character of this exhibition is also a way of consolidating peace in this part of the world. Communication and collaboration are essential. And sharing the monuments and the memories of their suffering with other people is essential as well. Suffering must not fall into oblivion; otherwise, we would live without knowing who we are, and peace could never be conceived around any humanist principle.

Thank you very much.

GLOSSARY

Accessibility: in the terms of reference of this book, increasing accessibility to heritage sites means both physical accessibility, for example to people with disabilities; or intellectual accessibility, which involves making the interpretation of the site comprehensible to the general public.

Aggregate 4: A name for the V2 Rocket, a German ballistic missile weapon of the Second World War, the forerunner of modern intercontinental ballistic missiles.

Agora: literally Classical Greek for a market place. In the context of the resistance of local people to the demolition of the former Carabanchel prison, Madrid, Spain, the word agora was used to mean a communal meeting place.

AWRE: the Atomic Weapons Research Establishment, a research station located at Orford Ness, Suffolk, England.

Bathymetric: pertaining to measurement of sea depths and submerged sea-floor contours

Bombe/bomba: an electro-mechanical decoding machine pioneered by Polish intelligence services and further developed by British intelligence during the Second World War. It worked using a "menu" of "cribs" or guesses to arrive at decoding by a process of elimination. It belongs to the group of RAMs – see also **Rapid Analytical Machines**.

Border Wall 75: An element of the main "blocking" part of the Berlin Wall confronting the west; so called because this building phase was completed in 1975.

Bottom profiler/ sub bottom profiler: Underwater survey echo-sounding technique which can be used to detect submerged features or wrecks which are buried under deposits by means of a transducer.

Chirp sonar: A type of sonar using a Compressed High Intensity Radar Pulse; the techniques were initially pioneered in terrestrial military radar applications.

Cobra Mist: the code name for a type of experimental "over the horizon radar" system, set up at Orford Ness, Suffolk, England, between 1967–73. See also **Over the Horizon Radar**.

Colossus: a forerunner of the modern computer used to break enemy codes during the Second World War at Bletchley Park, England.

Community archaeology: a method of archaeology that seeks to involve local communities as fully as possible in projects, whether directly through excavations or by gathering oral knowledge about the site; the community is thus placed at the centre of the project, rather than being merely a source of potential data, or being excluded entirely. Community archaeology is intended to have social as well as academic value. An example of community archaeology explored in this volume is the Shoreditch Park community project in east London – an area of park that was formerly housing destroyed during the Second World War.

Conflict Archaeology: A sub-discipline of archaeology dealing with armed conflict between groups; its scope is wider than the allied discipline of battlefield archaeology in that it takes in all aspects of the conflict, not only the areas where combatants clashed.

CoNISMa: the National Inter-University Consortium for Marine Sciences, a maritime research organisation based in Rome, Italy, a partner in the Landscapes of War Project.

Contested sites, contested landscapes: A space which may have been fought over in the past and /or whose meaning, perception or use is debated and controversial.

CVC: Consell Valencià de Cultura: (Council of Valencian Culture) Consultation and advisory institution of the Valencian Regional Government for heritage and cultural affairs, based in Valencia, Spain, and partner institution of the Landscapes of War project.

East Side Gallery: A name for an element of the Hinterland Wall near the Ostbahnhof in Berlin. See also **Hinterland Wall.**

English Heritage: the British Government's statutory adviser on the historic environment in England and a partner in the Landscapes of War project.

Enigma: an electro-mechanical encryption machine designed by the German Wehrmacht that used a series of keys on a keyboard and wheels to produce a vast number of possible codes. See also **Lorenz.**

Federal Republic of Germany: the Bundesrepublik Deutschland or West Germany, formed from the American, British and French zones, mainly in the western half of the country but also including an enclave in Berlin.

Fish: in the context of this volume, a type of underwater survey equipment, a torpedo/ fish-shaped device for transmitting and receiving sonar signals, towed from a research vessel, see also **side scan sonar.**

FVMP: Federación Valenciana de Municipios y Provincias. (Valencian Federation of Municipalities and Provinces): a non-profit association integrating municipalities, provinces and other local administrations of Valencia Region, who can join on a voluntary basis. The principal aim of the organisation is the representation, defence and promotion of the interests of local administration. FVMP is also a co-organising partner of Landscapes of War project.

FWA: Fondazzjoni Wirt Artna: the Malta Heritage Trust – a voluntary non-governmental organisation dedicated to preserving and interpreting Maltese heritage, particularly through "living history" or re-enactment events.

GCCS Government Code and Cipher School: a code-breaking section set up in 1919 by the British government, comprising former Admiralty (Royal Navy) section known as "Room 40" and War Office teams. See also **Room 40**

GDR: Abbreviation of the German Democratic Republic (Deutsche Democratische Republik); also known as "East Germany", the Soviet-dominated eastern half of Germany after its partition following the Second World War.

Geometric characterisation: a technique used in marine survey, meaning the three-dimensional measurement of submerged layers.

GIS: Geographic Information System. A computer system enabling the user to display the spatial position and extent of features such as monuments, archaeology, landscapes or administrative boundaries against a map, information may be divided into different "layers" (commonly confused with *GPS* see also **GPS**)

GPS: Global Positioning System. A computer application that allows the user to ascertain their position at a given point via satellite technology. (Commonly confused with *GIS*: see also **GIS.**)

Hardstanding/ hard standing: a purpose built area on a military site, such as an airfield or a military research site, which is provided with a hard surface in order for structures or vehicles to be positioned there.

Hinterland Wall: a rear element of the Cold War Berlin Wall complex facing the GDR.

Historic Landscape Characterisation (HLC): an holistic approach to landscape interpretation , using GIS, which maps diversity of landscape character as a means of managing future change in ways that are appropriate and sustainable.

Historical Memory Law (ley de la memoria histórica): legislation passed in 2007 by the Spanish government. It recognises the victims of political, religious and ideological violence on both sides of the Spanish Civil War and of the dictatorship of General Franco and promotes the moral restitution and recovery of their personal and family memory.

Historiography: The writing of history itself – the study of how history has been written; in the broadest sense, recognition that there are various ways to engage in history

Lidice: a village in the Czech Republic which was destroyed in 1942 as a reprisal against the assassination of Reinhard Heydrich, the brutal Nazi governor of the country; the adult male population was massacred and the women and children sent to concentration camps.

Lorenz: a German code-producing machine, larger and more complicated that Enigma, using international teleprinter code as its basis. (See also **Enigma**)

Memorialisation: in the context of conflict archaeology, the process by which events, people or sites are commemorated.

MEPA: the Malta Environment and Planning Authority, encompassing the natural, cultural and architectural environment.

Mnemonic/Mnemonics: literally an aid to memory, in this context memory evoking, memory-studies.

Nacht und Nebel [prisons]: – 'night and fog' in German, indicating covert action, in this context – the practice during the Second World War of spiriting away people in occupied countries suspected by the Nazis of opposition, to prisons, in some cases potentially to be held as hostages.

NATO: The North Atlantic Treaty Organisation, formed in 1949, an international security organisation, primarily in the Cold War period an alliance of North American and Western European states. It acted as a counterpoise to the

Warsaw Pact. After the end of the Cold War and the break up of the Soviet sphere of influence many former Warsaw Pact countries joined NATO. (See also **Warsaw Pact**)

No Mans Land Group: A pan-European group of experts set up in 2003, interested in the study of the archaeology of the Great War, particularly active on the former Western Front in northern France and Belgium.

NVA: Nationale Volksarmee the National Peoples Army – the army of the former East Germany or GDR/DDR (See also **GDR**)

OP-20-G: the United States Navy signals intelligence and decryption section during the Second World War.

Organisation Todt: often abbreviated as OT; the paramilitary construction and engineering organisation of the German "Third Reich", founded in 1938. It grew out of Reichsarbeitsdienst (compulsory state labour service) programmes, such as the building of motorways. During the Second World War it was used to build defences, such as the Atlantic Wall. Named after its founder, Fritz Todt (a senior Nazi and engineer) – it was controlled, after Todt's death in 1942, by Albert Speer, an architect who was Hitler's protégé. Towards the end of the war the organisation made increasing use, often under brutal conditions, of forced labour; this comprised mostly prisoners of war or civilian forced labourers from occupied countries, but also a number of prisoners from concentration camps.

Over the Horizon Radar: A type of radar used for ealy warning purposes, which can operate over the curvature of the earth.

RAF: Royal Air Force. The British air force, established in 1918, its former incarnation was the RFC or Royal Flying Corps (See also **RFC**).

RAMs: Rapid Analytical Machines designed to speed up decryption, such as the bombe or Colossus (see also **bombe** and **Colossus**)

Rectified Photography: a technique whereby photographs are enhanced to emphasise particular architectural or archaeological features more clearly; this may be achieved manually or by use of computer applications.

RFC: Royal Flying Corps The British air force of the First World War (actually formed in 1912). In 1918 it became the Royal Air Force.

Room 40: the British Admiralty's code-breaking section, set up during the First World War, later merged with other agencies into the GCCS (See also **GCCS**)

ROV: a remote operated vehicle, in the context of this volume used in underwater survey in conjunction with other survey equipment, cameras etc.

Side scan sonar: A sideward looking sonar technique used in underwater survey (see also **fish**).

Sigint: abbreviation for intelligence signals analysis, ie the interception and analysis of coded messages, rather than human intelligence.

SIS: the British Secret Intelligence Service, sometimes in the past also known as MI6. This organisation has a wider remit than the Security Service MI5 which is concerned with internal security.

Soldatenheim: A German military term meaning a centre for rest and recreation – for troops, for example, in commandeered buildings in occupied countries (including the Channel islands) during the Second World War.

Stereographic photography: a technique whereby two images are combined to produce a three-dimensional view.

The National Trust: A large and well-established British conservation body (for England, Wales and Northern Island).

Transducer: the "antennae" of a sonar system which converts electricity into sound waves and vice versa.

Trench art: the wider definition used here is taken from Saunders – "any object made by any person from any material, as long as it and they are associated in time or space with armed conflict or its consequences". Saunders, N 2003 *Trench Art: materialities and memories of war*. p11; Oxford and New York: Berg.

Ultra: Codename given to the code-breaking activities centred at Bletchley Park during the Second World War.

Warsaw Pact: the name given to the Cold War forces of the Soviet Union and its satellite countries in Eastern Europe, founded in 1955 and formally disestablished in 1991.

Y-Stations: British signals intelligence collection and analysis centres during the Second World War.